The International Criminal Court and Global Social Control

The International Criminal Court was established in 2002 to prosecute war crimes, crimes against humanity, and genocide. At its genesis the ICC was expected to help prevent atrocities from arising or escalating by ending the impunity of leaders and administering punishment for the commission of international crimes. More than a decade later, the ICC's ability to achieve these broad aims has been questioned, as the ICC has reached only two guilty verdicts. In addition, some of the world's major powers, including the United States, Russia and China, are not members of the ICC. These issues underscore a gap between the ideals of prevention and deterrence and the reality of the ICC's functioning.

This book explores the gaps, schisms, and contradictions that are increasingly defining the International Criminal Court, moving beyond existing legal, international relations, and political accounts of the ICC to analyse the Court from a criminological standpoint. By exploring the way different actors engage with the ICC and viewing the Court through the framework of late modernity, the book considers how gaps between rhetoric and reality arise in the work of the ICC. Contrary to much existing research, the book examines how such gaps and tensions can be productive as they enable the Court to navigate a complex, international environment driven by geopolitics.

The International Criminal Court and Global Social Control will be of interest to academics, researchers, and advanced practitioners in international law, international relations, criminology, and political science. It will also be of use in upper-level undergraduate and postgraduate courses related to international criminal justice and globalization.

Nerida Chazal is a Lecturer in Criminology at Flinders University, Australia. Her research examines the aims and functioning of international criminal justice in a complex and increasingly global world. Nerida has previously worked as a Research Fellow with the Centre for Crime Policy and Research at Flinders University. She is co-editor (with W. De Lint and M. Marmo) of *Criminal Justice in International Society* (Routledge, 2014), and co-author (with M. Marmo) of *Transnational Crime and Criminal Justice* (Sage, 2016).

Routledge Research in International Law

Available:

International Law and the Third World
Reshaping Justice
Edited by Richard Falk, Balakrishnan Rajagopal and Jacqueline Stevens

International Legal Theory
Essays and Engagements, 1966–2006
Nicholas Onuf

The Problem of Enforcement in International Law
Countermeasures, the Non-Injured State and the Idea of International Community
Elena Katselli Proukaki

International Economic Actors and Human Rights
Adam McBeth

The Law of Consular Access
A Documentary Guide
John Quigley, William J. Aceves and S. Adele Shank

State Accountability under International Law
Holding States Accountable for a Breach of Jus Cogens Norms
Lisa Yarwood

International Organizations and the Idea of Autonomy
Institutional Independence in the International Legal Order
Edited by Richard Collins and Nigel D. White

Self-Determination in the Post-9/11 Era
Elizabeth Chadwick

Participants in the International Legal System
Multiple Perspectives on Non-State Actors in International Law
Edited by Jean d'Aspremont

Sovereignty and Jurisdiction in the Airspace and Outer Space
Legal Criteria for Spatial Delimitation
Gbenga Oduntan

International Law in a Multipolar World
Edited by Matthew Happold

The Law on the Use of Force
A Feminist Analysis
Gina Heathcote

The ICJ and the Evolution of International Law
The Enduring Impact of the Corfu Channel Case
Edited by Karine Bannelier, Théodore Christakis and Sarah Heathcote

UNHCR and International Refugee Law
From Treaties to Innovation
Corinne Lewis

Reciprocity in International Law
Its Impact and Function
Shahrad Nasrolahi Fard

Asian Approaches to International Law and the Legacy of Colonialism
The Law of the Sea, Territorial Disputes and International Dispute Settlement
Edited by Jin-Hyun Paik, Seok-Woo Lee and Kevin Y. L. Tan

The Right to Self-determination Under International Law
"Selfistans", Secession, and the Rule of the Great Powers
Milena Sterio

Reforming the UN Security Council Membership
The Illusion of Representativeness
Sabine Hassler

Threats of Force
International Law and Strategy
Francis Grimal

The Changing Role of Nationality in International Law
Edited by Alessandra Annoni and Serena Forlati

Criminal Responsibility for the Crime of Aggression
Patrycja Grzebyk

Regional Maintenance of Peace and Security under International Law
The Distorted Mirrors
Dace Winther

International Law-making
Essays in Honour of Jan Klabbers
Edited by Rain Liivoja and Jarna Petman

Resolving Claims to Self-Determination
Is There a Role for the International Court of Justice?
Andrew K. Coleman

The Rise of Tamil Separatism in Sri Lanka
From Communalism to Secession
Gnanapala Welhengama and Nirmala Pillay

The United Nations and Collective Security
Gary Wilson

Justice for Victims before the International Criminal Court
Luke Moffett

Public-Private Partnerships and Responsibility under International Law
A Global Health Perspective
Lisa Clarke

Cultural Diversity in International Law
The Effectiveness of the UNESCO Convention on the Protection and Promotion of the Diversity of Cultural Expressions
Edited by Lilian Richieri Hanania

Incitement in International Law
Wibke K. Timmermann

The Cuban Embargo under International Law
El Bloqueo
Nigel D. White

Resisting United Nations Security Council Resolutions
Sufyan Droubi

The Changing Nature of Customary International Law
Methods of Interpreting the Concept of Custom in International Criminal Tribunals
Noora Arajärvi

Power and Law in International Society
International Relations as the Sociology of International Law
Mark Klamberg

Reciprocity in International Law
Its Impact and Function
Shahrad Nasrolahi Fard

International Law and Boundary Disputes in Africa
Gbenga Oduntan

Means of Transportation and Registration of Nationality
Transportation Registered by International Organizations
Vincent P. Cogliati-Bantz

Forthcoming titles in this series include:

Technology and the Law on the Use of Force
New Security Challenges in the Twenty-First Century
Jackson Maogoto

Seeking Justice in International Law
The Significance and Implications of the UN Declaration on the Rights of Indigenous Peoples
Mauro Barelli

The International Criminal Court in Search of its Purpose and Identity
Edited by Triestino Mariniello

The Responsibility to Protect in International Law
An Emerging Paradigm Shift
Susan Breau

Legal Accountability and Britain's Wars 2000–2014
Peter Rowe

Fragmentation vs. the Constitutionalisation of International Law
A Practical Inquiry
Edited by Andrzej Jakubowski and Karolina Wierczyńska

The International Criminal Court and Global Social Control

International Criminal Justice in Late Modernity

Nerida Chazal

Routledge
Taylor & Francis Group
LONDON AND NEW YORK

First published 2016 by Routledge

2 Park Square, Milton Park, Abingdon, Oxfordshire OX14 4RN
711 Third Avenue, New York, NY 10017

Routledge is an imprint of the Taylor & Francis Group, an informa business

First issued in paperback 2018

British Library Cataloguing in Publication Data
A catalogue record for this book is available from the British Library

Library of Congress Cataloging-in-Publication Data
Chazal, Nerida, 1983- author.
The International Criminal Court and global social control : international criminal justice in late modernity / Nerida Chazal.
pages cm. -- (Routledge research in international law)
Includes bibliographical references and index.
ISBN 978-1-138-82090-6 (hbk) -- ISBN 978-1-315-74361-5 (ebk) 1. International Criminal Court. 2. International criminal courts. 3. Criminal procedure (International law) 4. Criminal liability (International law) 5. Globalization. I. Title.
KZ7312.C43 2015
345'.01--dc23
2015023807

ISBN: 978-1-138-82090-6 (hbk)
ISBN: 978-1-138-61459-8 (pbk)

Typeset in ITC Galliard by
Servis Filmsetting Ltd, Stockport, Cheshire

Contents

Acknowledgements

This book has evolved over the past five years, beginning as a PhD thesis and progressing during a post-doctoral position with the Centre for Crime Policy and Research at Flinders University. As such, many people have helped me to bring this book to fruition. I was fortunate to have two wonderful supervisors, Associate Professor Marinella Marmo and Associate Professor Derek Dalton, who have both been extremely generous with their time, advice, and feedback. Thank you, Marinella and Derek, for always pushing me to reach my goals and for your wise advice and valued friendship along the way.

Many other colleagues have also supported and encouraged me throughout this project. I extend my sincere thanks to: Professor Dawn Rothe; Professor Philip Stenning; Professor Willem de Lint; Dr Maria Giannacopoulos; Professor Andrew Goldsmith; Dr Russell Brewer; Dr Andrew Groves; Sue Jarrad; Jessica Viven; Rhiannon Bandiera; Jeremy Ryder; and Adam Pocrnic. Thank you, Sian Davy, for all your hard work and for your excellent research and editorial assistance; I couldn't have finished the book without you! Thank you to Flinders University Law School and the Centre for Crime Policy and Research for providing a supportive and collegial environment conducive to research.

During my fieldwork in Europe, I met many enthusiastic and generous individuals who contributed to the project. I was welcomed by academics in Europe, particularly the VU University, Amsterdam, who provided feedback on my ideas and helped me to develop my work. I met many passionate individuals who work in the field of international criminal justice. Thank you to these individuals who participated in interviews and provided me with information and an understanding of the International Criminal Court that I could not have achieved without their assistance.

Thank you to my family and friends who have always been there for me: Mum and Dad; Carmel and Colin Langley; Ryan Langley; Claire Wright; Luke Wright; Emma and John Warne; Chloe Kosmina; Chrissy Pavlakis; Andrea Matthews; Courtney Semmler; Chelsea Grahame; and Kendall Carracher. Finally, I've saved the biggest thank you of all for my two biggest cheerleaders: my husband, Lionel, and my son, Oliver – you both light up my world.

Abbreviations

ADFL	Alliance of Democratic Forces for the Liberation of Congo-Zaire (Alliance des forces démocratiques pour la libération du Congo-Zaïre)
ASF	Avocats Sans Frontières
ASP	Assembly of States Parties
AU	African Union
BIA	Bilateral Immunity Agreement
CICC	Coalition for the International Criminal Court
CNDP	National Congress for the Defence of the People (Congrès national pour la défense du peuple)
DRC	Democratic Republic of the Congo
FARDC	Congolese Armed Forces (Forces armées de la République démocratique du Congo)
FAPC	People's Armed Forces of Congo (Forces armées du peuple congolais)
FDLR	Democratic Forces for the Liberation of Rwanda (Forces démocratiques de libération du Rwanda)
FIDH	International Federation for Human Rights (Fédération internationale des ligues des droits de l'homme)
FNI	The Nationalist and Integrationist Front (Front des nationalistes et intégrationnistes)
FPLC	The Patriotic Forces for the Liberation of the Congo (Forces patriotiques pour la libération du Congo)
FRPI	The Front for Patriotique Resistance in Ituri (Force de résistance patriotique en Ituri)
HRW	Human Rights Watch
IBA	International Bar Association
ICC	International Criminal Court
ICTR	International Criminal Tribunal for Rwanda
ICTY	International Criminal Tribunal for the former Yugoslavia
ILC	International Law Commission
LMG	Like-Minded Group of states
LRA	Lord's Resistance Army (Uganda)

MNC	Congolese National Movement (Mouvement National Congolais)
MONUC	United Nations Organization Mission in the Democratic Republic of the Congo
MONUSCO	United Nations Organization Stabilization Mission in the Democratic Republic of the Congo (formerly MONUC)
NATO	North Atlantic Treaty Organization
NGO	Non-governmental organization
NRA	National Resistance Army (Ugandan Government)
PTC	Pre-Trial Chamber
OTP	Office of the Prosecutor
PUSIC	Party for the Unity and Safeguard of Integrity in Congo
RCD	Rally for Congolese Democracy
UN	United Nations
UNHRC	United Nations Human Rights Council
UPC	Union of Congolese Patriots (Union des patriotes congolais)
UNSC	United Nations Security Council

1 Introduction

Speaking at a ceremony to celebrate the ten-year anniversary of the International Criminal Court (herein the ICC or the Court) in 2012, the then president of the Court, Judge Sang-Hyun Song, declared: 'Impunity for atrocity crimes must end. Accountability must prevail. Always and everywhere' (Song 2012). At the time of this celebration the ICC had only successfully prosecuted one individual, Thomas Lubanga from the Democratic Republic of the Congo, while 11 trials continued and 13 arrest warrants remained outstanding. One of the most notable suspects on this wanted list, the president of Sudan, Omar al-Bashir, dismissed his arrest warrant saying, 'we are telling them to immerse it in water and drink it' (James 2009). Al-Bashir continued to act as the country's active president while describing the Court as 'a tool to terrorize countries that the West thinks are disobedient' (Dealy 2009b).

Further to this, at the time of the celebratory event, widespread violence continued in Syria (Greenwood 2012), tensions intensified in Gaza (Barzak and Teibel 2012), and commentators warned of potential violence at the 2013 elections in Kenya, despite the ICC's ongoing investigation and prosecution of the 2008 election violence (Cummings 2012). Similarly, conflict in eastern Congo escalated with over 320,000 people affected by violence (CARE 2012), even though the ICC found Thomas Lubanga guilty of war crimes in March 2012 (ICC 2012a). In the face of these challenges, Judge Sang-Hyun Song affirmed that for the Court to succeed 'we must remain determined and united' (Song 2012), yet some of the world's major powers, including the United States, Russia and China, are not parties to the ICC, relatively few Asia-Pacific countries have signed the Rome Statute of the Court (Freeland 2013), and Africa remains divided over the role of the ICC (Keppler 2011). A prominent example of this division is the complicity of Chad, Kenya, and Djibouti with ICC suspect Omar al-Bashir. These countries have all hosted al-Bashir without enforcing his outstanding ICC arrest warrant, despite their status as States Parties to the ICC (du Plessis and Louw 2011).

Such contradictions define the International Criminal Court after more than a decade of existence. Established in 2002 as the world's first permanent court to prosecute war crimes, crimes against humanity, genocide, and aggression, the ICC was given the task of achieving a broad array of aims. These aims are reflected in the United Nations' overview of the Rome Statute of the ICC, which states that the Court was developed:

> to achieve justice for all; to end impunity; to help end conflicts; to remedy the deficiencies of ad hoc tribunals; to take over when national criminal justice institutions are unwilling or unable to act; and to deter future war criminals.
>
> (UN 1999, n.p.)

It would be difficult for any justice institution to achieve such broad and lofty aims, let alone a nascent court still striving to assert its legitimacy and develop its identity while operating within a fragmented, highly political milieu. Unsurprisingly, then, disparities between the ICC's aims and its functioning have developed, which have been described as expectation gaps and impunity gaps (Gibb 2010). These disparities have disappointed victims, created scepticism over the role of the Court, and undermined the power and influence of the ICC. Despite these gaps, rhetoric surrounding the Court continues to rely on lofty goals, meaning the Court's formative years have been marked by schisms between inspirational narratives that exalt the Court's potential and criticisms that warn of the Court's dangers and shortcomings. This book takes the contradictions and gaps between the ICC's aims and its reality as the starting point to explore the role and position of the Court in international society and its ability to be used as a tool of social control.

1.1 The contradictory aims of the International Criminal Court

A quick search of discourse surrounding the ICC will reveal that the Court is, among other things, designed to: end impunity, add accountability to the international system, prevent international crimes from occurring, halt the escalation of conflict, ensure peace, bring a sense of justice to victim communities, provide reparations for victims, punish human rights abusers, highlight areas where human rights abuses are occurring, and set standards of rights and justice. As Damaška (2008) highlights, the goals proclaimed by international criminal courts go beyond the traditional aims of retribution, deterrence, incapacitation, and rehabilitation ascribed to domestic criminal justice systems. On top of these aims, international courts seek to produce a historical record of the context of international crimes, give victims of mass atrocities a voice, and promulgate human rights norms (Damaška 2008). International courts, and in particular the ICC, must achieve these aims despite lacking a system of enforcement to assist in the investigation and adjudication of especially complex crimes. This creates a paradox where 'intrinsically powerless institutions aspire to achieve objectives whose attainment would be a serious challenge to even their most powerful national counterparts' (Damaška 2009, p. 23). Considering the limitations of the ICC and its reliance on outside support, we could expect the ICC to espouse more modest ambitions, yet the Court continues to set lofty, unachievable aims for itself which creates disparity between the ICC's rhetoric and the reality of its operation.

In addition to the overabundance of highly ambitious goals, many of the ICC's stated aims clash with each other, creating tensions and contradictions in the functioning of the Court. Damaška (2008) outlines some of these tensions: the desire to stop ongoing conflict can be hampered by bringing prominent leaders to justice; the aim of producing an accurate historical record cannot be achieved through the narrow juridical framework of individual responsibility and adversarial proceedings; the ideal of protecting the rights of the accused clashes with the desire to provide satisfaction to victims; and the aspiration to propagate human rights conflicts with the ICC's model of narrow and selective prosecutions and the disparate effects of the ICC in local and international contexts. Adding to these tensions is the lack of ranking order to prioritize the conflicting aims and the ICC's limited institutional capacity to achieve these aims given its reliance on outside support, its finite resources and the complex nature of the international crimes that it deals with (Damaška 2009).

Damaška's (2008, 2009) work on the aims of international criminal justice provides a useful foundation to think about the multiple aims of the ICC and the many tensions and contradictions that are inherent in the functioning of the Court. His work is joined by other literature that examines the aims of sentencing at an international level (Drumbl 2005; Henham 2002, 2005, 2007a, 2007b; Henham and Findlay 2005) and explores the complex and often contradictory role of international criminal justice in international society (Smeulers and Haveman 2008; De Lint, Marmo and Chazal 2013; Rothe and Mullins 2006a). This book explores these contradictions and tensions, categorizing the multiple goals into aims of prevention and aims of persuasion, using a social constructivist perspective to explore the role of actors in constructing the ICC's aims, examining how idealpolitik and realpolitik shape the ICC, and adopting the theoretical framework of late modernity to understanding how the ICC's conflicting aims allow it to act as an institution of global social control. These conceptual tools are briefly outlined below and elaborated on throughout the book.

Aims of prevention and persuasion

To assist in better understanding the development and operation of the multiple aims of the ICC, a schematic for simplifying the aims is needed. This book groups the aims of the ICC into two broad, overarching categories: aims of prevention and aims of persuasion. These categories capture the two core roles that the ICC plays and encapsulate the variety of aims as defined in both discourse surrounding the Court and by those who work closely with the ICC.

Preventative aims are often articulated through the catch cries of 'ending impunity' and 'adding accountability' to the international system. Aims of prevention include criminal justice goals of general and specific deterrence and retribution. These aims seek to stop international crimes from occurring or from escalating and in doing so contribute to peace (UN 1999). Persuasive aims view the Court as an important normative body that exists to reinforce human rights norms and improve legislation and justice processes at both international and domestic levels. Persuasive aims construct the Court as a catalyst for action and change at a national level and highlight the importance of the ICC in establishing appropriate procedural justice precedents in response to international crimes. Persuasive aims capture the didactic role of the ICC and construct the Court as a model of justice.

The aims of prevention and persuasion come to the fore in discourse surrounding the ICC and in actors' descriptions of the aims of the Court. Of course, this schematic is conceptual and is somewhat contrived as, in reality, aims are multiple, fragmented, and complex. However, viewing the multiple aims of the ICC as fitting under these two overarching paradigms is useful in understanding the work of the Court. Aims that often appear central to the operation of the ICC, such as providing satisfaction and reparation to victims, are exposed as secondary to more control-based aims of preventing international crimes and establishing a persuasive, normative framework for international society. As this book will explore, it is these aims that dictate the reality of the ICC.

The social construction of the ICC

This book uses a social constructionist perspective to examine the role that actors play in constituting the aforementioned aims of the ICC. It argues that the multiple aims of the Court are socially constructed by the broad range of actors that interact and engage with the Court. Throughout the book, the terms 'actors' and 'groups' are used to refer to the different agents that construct international society. Individual actors can act reflexively and this reflexivity is particularly heightened in late modernity (as explored in Chapter 4), but in doing so they are significantly constrained by the structures in which they operate. The individual human rights actor, for example, can shape international criminal justice discourses, but will often reproduce the narratives of the group they are connected to, for example, the NGO Human Rights Watch (Chapter 3 examines the social constructivist perspective in greater depth).

Groups are similarly constrained by the wider structures in which they operate, such as the assumptions that guide the field of human rights or the norms and principles of the field of international law (Chapter 5 uses Bourdieu's concept of fields to explore how actors are constrained by norms of the area in which they operate). The vast numbers of groups that make up international society, including the United Nations, states, and NGOs, means that there are many different interests that are articulated through engagements with the ICC and, therefore, many different aims set out for the Court. Groups use the Court for a variety of reasons and to support their own interests and identities. This creates polarized discourses surrounding the ICC and multiple, contradictory aims for the Court.

Realpolitik and idealpolitik

One way of conceptualizing the contradictory aims of the ICC and the gap between the Court's rhetoric and its reality is through the framework of idealpolitik and realpolitik. Idealpolitik refers to circumstances where 'behaviour is dictated by "principles of legitimacy" and conditions where normative principles are privileged over simple power politics' (Atkinson 2011, p. 101). The ideas that underpin idealpolitik are predominately normative or ideal-based. Realpolitik is equally constituted by ideas; however, these ideas focus on power politics and strategic political interests (Rudolph 2001). As this highlights, both idealpolitik and realpolitik are constituted by ideas; it is the premise of the ideas as based on normative and ideational frameworks or political strategies and power politics that differentiates the two. Idealpolitik can, therefore, be defined as the mobilization of normative ideals, and realpolitik as the mobilization of instrumental ideals and practical interests.

The ICC is constructed by both idealpolitik and realpolitik. Some groups use idealpolitik to support the Court and align their identities and interests with the ICC, while others are driven by realpolitik and construct their interests and identities through their negative interactions with the Court in order to reinforce power structures and political interests. A key example of the use of idealpolitik in the construction of the Court is the international NGOs that support the work of the Court and use ideals based on human rights to construct the Court as a positive institution that can end impunity, achieve peace, and bring justice to victims. At the same time as engaging with such idealpolitik, the ICC also interacts with groups whose ideas are based on realpolitik. A primary example is engagement between the United States and the ICC. The United States has been opposed to the ICC and has had a series of negative interactions with the Court, as explored in Chapter 3. As both realpolitik and idealpolitik are used to construct the ICC, it becomes apparent that tensions and conditions of the ICC are an inherent part of the operation of the Court.

Late modernity and social control

The contradictions, schisms, and tensions that define the aims of the ICC can also be considered symptomatic of the ICC's desire for control in an international environment that is complex and fragmented. This corresponds to criminological theories of social control in late modernity (Garland 2001; Young 1999). Although the convergence of crime and justice discourses and the concept of control have been used to examine the contradictions of criminal justice at a national level (amongst others Garland 1996, 2001; Hudson 2003b; Young 1999, 2007), these concepts are yet to be used to explain the contradictory nature of emerging international criminal justice institutions. From the late-modern perspective, the Court's contradictions and ambivalences are beneficial as they assist the Court in responding to the simultaneous desire for unity, pluralization, flexibility, and control that are characteristic of the late-modern environment in which the Court is acting (Bauman 1990, 1991 and 2000).

This flexibility can also be negative, however, as it means more powerful actors can use the Court according to their own realpolitik. The ICC has the power to selectively criminalize particular situations, mirroring pre-existing geopolitical divisions, inequalities, and disadvantages in the process. As Roberts and McMillan (2003, p. 321) highlight, 'processes of social censure and criminalization are today being replicated in supranational contexts'. Similarly, Michalowski (2009) highlights that transnational structures of power create and use the 'criminal other' to facilitate control at an international level. Adopting this outlook, this book considers how the contradictions and schisms of the ICC are both useful in allowing it to navigate the complex terrain of late modernity and detrimental in reproducing existing geopolitical divides.

1.2 Aims, methods, and structure of the book

The overarching aim of this book is to examine how and why gaps between the ideal and reality occur and to understand how they influence the functioning of the Court, the construction of the Court's identity, and the position of the ICC in international society as an institution of social control. The book examines how the many different actors construct the ICC through their interactions with it and considers how the broad aims of the Court can be useful, as they allow these varied actors to engage with and support the Court while simultaneously pursing their own unique interests and goals.

This book examines the ICC from a critical and theoretical perspective. The theoretical examination of the ICC seeks to clarify broader trends in the work of the Court and understand how these trends influence its functioning within international society. Any critical examination of the ICC has not been undertaken in the spirit of undermining the Court. As Shklar (1986, pp. 122–23) highlights, 'to show that justice has its practical and ideological limits is not to slight it. . . . The entire aim is rather to account for the difficulties which the morality of justice faces in a morally pluralistic world.' By examining the pluralities of ICC through a critical lens, this book seeks to illuminate the Court's position in international society as an adaptable institution of social control.

Methods

To achieve these goals, the book examines documents surrounding the ICC, analyses interview data from a series of semi-structured interviews with individuals who work closely with the Court, and explores a case study of the trial of Thomas Lubanga. The interviews were designed to examine how actors working closely with the ICC construct the Court's aims, explore the use of realpolitik and idealpolitik in the construction of the ICC, and illuminate the tensions between different perspectives on the ICC. By interviewing those who work closely with the Court, the semi-structured interviews offer first-hand accounts of how experts view the Court and how their perceptions of international criminal justice and their interactions with each other shape the Court's aims and contradictions. Throughout the book, interview quotes are attributed to participants (for example, Participant A), and an interview schedule is provided in Appendix A. To complement this data, the use of a case study exemplifies how the contradictions and ambivalences of the ICC operate in the trial setting.

Structure

Following this introduction, Chapter 2, 'The development and aims of the International Criminal Court', examines the Rome Statute Preamble, ICC documents, and broad discourses surrounding the Court to understand how the aims of the ICC have developed. This includes historical contextualization of the ICC's aims and narratives, such as 'never again', which have matured over the past century. This chapter highlights how the aims of the ICC are multiple, competing, and broad. It contrasts the ideals of the ICC with the reality of its functioning, using the oppositional framework of idealpolitik and realpolitik to examine the gaps between what the ICC says it will achieve and what the Court has actually achieved. The chapter highlights that the Court is often characterized simultaneously as a positive tool that can end impunity and enforce human rights standards, and a negative weapon that can amplify political struggles and reinforce geopolitical divides.

Chapter 3, 'Tensions in the pursuit of justice', explores how the gaps and tensions between the ideal and reality of the ICC are socially constructed. To do this, the chapter compares the ICC's tensions, as outlined in Chapter 2, with the tensions inherent in the operation of domestic justice systems. It uses socio-legal and criminological literature and understandings of domestic criminal processes and systems (such as Duff et al. 2004a), gaps between law on the books and law in action (Ewick and Silbey 1999), and theories of social construction to explore common factors that contribute to justice systems failing to meet their aims. While this comparison acknowledges that the ICC is not unique in producing tensions and competing aims, the chapter also seeks to identify and understand factors that are specific to the ICC and result in significant gaps and failings of the Court. This involves exploring the limitations inherent in the structure of the ICC and the constraints imposed by the Rome Statute, the plethora of actors who engage with the ICC, and the unique nature of the international environment, which is considerably shaped by geopolitics while lacking broader systems of accountability, justice and governance.

Chapter 4, 'Late modernity, social control, and the ICC', introduces the framework of late modernity to better understand the context in which the ICC's tensions are produced and used. The chapter argues that this late-modern environment means that the ICC embraces ambiguity and ambivalence through its articulation of broad aims, which may cause tensions, but also allows many different actors to engage with the Court and use it as a tool of social control. By embracing ambiguity, the ICC remains flexible enough to constantly redefine its aims and respond to the unpredictability of the international environment. The malleability of the Court's aims allows the ICC to adapt to events as they unfold, meaning the Court can capture and respond to a wider range of situations in an unpredictable and complex environment. This framework explains how contradictions can be useful for the Court to enable it to respond to, and thrive in, the complex environment that is late modernity.

Chapter 5, 'The role of actors', examines how those working closely with the Court construct the aims and roles of the ICC and view the Court's identity and functioning in international society. This chapter analyses how those who work closely with the Court use idealistic rhetoric based on broad, common aims while also pursing their own, individual objectives. Based on interview material, the chapter reflects on the perceptions and attitudes of those who work closely with the ICC and examines the relationships between those who interact with the Court and the structures and fields within which these actors operate. This deepens the theoretical examination of Chapter 4 by illustrating the multiple and competing tensions that occur as many actors attempt to engage with and use the ICC.

Chapter 6, 'The trial as a site of contest: the DRC and Thomas Lubanga', examines how the aims and contradictions that define the ICC influence the trials that come before the Court, using the trial of Thomas Lubanga as a case study. Lubanga was charged with war crimes for his participation in the conflict in the Democratic Republic of Congo. His trial was the first to come before the Court and it is currently one of only two guilty verdicts to have been reached by the ICC (ICC 2012a). As such, this trial provides an excellent case study to examine the articulation and use of a variety of contradictory aims. The objective of this chapter is to analyse how contradictions and tensions shape the direction of the court trial and explore how the ICC uses contradictory aims to achieve unity and momentum during trials while also remaining flexible and able to respond to unpredictable circumstances as they arise.

Chapter 7, 'The ICC as a tool', reflects on the broader outcomes of the Court's flexible aims by examining how they construct the Court as a model of justice and a tool that can be used by a range of actors in a variety of situations. The chapter looks at how the ICC is used to achieve political goals: it explores how the Ugandan government used the ICC to maintain political power within Uganda, and how the international community mobilized the Court to achieve certain outcomes in Libya. As these examples highlight, the broad aims of the ICC mean that it can be used from the bottom up or the top down to achieve different forms of social control. The chapter highlights the potential for the ICC to reproduce existing inequalities and geopolitical divides through its differential application of crime and justice narratives and labels.

Chapter 8, the conclusion, discusses how the gaps, tensions, and contradictions of the ICC can be useful, as they arise from the ICC's broad and flexible aims, which enable many actors to engage with and use the Court. This ensures the ICC can respond to many different situations in the unpredictable environment of late modernity, thereby creating a resilient institution. The negative consequences of the Court's broad and flexible aims (namely the gaps between the Court's rhetoric and reality and its potential to be used as a tool of social control and thus reproduce existing inequalities and divides) become 'negative externalities' (Mackenzie 2010) in the Court's quest for legitimacy and resilience in a complex and fragmented international environment. This chapter draws conclusions about what the functioning of the ICC can tell us about the shape and role of criminal justice, in international society, during late modernity. It concludes by considering how a broader range of individuals may engage with and use the ICC to have their claims for justice heard and in doing so counter the inequality that currently defines ICC prosecutions and the international landscape.

1.3 Concluding comments

The ICC's multiple and idealistic aims produce many tensions and gaps. While these tensions and the continued espousal of such idealistic aims appears illogical, the exploration in this book will highlight that such broad and ambiguous aims serve several productive purposes, encouraging flexibility and engagement with the Court. This is important in the fragmented and complex environment of late modernity in which many actors seek to engage with the Court while pursuing their own interests. By examining multiple effects of the ICC's contradictions, we can see that while proclamations such as 'impunity for atrocity crimes must end. Accountability must prevail. Always and everywhere' (Song 2012) are not necessarily *realistic* goals for the ICC, they are useful sentiments that allow the ICC to become an institution of global social control in a late-modern environment.

2 The development and aims of the ICC

The idea of a permanent international criminal court has a long and chequered history. Today's International Criminal Court is the product of a myriad of historical, political, and social forces that span the past century.[1] The Rome Statute, establishing the ICC, was drafted at the historic Rome Conference in 1998 (Tallgren 1999). Four years later, on 1 July 2002, the ICC entered into force after the requisite number of 60 ratifications of the Rome Statute was reached. The threshold of 60 ratifications, needed to bring the Court into existence, was achieved much faster than most people expected, showing an unexpected sense of support for the Court and the principles enshrined in the Rome Statute (Schiff 2008). However, this significant success was preceded by several false starts, as well as deviations, with the development of other international tribunals and justice mechanisms (Bassiouni 1995). From its conception in 1998, through to its establishment in 2002, and during its first decade of existence, there has been much debate and negotiation concerning the shape, structure, aims, and functioning of the ICC.

This chapter explores how the aims of the ICC have developed over time by examining the establishment of the Court and the articulation of the Court's aims in the Rome Statute Preamble, ICC documents, and broad discourses surrounding the Court. The chapter provides a brief introduction to the development, jurisdiction, and functioning of the ICC and explores how its aims are multiple, competing, and broad. Using the framework of idealpolitik and realpolitik, the chapter contrasts the ideals of the ICC with the reality of its functioning to examine the gaps between what the ICC says it will achieve and what the Court has actually achieved. As Rudolph (2001, p. 656) explains:

1 There is considerable literature on the development of international criminal law and the ICC. For example, Schiff (2008) provides an excellent overview of the development of the Court using the metaphor of the 'river of justice' to examine how different 'streams' and 'norm cascades' have flowed and converged to produce the international criminal law that has shaped the ICC. There are also several other good introductory texts to the International Criminal Court, including: Broomhall (2003); Bekou and Cryer (2004); Rowe, McGoldrick, and Donnelly (2004); Sadat (2002); and Schabas (2007b). These texts present an overview of the key issues facing the Court, primarily from a legalistic viewpoint.

> although liberal humanitarian ideas have created the demand for political action [in response to international crimes], the process of dealing with brutality in war has been dominated by realpolitik—that is, furthering the strategic interests of the most powerful states.

The impetus for the ICC resides in idealistic, liberal, humanitarian discourses (idealpolitik) which construct the Court as a positive 'tool' that can end impunity, add accountability to the international system and bring justice to victims. However, the reality of the ICC's functioning is considerably defined by realpolitik which sees the ICC acting as a negative 'weapon' that can disrupt peace processes and reinforce power imbalances at a supranational level. This chapter explores how the aims of the ICC are structured through both idealpolitik and realpolitik to demonstrate the contradictions inherent in the preventative and persuasive aims of the ICC.

2.1 The historical development of the ICC

The first calls for the creation of a permanent international criminal court came in 1872 when Gustave Moynier, one of the founders of the International Committee of the Red Cross, proposed an international criminal court to deal with the crimes committed during the Franco-Prussian War (Moynier 1872). The next serious call for an international criminal court arose in 1919 when the drafters of the Treaty of Versailles envisaged an ad hoc court to try the Kaiser and German war criminals of World War I (Bassiouni 1995). After World War II, allied forces created the International Military Tribunal, known as the Nuremberg Tribunal, to prosecute key leaders of the Nazi Regime. The Nuremberg Tribunal was followed by the International Military Tribunal for the Far East, which was established in Tokyo to deal with similar war crimes. Both of the post-World War II tribunals were marred by criticism for the 'victor's justice' they exemplified in the face of the allies' success in the war (Peskin 2005; Totani 2008). Despite their limitations, these tribunals brought the idea of international criminal justice into the spotlight of the international arena (Bassiouni 1997).

Following these tribunals, the General Assembly of the United Nations mandated the International Law Commission (ILC) to prepare a draft code for a permanent international criminal court to deal with similar crimes in the future (Nuremberg Human Rights Centre 2007). The initial attempts by the ILC to reach an agreement on a draft statute were unsuccessful due to the difficulty of adequately defining the crime of aggression (Schabas 2004). Following the ILC's attempt to create a permanent international criminal court, the topic of international criminal justice fell into the background throughout the Cold War. There were periodic attempts to draft a statute for a permanent international criminal court; however, it was not until 40 years later and the end of the Cold War that the ILC again attempted a draft statute. These attempts were prompted by calls from Trinidad and Tobago in 1989 to develop an international court to deal with the increasing problem of transnational drug trafficking (Scarf 1994).

The 1990s saw the increase of human rights movements which impelled 'a victim-oriented discourse that required states to ensure that perpetrators of atrocities were brought to justice' (Schabas 2006, p. 422). These human rights and victim-oriented discourses caused the United Nations Security Council to react to the atrocities in the Balkans by setting up the ad hoc tribunal known as the International Criminal Tribunal for the former Yugoslavia (ICTY) in The Hague (Swart, Zahar, and Sluiter 2011). Closely following this tribunal, the 1994 genocide in Rwanda and the failure of international society to react to the horrors as they unfolded prompted the introduction of another ad hoc tribunal, the International Criminal Tribunal for Rwanda (ICTR), in Arusha (Cruvellier 2010). The logistics of setting up these two ad hoc tribunals proved time-consuming and resource intensive for the United Nations and a sense of 'tribunal fatigue' coincided with renewed attempts by the ILC to establish a permanent court to deal with such atrocities in the future (Bassiouni 1995, p. 57).

In 1994, when the ILC completed its final draft statute for an international criminal court (UN General Assembly 1994), the United Nations established the Preparatory Commission on the Establishment of the ICC to prepare a consolidated draft text leading up to the Rome Conference in 1998 (CICC 2015). The historic Rome Conference was attended by thousands of individuals and groups representing States Parties, international bodies, such as the United Nations, and, notably, many representatives of global civil society, including advocates for human rights and victims' rights and media organizations (Glasius 2006). Over the course of the conference, these actors negotiated the Rome Statute that created the International Criminal Court (Kirsch and Holmes 1999; Tallgren 1999). In 2002, when 60 countries ratified the Rome Statute, the ICC was born.

As of 2015, 123 countries have ratified the Rome Statute of the International Criminal Court and 139 countries have signed the Statute (CICC 2015). When compared with the 193 member countries of the United Nations, it becomes apparent that the ICC is still not a universal institution (UN 2015). There are several countries who oppose the Court, most notably and vocally the United States (Casey 2002; Goldsmith 2003). There has also been limited participation in, and engagement with, the Court from Asian countries, with only nine out of 24 having ratified the Rome Statue (CICC 2015). The bid for 'universality' is ongoing with the ICC and supporting organizations, such as the Coalition for the International Criminal Court, rallying countries to sign and ratify the Rome Statute (CICC 2015).

The criminal jurisdiction of the ICC

The International Criminal Court has limited scope in terms of its criminal jurisdiction. The Court is mandated to deal with the 'worst crimes known to mankind', defined as genocide, war crimes, crimes against humanity, and aggression (Rome Statute 1998, Article 5). The inclusion of these crimes in the Rome Statute reflects the types of crimes that have been prosecuted by previous tribunals, such as the Nuremberg tribunals, the ICTY, and the ICTR, in which war crimes, genocide, and crimes against humanity were central to prosecutions (see Bassiouni 1999a and 1999b; Ratner, Abrams, and Bischoff 2009; Roberston 2006).

The crime of aggression has been an elusive crime to define and, at the drafting of the Rome Statute, the inability to arrive at a consensual definition of aggression resulted in a delay of the prosecution of crime before the ICC (Nesi and Politi 2004). Many countries have been reluctant to include aggression in the Rome Statute due to the potential political ramifications (see Drumbl 2009; Nesi and Politi 2004; Mullins, Kauzlarich, and Rothe 2004 for a discussion of the development of aggression). Despite this difficulty, during the Kampala Review Conference of the Rome Statute in 2010, a consensus on the definition of aggression was reached and the ICC's jurisdiction over the crime was confirmed (Heinsch 2010; Trahan 2011; Wenaweser 2010).[2] However, the ICC will not prosecute aggression until after 2017 when a decision is made by States Parties to activate the jurisdiction (ICC 2010a).

There has also been considerable debate over the inclusion of other prominent crimes of an international and transnational nature in the Rome Statute, including terrorism (Goldstone and Simpson 2003) and drug and human trafficking (McConville 2000; Obokata 2006). While these crimes are not explicitly covered in the Rome Statute, some have argued that the broad category of 'crimes against humanity' gives the ICC the potential to prosecute these crimes (see, for example, Obokata 2006; and Proulx 2004). The Court's focus on genocide, war crimes, and crimes against humanity illustrates the historical and contextual influences on the creation of the ICC (these crimes were the crimes prosecuted by the Nuremberg Tribunals), as well as the process of negotiations and concessions that defined the Rome Conference (Tallgren 1999). This process of negotiation meant that although some countries argued for the inclusion of crimes such as the use of nuclear weapons (India) and drug trafficking (e.g. Egypt, Algeria, Turkey, Sri Lanka, and Caribbean states), these crimes were not covered in the Rome Statute due to concessions made to other countries (Kirsch and Holmes 1999).

There are three ways in which a case can be brought before the Court. First, a country can refer their situation to the ICC and ask the Court to prosecute due to an inability to achieve legitimate or effective national prosecutions (Rome Statute 1998, Article 14). This mechanism of self-referral occurred in the situations of the Democratic Republic of the Congo (DRC), Uganda, and the Central African Republic (CAR). The second way in which a case can come before the ICC is through the chief prosecutor of the Court mobilizing their *proprio motu* powers

2 Article 8 *bis* adopted in Kampala defines the individual crime of aggression as the planning, preparation, initiation, or execution by a person in a leadership position of an act of aggression. Importantly, it contains the threshold requirement that the act of aggression must constitute a manifest violation of the Charter of the United Nations (see Rome Statute Article 8 *bis* and http://www.iccnow.org/?mod=aggression).

to initiate an investigation and prosecution (Rome Statute 1998, Article 15).[3] The former Chief Prosecutor, Luis Moreno-Ocampo, started prosecutions in this manner in Kenya. The third and final way in which a situation can be brought before the ICC is through referral by the United Nations Security Council (Rome Statute 1998, Article 13(b)). The United Nations Security Council (UNSC) can refer a situation to the ICC acting under Chapter VII of the Charter of the United Nations. The UNSC controversially referred ongoing conflicts in Libya and Darfur to the ICC.

2.2 The symbolic role of the victim

Throughout the development of international criminal justice and the ICC, as detailed above, the image of the victim has played a strong, symbolic role. The language of victim-oriented human rights is woven throughout the discourses surrounding the ICC and 'bringing justice to victims' (TRIAL 2012) is often cited as one of the core goals of the ICC. For example, the Preamble to the Rome Statute of the ICC (1998, p. 1) provides that the States Parties are 'mindful that during this century millions of children, women and men have been victims of unimaginable atrocities that deeply shock the conscience of humanity'.

The focus on victims is reflected in the ICC's decision to make victims a part of its proceedings through the inclusion of victims as parties to trials—a pioneering aspect of the ICC which is defined under Article 68(3) of the Rome Statute (see Gillett 2009 for a discussion of victim participation in ICC trials). Victims are also supported in providing testimony in The Hague and victims who participate in trials have access to repatriation funds and options which can help them to recover after international crimes (ICC 2012e). Additionally, the ICC has developed an independent fund, the Trust Fund for Victims, which supports the restoration and rehabilitation of victim communities in situations that are prosecuted by the ICC (The Trust Fund for Victims 2012). The victim-oriented focus also generates several aims that fall under a transitional justice paradigm. From this perspective the ICC trials form a spectacle that plays a cathartic role, creates collective memory, allows for the witnessing of traumatic events (Oisel 2000), and has an educative function (Henham 2005). Through its international trials the ICC seeks to play a role in such processes by witnessing international crimes—this allows for acknowledgement and validation of victims and victim communities (Steele 2005). In this capacity the ICC seeks to ensure that international crimes are 'inscribed in collective memory' (Fournet 2007, p. 128) at both a national and international level.

3 The chief prosecutor's *proprio motu* powers are a contentious issue in the development of the Court. Many argue for the prosecutor to be independent and have the ability to initiate investigations (Goldstone and Fritz 2000) while others argue that the prosecutor should be held more accountable and should be more closely linked to the United Nations Security Council (Goldsmith 2003; Schabas 2004). These debates are linked to prosecutorial discretion, which has been extensively examined (Danner 2003; Goldstone 2010; Greenawalt 2007; Takemura 2007).

The ICC's capacity to achieve these restorative justice aims is significantly limited by its structure and functioning. The selectivity of the ICC's prosecutions means that the person who is punished may have no direct relation to the perpetrator of the violence that the victim actually experienced. Similarly, the ICC's selectivity, in terms of the crimes it focuses on within a particular region, may exclude a large group of victims—as with the example of the focus on child soldiers instead of rape as a war tool. The length of the trial can also be disappointing as victims may wait years to see a verdict.

Even if a guilty verdict is reached, victims may view the punishments that are enforced by the tribunal as inadequate in relation to the trauma of the genocide (Afflitto 2000). As Hannah Ardent (see Köhler and Saner, p. 54) explains, 'this guilt, in contrast to all criminal guilt, oversteps and shatters any and all legal systems'. For many, there is no punishment that can equal the extreme trauma and losses caused by international crimes (Stover and Weinstein 2004) and the framework of individual criminal responsibility cannot equate to the gravity of international crimes. Victims may have little knowledge of the ICC trials, as the Court is both culturally and geographically removed from the site of atrocities (Sriram and Ross 2007). These factors create an expectation gap between what the ICC promises victims and the reality of the functioning of the Court, and illustrates the need for multiple 'tools' to achieve the multifaceted aims of justice in the wake of mass atrocities (Simpson 2008). Finally, the ICC's selectivity and narrowness prohibits an accurate, contextualized historical account from being developed through ICC trials. The record that the ICC creates is filtered through strict procedural rules and the contests of adversarial parties, giving the trial a marginal role in creating collective memory. As Damaška (2008, p. 338) highlights, the best that can be expected of international courts is 'to provide fragmentary material as a scaffolding for subsequent historical research'.

Given these limitations, aspirational, transitional justice goals are often subordinate to the ICC's more prominent goals of prevention and persuasion. Instead of working towards restorative goals, the ICC often conceives the aim of bringing justice to victims through a retributive paradigm. This approach follows the logic of the ICTY, which stated, 'thwarting impunity even to a limited extent would contribute to appeasement and give the chance to the people who were sorely afflicted to mourn those among them who had been unjustly killed' (Trial Chamber ICTY, quoted by Tallgren 2002, p. 593). By focusing on retributive paradigms, aims of punishment, such as rehabilitation, are constructed as unsuitable for international crimes. The idea of rehabilitation does not fit within the human rights and victim-oriented framework, where victims are used as symbolic currency to reinforce the more punitive aims of prevention, deterrence, and retribution.

It follows that the victim-oriented focus of the ICC often comes at the expense of the rights of the defence, such as the right to an expeditious trial. Those accused of international crimes are often represented as 'warlords' or 'criminals' prior to being judged. This is typified in a headline from *The Guardian* that read 'Judges urged to convict Congo warlord Thomas Lubanga' (Associated Press 2011). Such demonization can compromise the right of the defence to a fair and expeditious trial, and skews the principle of equality of arms. Damaška (2008) similarly highlights that the ability of victims to act as parties to proceedings may cause judges to attribute to the defendant a greater role in atrocities that are widespread and complex. Interestingly, Damaška (2008, p. 343) convincingly argues for victim-related goals to be removed from the ICC's list of aspirations, as 'effective measures to provide victims with satisfaction require that elements of restorative justice be injected into criminal proceedings, and, as is well known, retributive and restorative forms of justice do not mix very well'.

The continued prevalence of a victim-oriented human rights discourse, despite the problematic outcomes, can be explained by the persuasive power that the image of the valorized victim presents. As Clarke (2009, p. 13) highlights, 'the victim is both central yet marginal to the justice project itself'. Images of victims provide popular and visible currency for the promotion of the retributive aims of ending impunity and deterrence, and justify the ICC's role as a persuasive institution that can set standards, enforce human rights, and develop a normative framework for international society. However, this is a narrow conception of restorative justice and the underlying retributive paradigm of the ICC means that it is 'erroneous to presume that internationalised principles of criminal justice will remain anything other than partial, relativistic and profoundly undemocratic' (Henham 2002, p. 268).

2.3 Aims of persuasion

The victim-oriented discourse of the ICC constructs the Court as a norm-building and enforcing institution based on human rights standards and assumptions. The ICC is a tool that can cement and enforce human rights standards at a local and international level. These aspirations come under the persuasive goals of the Court, which involve defining international crimes, asserting standards for protecting human rights, and encouraging domestic jurisdiction to implement and adhere to ICC standards of justice.

The idealpolitik of persuasion

The International Criminal Court embodies cosmopolitan sentiments which decouple law from territorial confines and discursively minimize the role of sovereign powers in determining claims to human rights and justice. The ICC seeks to transcend state borders by constructing universal morals and enforcing inalienable human rights norms through criminal justice prosecutions. Under this framework, rights are held by citizens of the earth rather than citizens of particular states, meaning that the ICC, as a supranational institution, is justified in prosecuting those accused of impinging upon victims' rights. Teitel (2002) argues that what he terms 'humanity's law' has growing reach, due to the merging of humanitarian law and international human rights law, which has created a global rule of law. The idea of a global rule of law or 'humanity's law' resonates with Kant's (1991, pp. 107–108) treatise that:

> the peoples of the earth have entered in varying degrees into a universal community, and it is developed to the point where a violation of laws in one part of the world is felt everywhere. The idea of a cosmopolitan law is therefore not fantastic and overstrained; it is a necessary complement to the unwritten code of political and international law, transforming into a universal law of humanity.

The International Criminal Court enacts this vision of cosmopolitanism through its claims of universal justice. Kleingeld and Brown (2006, p. 10) describe the ICC as an innovative form of cosmopolitanism in which 'individuals are now the bearers of certain rights under international law, and they can be held responsible for crimes under international law in ways that cut through the shield of state sovereignty'. The cosmopolitan underpinnings of international criminal justice are reflected in much discourse surrounding the ICC—for example, the opening phrases of the Rome Statute Preamble, the founding document of the ICC, declares States Parties to be 'conscious that all peoples are united by common bonds, their cultures pieced together in a shared heritage, and concerned that this delicate mosaic may be shattered at any time'. The Preamble also recognizes 'that such grave crimes threaten the peace, security and well-being of the world'. Such idealistic prose highlights the collectivity of the world and invokes the concept of humanity which must be protected through international law and justice. As this rhetoric illustrates, the Court relies on cosmopolitan values of universality and collectivity and thus plays into the 'space-less and neutral universalism of post-war global institutions' (Minca and Vaughan-Williams 2012, p. 765). This constructs one of the core roles of the ICC—to act as a norm-building institution that can develop and enforce a global rule of law and set international standards of justice.

Paradoxically, although the ICC relies heavily on cosmopolitanism and going beyond the sovereign state, the Court exists within, and must navigate, a state-based system and is reliant on states as its constitutive members and for support in its investigations and prosecutions. The Court must, therefore, continue to respect the sovereignty of states, which is why it was designed to be a court of last resort. The role of the ICC as a court of last resort is reflected in the principle of complementarity, which means that the Court can only act in situations where national jurisdictions are unwilling or unable to do so. The principle of complementarity is mentioned throughout the Rome Statute Preamble, as follows:

> Affirming that the most serious crimes of concern to the international community as a whole must not go unpunished and that their effective prosecution must be ensured by taking measures at the national level and by enhancing international cooperation, . . . Recalling that it is the duty of every State to exercise its criminal jurisdiction over those responsible for international crimes, . . . Emphasizing that the International Criminal Court established under this Statute shall be complementary to national criminal jurisdictions.

Through these phrases the Court asserts the responsibility of national jurisdictions to prosecute the international crimes codified in the Rome Statute. The Court can thus act in a persuasive manner by threatening to investigate situations if a nation state does not undertake appropriate judicial action. The threat of the ICC rests in its potential for prosecutions in these situations, and this mechanism is designed to persuade local jurisdictions to act in a manner consistent with the international standards and norms defined by the ICC. Such a persuasive role was played by the ICC in its warnings to countries such as the Côte d'Ivoire and Kenya. In such situations the ICC envisages its role as encouraging national prosecutions, which must comply with the ideas of justice embodied in the Rome Statute. Thus the Rome Statute is held as a standard which national jurisdictions must adhere to and this gives the Court the capacity to 'catalyse' national prosecutions (HRW 2011b) and encourage the implementation of criminal justice standards in nation states.

Often the implementation of legislation in line with the Rome Statute is encouraged by NGOs and human rights organizations that campaign for countries to ratify the Rome Statute and implement appropriate legislation. Here, the ICC is characterized as a valuable tool that can be used by a variety of actors to encourage the implementation of national legislation and adoption of liberal principles of criminal justice. In addition to implementing new legislation, the ICC is also considered a tool that can be used to develop human rights standards in developing countries. One area in which the ICC is used to bring about changes in human rights standards is the issue of women's rights. Several NGOs have used the ICC and the Rome Statute to try to influence the treatment of women in developing countries. This use of the ICC as a tool illustrates the close connection between the ICC and human rights. Here the threat of punishment is used, but the Court plays more of a persuasive role and attempts to enforce a normative framework for international society, based on human rights standards.

This construction of the Court's persuasive and denunciatory aims reflects Durkheim's (1960, 1984) conceptualization of punishment as a means of creating social solidarity and establishing and reinforcing the conscious collective (see also Hudson 2003a and Garland 1990 for further analysis of Durkheim's theories of punishment). Viewed from this perspective, the ICC seeks to build an international society through the denunciation of crime and the development of an international conscious collective. Thus, rather than representing a pre-established normative order, the ICC's symbolic prosecutions seek to build one.

Realpolitik: issues with the ICC's normative role

There are several issues associated with the ICC's aim of creating a normative framework for international society. This conceptualization considers the Rome Statute to reflect the consensus of an international community. Instead, the creation of the Rome Statute and the ICC was a process of negotiation, contestation and concession (Kirsch and Holmes 1999), reflecting divisions, realpolitik, and the material interests of states (Rudolph 2001), rather than the interests of humanity as a whole. Of the countries that were involved in the creation of the Rome Statute, many disagreed with some aspects of the Rome Statute and therefore refused to support the final proposal for the Court. For example, India did not support exclusion of the use of nuclear weapons as an international crime, while Israel objected to the definition of occupation of territory, with both countries refusing to accept the Statute. Although many countries argued for terrorism to come under the purview of the Court, there was no consensus on this issue and terrorism was not included in the Statute. Similarly, there was much disagreement over the definition of the crime of aggression, meaning that even though aggression was included in the Rome Statue, it was not able to be prosecuted until adequate consensus over the definition of aggression was achieved.

The shape of the ICC and the types of crimes it prosecutes is also vastly different to how some envisaged. For example, when Trinidad and Tobago first resurrected the idea of an international criminal court, they intended for it to prosecute transnational crimes, such as drug trafficking and money laundering (Schiff 2008); however, such crimes are not included in the Rome Statute. Even the structure of the Court was a concession, with the merging of civil and common law systems forming the ultimate shape of the Court. These are clear examples of the influence of realpolitik on the creation of the Rome Statute and the ultimate shape of the ICC. For these reasons the Rome Statute can be considered a package deal (Kirsch and Holmes 1999) 'marked by concessions made to great power interests' (Rudolph 2001, p. 678), rather than a reflection of the consensus of an international community. This delegitimizes the ICC's assertion of impartially enforcing a normative framework for the international community. The ICC's assertion of a consensus-based moral code is made more problematic by the Court's lack of accountability. As opposed to national courts, the ICC is an independent institution lacking the support of a broader system of justice, meaning it lacks a crucial system of checks and balances (Laughland 2008). In recent literature, the issue of accountability has been raised in regard to the chief prosecutor and his power to initiate and undertake investigations with little accountability (Danner 2003; Stenning 2013). The development of a normative framework, in conditions of unaccountability, is problematic, particularly as the development of the Court represents partial interests.

Today, the Court is still far from being universal; currently, 123 states have ratified the Rome Statute, just a third of UN member states. The ICC lacks support from powerful countries, such as the United States—which has vehemently opposed the ICC—Russia and China. Many less powerful nations also reject the authority of the ICC. Without universality the Court remains a partial institution that does not embody international consensus, but rather serves to reinforce geopolitical divides through selective prosecutions and narrow definitions of crime. Thus, instead of reflecting international collectivity, the ICC seeks to build international consensus through the enforcement of its standards and the use of the ICC and the Rome Statute as tools to change domestic legislation.

Cosmopolitan justice or lawfare?

The Court embodies the term 'lawfare' where the threat of law and prosecution is used in place of the threat of war (Scheffer 2010). The term 'lawfare' parallels with ideas of the Court as a weapon that can be used to threaten or persuade certain types of behaviour in particular situations. The United States has applied the term to the ICC (Scheffer 2010); however, the United States' fears that it could be the target of the ICC are misplaced, as it has instead been less powerful countries, particularly African countries, that have been brought before the Court. This concept is exemplified by the situation in Sudan. Here, powerful countries, such as Britain, have publicly backed the indictment of Sudan's president Omar al-Bashir (Economist 2011). However, a recent document published by WikiLeaks exposed that Britain regards the ICC's indictment of al-Bashir as 'unhelpful', and instead sees the ICC as a 'chip to be exchanged for setting south Sudan free and making peace in Darfur' (Economist 2011, n.p.). As *The Economist* highlights, it 'does nothing for the ICC's credibility to be seen as a pawn in a foreign power's chess game' (Economist 2011, n.p.). Such characterizations problematize the ICC's ideal of enforcing a normative framework and being used impartially as a tool for development and legislative change. Instead, by labelling particular cases and situations as crimes, the ICC serves to define the enemies of mankind (Nouwen and Werner 2011) and in this sense is used as a weapon to achieve realpolitik objectives in the uneven terrain of the international environment.

Although the ICC aims to enforce human rights standards and set a normative framework for dealing with mass atrocities, in order to do so the Court is forced to negotiate many political obstacles and navigate through the complex normative and strategic terrain of international society (Ruldolph 2001, p. 657). In the fragmented international environment, the ICC's ability to implement a normative framework is problematic, due to the ICC's lack of accountability, and limited, due to the lack of consensus on international criminal justice and the domination of realpolitik (Ruldolph 2001, p. 656). As this illustrates, it is difficult for the ICC to escape being used as a political weapon. This is because 'determining who is "on the political side" or not is inherently political, especially when it involves the labelling of groups and individuals as international criminals' (Nouwen and Werner 2011, p. 962) and no consensus exists in the international community; even the idea that an international community exists is itself problematic.

2.4 Aims of prevention

Alongside the ICC's persuasive aims, preventative aims of 'ending impunity' and deterring international crimes are also prominent for the ICC. The preventative aims of the ICC are influenced by the historical contexts and narratives that shape international criminal justice. One such narrative is the notion of 'never again', which can be traced back to discourse surrounding the Nuremberg Tribunals. The mantra of 'never again' captured the sentiment of the international community that mass atrocities, such as the Holocaust, should never be repeated.

The Nuremberg Tribunals embodied this spirit of non-repetition, as judicial/legal responses to Nazi war crimes were constructed as a decisive stand against international crimes and a means of reinstating order (Chesterman 1997). The principle of 'never again' was a strong justificatory foundation for Nuremberg, as demonstrated by Justice Jackson (1946), Chief of Counsel for the United States at Nuremberg, who stated in his opening address to the tribunal, 'The wrongs we seek to condemn and punish have been so calculated, so malignant, and so devastating that civilization cannot tolerate their being ignored, because it cannot survive their being repeated.'

Since Nuremberg, there have been many mass atrocities around the world, yet the spirit of 'never again' has remained and has provided the impetus for the creation of the two ad hoc tribunals, the ICTY and the ICTR, as well as the ICC. Indeed, 'never again' featured prominently in Rome Statute negotiations for the ICC. Kofi Annan (cited in UN Information Service 2002, n.p.) declared that the message from the international community in negotiating an ICC was clear: 'Never again would it stand aside and let the fabric of humanity be torn asunder by those who commit genocide, crimes against humanity, war crimes and the crime of aggression.' The idea of 'never again' continues to infuse the rhetoric of the Court. At the Review Conference of the ICC in Kampala, in 2010, the then Chief Prosecutor of the ICC, Luis Moreno-Ocampo (2010, p. 2), stated:

> The Rome Statute . . . transformed the words 'never again' from a moral promise to the victims, into a legal duty. . . . Never again will victims of atrocities be ignored. This is the time of action, to show how the law is implemented.

As this remark illustrates, there is a close link between the rhetoric of 'never again' and calls for legal action and intervention in response to emerging atrocities. The repetition of 'never again' provides a primary rationale for the ICC and demonstrates the provenance of the ICC's preventative aims of deterrence and 'ending impunity'.

The idealpolitik of ending impunity

The overarching aim of prevention is often expressed by the ideal of 'ending impunity', a mantra which is ever-present in discourses surrounding the ICC. For example, the Rome Statute Preamble states, 'Determined to put an end to impunity for the perpetrators of these crimes and thus to contribute to the prevention of such crime.' This reference to 'ending impunity' explicitly constructs prevention as the primary aim of the Court and this is mirrored in many discourses surrounding the ICC. At the Rome Conference, numerous participants asserted ending impunity and preventing international crimes as the primary rationales for the Court—for example, Mary Robinson, UN High Commissioner for Human Rights (1998, n.p.), stated, 'When I am asked what an International Criminal Court would do, I have a very simple answer. It would fight impunity. I can think of no greater contribution to the promotion or protection of fundamental human rights.' Similarly, William Pace, (President of the NGO Coalition for an ICC (the CICC)) claimed that:

> the establishment of an international criminal court would represent a monumental advance, acting as a deterrent and strengthening national legal systems for prosecuting crimes against humanity. It would save millions of humans from suffering unspeakably horrible and inhumane death in the coming decades.
>
> (UN 1998, p. 192)

Such aspirational statements continue to infuse discourse surrounding the Court. The Office of the Prosecutor (OTP) (ICC 2009b, p. 1) states, that the aim of the Court is 'to help end impunity for the perpetrators of the most serious crimes, of concern to the international community as a whole, and thus, to contribute to the prevention of such crimes'. Recently, at the Kampala Review Conference, Ban Ki Moon (cited in UN 2010, n.p.) proclaimed:

> The old era of impunity is over. In its place, slowly but surely, we are witnessing the birth of a new Age of Accountability. . . . In this new age of accountability, those who commit the worst of human crimes will be held responsible. Whether they are rank-and-file foot soldiers or military commanders, whether they are lowly civil servants following orders, or top political leaders, they will be held accountable.

Such quotations characterize the ICC as a positive and powerful weapon in the fight against impunity. The conceptualization of the ICC as a 'weapon' implicitly underpins much of the idealistic discourse on ending impunity and this idea is also often stated explicitly—for example, during the Rome Conference:

> We must admit that the international community, through the United Nations, has a poor record in preventing and stopping such acts. We have lacked means, lacked political will and we have lacked an effective weapon against the culture of impunity
>
> (UN High Commissioner for Human Rights 1998, n.p.)

> Our task is to take this text and turn it into a court room made of bricks and mortar that will give our children a weapon with which to fight the malevolent tendencies that have stained this century.
>
> (Alexander Downer, Australian Minister for Foreign Affairs 1998, n.p.)

Characterizations of the Court as a powerful weapon demonstrate a strong belief in the deterrent capacity of the Court (Mullins and Rothe 2010). This belief in deterrence and prevention, coupled with the permanency of the Court, allows the ICC to be characterized as a weapon that can be wielded at any time against any person, regardless of their rank or status, and thus end impunity.

Prosecutorial strategies to end impunity

Although the ICC has adopted a framework of individual criminal responsibility, transplanted from national conceptions of criminal justice (Robinson 2008), the Court does not have the resources to prosecute every actor who contributes to mass atrocities and widespread violence in the situations it investigates (O'Donohue 2005). Accordingly, the Court has adopted the prosecutorial strategy of pursuing the 'big fish' (Takemura 2007), where the Prosecutor focuses 'on those who bear the greatest responsibility, such as the leaders of the State or organisation allegedly responsible for those crimes' (ICC OTP 2003a, p. 7).

The strategy of prosecuting 'those most responsible' uses highly visible cases as symbolic exemplars to demonstrate the potential punishments for international crimes and thus achieve general deterrence. The OTP argues that high-ranking officials act in a calculated and rational manner when orchestrating and commanding international crimes, and thus the threat of punishment can be an effective deterrent for rogue leaders (Akhavan 2001). Through this strategy the ICC seeks to end conflict and contribute to peace by incapacitating leaders in the midst of ongoing conflict and by achieving specific deterrence. The ICC also uses the principle of general deterrence to contribute to peace by undertaking highly visible and symbolic prosecutions in order to deter other individuals from perpetrating similar violence (HRW 2009b; Mullins and Rothe 2010). For example, when the ICC focused on Lubanga's use of child soldiers in Uganda, there were claims of a 'Lubanga effect' with Radhika Coomaraswamy, UN special envoy for children and armed conflict, highlighting the enormous impact of the ICC indictments, which have driven home the message that recruiting child soldiers was a serious offence (IRIN 2011). However, these claims are anecdotal and the deterrent effect is notoriously difficult to measure or prove (Mennecke 2007).

In a similar bid to prevent conflict, the ICC has issued early warnings or threats in its preliminary investigation stage to countries where violence has threatened to escalate (HRW 2011b). The prosecutor also used this strategy following election violence in Kenya in 2007–2008. In 2008, the prosecutor reminded Kenya that they were under the jurisdiction of the ICC and that the OTP carefully monitors such situations (ICC OTP 2008) in an effort to curb further incitement to violence (International Crisis Group 2012). In 2009, the prosecutor stated, 'the OTP continues to follow-up whether national proceedings into the post-election violence in Kenya in early 2008 are being conducted' (ICC OTP 2009a, p. 1).

Similarly, other groups or agencies have used the ICC as a warning to stop the escalation of violence—for example, in the Côte d'Ivoire, the UN special advisor on the prevention of genocide warned that the situation involving hate speech and incitement to violence on the government-controlled National Radio could be referred to the International Criminal Court (HRW 2009b). In 2011, the OTP also issued a statement (ICC 2011b). Recently, there have been similar warnings from diplomats labelling the violence in Syria as war crimes and threatening referral to the ICC (Goodman and Cumming-Bruce 2012). By acting as a weapon to end impunity, the ICC has been characterized as a positive tool in the peacemaker's toolkit (UN 1999).

The realpolitik of prevention

Despite the general belief in the deterrent capacity of the ICC, there are many political and practical realities that limit the ability of the Court to deter international crimes. First, the ICC's use of a framework of individual criminal responsibility inaccurately reflects the complex nature of international crimes and mass atrocities. The model of individual responsibility characterizes international crimes as perpetrated by several high-powered individuals and a small group of rational actors. Contrary to this, international crimes are committed in widespread manner with a range of actors, including militias, government officials, civilians, and international corporations playing a role in the commission of such crimes (Clarke 2009; Mullins and Rothe 2008a). Criminological literature suggests that in these conditions 'rationality can be overshadowed by the sentiments of ideology, religion, nationalism and at the most basic level, power and politics' (Rothe and Mullins 2010, p. 102). International crimes often engage powerful passions and self-transcending behavioural motives (Damaška 2008), in situations where the offender is likely to belong to a collective, sharing group values (Tallgren 2002), and are often committed out of passion or fear in anomic conditions in which violence has become normalized (Akhavan 2001). As the ICC is premised on liberalism's 'construction of the individual as the central unit of action' (Drumbl 2005, p. 542), it does not account for the 'organic' violence of international crimes. These realities undermine the concept of the rational actor, upon which deterrence is based, and thus limit the deterrent capacity of the Court.

Additionally, although in some cases the ICC has enacted its strategy of pursing high-profile individuals—most notable is the arrest warrant issued for Sudanese president Omar al-Bashir—often the ICC has targeted less powerful individuals, for example, Callixte Mbarushimana, alleged Executive Secretary of the Forces démocratiques de libération du Rwanda (FDLR) and alleged perpetrator of atrocities in the DRC. This contradicts the rhetoric of pursuing those most responsible for international crimes and instead produces scapegoats, who are held personally responsible for widespread and systemic crimes and are tenaciously pursued in order to produce maximum symbolic and deterrent effect. In this light, many individuals who come before the Court refuse to accept responsibility for the entirety of their charges. For example, during his initial appearance hearing Mbarushimana, who was charged with five counts of crimes against humanity and eight counts of war crimes relating to the situation in the DRC, stated:

> I understand the words that have been used in this reading of the charges, but I do not understand the basis upon which these accusations are made against myself because I was in no way involved in everything that has been said.
>
> (ICC 2011i, p. 8)

Another example is Thomas Lubanga in the DRC where some locals posed the question, 'Why is Lubanga on trial . . . when others who did the same thing are working within the government?' (Hochschild 2009, n.p.). Widespread crimes are thus attributed to a handful of individuals and this selectivity and inequity makes deterrence unlikely, as powerful leaders are able to evade prosecution by the ICC, as is seen with Omar al-Bashir.

Selectivity is not only present in the limited number of cases that come before the Court, but also in the types of crimes the ICC focuses on. In Uganda, the Lubanga case has been criticized for focusing heavily on the use of child soldiers as a war crime, while neglecting the prevalence of rape as a tool of war (Inder 2011). Such narrow prosecutions create an 'impunity gap' in which certain crimes are prosecuted while others remain unpunished (Gibb 2010). This selectivity can partly be explained by the Court's reliance on state support to enforce its arrest warrants, conduct investigations, and collect evidence, a situation which has seen the ICC perceived as a 'paper tiger' (HRW 2011b). The ICC's reliance on state support means that the Court has been unsuccessful in situations where it does not have the support of a situation country, as demonstrated by the indictment of Sudanese president Omar al-Bashir. In this case, the ICC attempted to enforce a symbolic, highly visible prosecution of a sitting head of state, with the aim of achieving both general and specific deterrence. However, this strategy failed and instead illustrated the weaknesses of the Court, as al-Bashir remains free, despite his known location and his travel to other African nations (BBC 2011b).

Following the UN Security Council's referral of the situation in Darfur to the ICC, Sudan characterized the Court as just another instrument in the toolbox of the United States and its allies to topple an Islamic regime of which they do not approve (Dealy 2009a). The Court's involvement in Sudan also caused the African Union to express hostility towards the Court for its exclusive focus on African countries and leaders (Kegoro 2011; Stearns 2011). In this situation, the ICC is depicted as a dangerous weapon that can be used by powerful countries against weaker countries or longstanding opponents (Dealy 2009a; Nouwen and Werner 2011).

Conversely, in situations where countries have referred their situation to the ICC, the Court becomes an inadvertent political actor as the prosecutor's decision on who to prosecute can be influenced by the political climate in the situation country, based on the need for state cooperation in facilitating prosecutions (Nouwen and Werner 2011). This is best exemplified by the situation in Uganda, where the government referred the situation involving the Lord's Resistance Army (LRA), its political opponents, to the ICC (ICC 2004). Here, the Ugandan government used the Court to prosecute opponents while asserting its own innocence, and the Court pursued members of the LRA as these prosecutions were more viable due to the support of the government (Nouwen and Werner 2011). As this illustrates, the necessity of state support makes the ICC vulnerable to realpolitik and to being used as a tool to cleave political divisions, or as a weapon to bring down opponents.

The ICC's weak deterrent capacity and potential to be used as a political weapon limits the ability of the Court to achieve its aim of ending violence and contributing to peace. Despite the prosecutor's early warnings and attempts to prevent the escalation of violence in Kenya and the Côte d'Ivoire, violence continued in these situations (ICC OTP 2009a; Chabas 2011). Additionally, in issuing too many precautionary warnings, the ICC risks further minimizing its deterrent capacity by creating a gap between what it threatens to do and what it can actually do, bearing in mind the political obstacles and limited resources it must work with. Considering this, critics question the role of justice in ongoing conflicts, arguing that, in order to achieve stability, diplomatic relations should take primacy over justice objectives to enable a region or country to be restored to relative peace (Astor 2008; Laughland 2008; Reynolds 2008).[4]

Practical prevention or symbolic deterrence?

The selectivity of the Court, based on local realpolitik and international geopolitics, significantly undermines the legitimacy of the ICC and its ability to achieve deterrence. The perceived threat of prosecution, crucial to the concept of deterrence (Mullins and Rothe 2010), is minimized by the selectivity of the cases and the necessity of state cooperation for arrest and surrender to the ICC. The ICC cannot pose a significant threat of prosecution if only a minimal number of individuals and selective crimes are prosecuted. Rothe and Mullins (2010, p. 110) highlight that 'if international law and its enforcement are not perceived as a real threat, general deterrence is negated'. The selective and minimal prosecutions of the ICC do not constitute a significant threat to a large number of individuals, meaning that the Court cannot be seen as a realistic or legitimate deterrence as 'the probability that the courts will realize the threat of punishment on their own is miniscule—unfortified by state support, they are powerless' (Damaška 2008, p. 345). Ban Ki Moon's bold declaration of the end of impunity in Uganda, a country still struggling to maintain peace with a government that has committed widespread mass atrocities (Mullins and Rothe 2008a), highlights the idealistic rhetoric which crowds discussions on the ICC.

This rhetoric leaves little space to consider the political realities of the international environment or the practical ability of the ICC to achieve these idealistic aims. It limits open discussion of alternative conceptions of international criminal justice, causing the perpetuation of the ubiquitous aims of ending impunity, deterrence, and prevention, largely due to a void of rational alternatives (Tallgren 2002). As Tallgren (2002, p. 561) argues, 'everybody knows that prevention does not work, . . . everybody knows, but the knowledge has no consequence'. The limited ability of the Court to achieve deterrence and prevention means that,

4 Of course, there is no guarantee that diplomatic measures are more successful and that justice should, therefore, be suspended until more stability is achieved. The fallibility of diplomatic measures was highlighted by the failed creation and signing of the ceasefire in 2006 in Darfur, since which violence has only worsened in the region (Steidle 2007).

instead of being a weapon against impunity, the ICC amplifies political struggles in the countries in which it intervenes, as is illustrated by the situation in Uganda, and also amplifies geopolitical divides on a global level, as is exemplified by the case of Sudan. The ICC is not universal and this means that more powerful countries face little risk of coming before the Court, while less powerful countries, such as Sudan, serve as symbolic and exemplary cases under the guise of general deterrence.

2.5 Concluding comments

This examination has illustrated the conflicting nature of the Court's aims and narratives. The ICC can be considered a positive weapon that can end impunity, achieve deterrence, prevent international crimes, contribute to peace, bring justice to victims, and proscribe and enforce human rights and normative standards. However, realpolitik limits each of these aims and makes the Court a weapon that can reinforce political divides and amplify political struggles at both a national and international level. Additionally, these aims are contradictory and by espousing such a wide range of aims the Court weakens its ability to achieve any of its aims, thus creating expectation and impunity gaps. The proliferation of multiple aims seeks to cover all discourses on international justice, from liberal principles of criminal justice and punishment, to human rights norms, to transitional justice imperatives. In doing this, the Court attempts to appease a fragmented and critical international society and address the multiple and polarized perspectives that surround it. This means that the Court uses idealpolitik to assert its legitimacy and authority on the international stage. This idealpolitik is a response to the contested international environment in which realpolitik limits the work of the Court and demands multiple aims, while at the same time limiting the ability of the Court to achieve these aims.

3 Tensions in the pursuit of justice

The ICC is increasingly defined by gaps between its ideals and its reality. There is a broad series of preventative and persuasive aims espoused for the ICC and the multiplicity of these aims, and the gaps between rhetoric and reality, create contradictions in the work of the Court, as demonstrated in Chapter 2. The fact that the ICC is beset by such contradictions and tensions does not make it unique: all justice systems are, to some extent, contradictory and partial arbiters of justice. Domestic justice systems are also plagued by gaps between ideal and reality and by conflicting and contradictory imaginings of what they should achieve and how they should achieve it. This chapter considers some of the tensions that occur at a domestic level and examines the qualities that differentiate international law and the ICC from domestic justice systems, making the embryonic system of international criminal justice particularly incongruous.

One of the main reasons that the ICC espouses multiple aims is that there are so many actors involved with the Court. Each of these actors has different ideas about the role of the ICC and its position in international society. The second half of this chapter considers how the ICC is socially constructed by a range of actors. As a nascent judicial institution, the ICC is seeking legitimacy and relevance on the world stage and has thus needed to be a flexible institution that can be many things to many different people. Viewed through this lens, the gaps and contradictions of the ICC become inevitable yet also productive as they result from the ICC's malleability, which allows it to be used by many different actors in many different settings. The idea that the ICC's contradictions could be productive mirrors Ewick and Silbey's (1999, p. 1037) theory that 'legality's power is sustained by its ability to mediate diverse normative aspirations'. The end of this chapter considers how the gaps and contradictions in law, and the ICC, ensure it is an enduring institution, a theme which is explored throughout the rest of this book.

3.1 Tensions in criminal justice systems

Criminal justice systems are often defined by multiple and conflicting aims. They are expected to deter future crimes, while punishing past crimes, and to uphold the rights of the accused, while also respecting the rights of victims and society.

They are tasked with responding to crime swiftly and efficiently as resources are finite and budgets are tightening; yet they must also ensure that investigations and trials are conducted thoroughly to avoid miscarriages of justice. Many of the core aims of criminal justice systems are fundamentally at odds with each other. Hudson (2003a), for example, highlights how utilitarian criminal justice aims, based on preventing future crime, clash with past-oriented retributivist aims that seek to punish offenders for their crimes. The goal of rehabilitating offenders may undermine the protection of society, which is often achieved through incapacitation. The desire to develop social norms by symbolically denouncing particular acts as criminal can clash with the goal of administering penalties that are specific to, and appropriate for, the individual circumstances of the offender.

In addition to these conflicting aims, the foundations and philosophical approaches to criminal justice can also differ within justice systems. For example, Hudson (2003a, p. 3) states that 'there is a perennial and unavoidable tension between protecting the rights of offenders not to be punished more than they deserve, and protecting the rights of the public not to be victims of crime'. Punitive and non-punitive approaches to criminal justice are also often contradictory and there is a clash between retributive and restorative paradigms (see Ashworth and Redmayne 2010 and Zedner 1994 for a discussion). Furthermore, there are tensions between different perspectives on how criminal justice systems should operate. Packer's (1964) theory on the 'Two models of the criminal process' highlights a division between the 'crime control' model of justice and the 'due process' model of justice. Under the crime control model, efficiency is paramount and the justice process can be viewed as a conveyer belt whereby cases are processed quickly to achieve law enforcement aims of preventing crime (Packer 1968). Conversely, the due process model emphasizes the importance of respecting judicial procedures and upholding the rights of the defendant (Packer 1968). Instead of a conveyer belt, the due process model can be likened to an obstacle course (Packer 1968). Packer's seminal work on these two conflicting models of justice has since been expanded by academics; for example, Roach (1999) proposes four models for the criminal justice system which includes two new models based on punitive and non-punitive ways of respecting victims' rights. Again, this highlights the tensions between retributive/punitive and restorative/non-punitive approaches to criminal justice.

In addition to these inherent tensions, criminal justice is particularly fragmented, incoherent, and contradictory in times of late modernity. Garland (2001, p. 138) examines governments' ambivalence in response to the high crime rates associated with late modernity, stating, 'Over the last two decades, populist, punitive, state-centre policies have accompanied and contradicted the strategies of normalising crime, responsibilising others and defining deviance down'. O'Malley (1999) suggests that incoherent criminal justice policies stem from contradictory elements of New Right politics, which involves both neo-conservative (nostalgic) state authoritarian strategies and neoliberal strategies, based on minimal state interference, private sector involvement, and the strategy of responsibilizing individuals. The coexistence of these two social structures results in criminal justice being defined through a series of dichotomies, such as 'disciplinary obedience versus enterprising autonomy, incapacitation and warehousing versus correctional reform, punishment and stigmatization versus reintegration, formal criminalizing versus informal victim/offender settlements' (O'Malley 1999, p. 176). Chapter 4 explores late modernity and its impact on crime control and the ICC in more depth. The point here is that broad social forces and structures contribute to contradictions in criminal justice systems at a domestic level.

Another primary reason for tensions in domestic justice systems is that justice is not administered through a coherent 'system', but rather through a collection of different agencies (e.g. police, prosecutors, magistrates and judges, and prison personnel), each of which has different aims, functions, and values (Daly 2012). Sarre (2012, p. 435) supports this point, stating that, while we may often refer to a criminal justice 'system', 'in truth, it is not a system at all, rather a convenient arrangement of a number of state-run bureaucratic institutions that deal with offending and offenders' (Sarre 2012, p. 435). Conflicts thus arise as different agencies seek to fulfil their particular functions and operate according to their own bureaucratic interests (Sarre 2012). This discussion raises an important theme that is explored throughout this book: there are many different actors who operate within the realm of criminal justice and these actors have different aims and interests, which create tensions and conflicts in the administration of justice (see Chapters 5 and 6 for an exploration of how different actors construct the aims of the ICC according to their own interests and functions).

Structure of the ICC

The above discussion introduces the idea that many of the contradictions in criminal justice aims stem from clashes between different agencies, as they work as part of a criminal justice 'system', while also trying to achieve their own unique goals in both an instrumental and symbolic capacity (Daly 2012). In contrast to domestic justice systems, the International Criminal Court does not have clearly separated powers and agencies to enforce its many aims, and it does not exist within a wider system of criminal justice that provides some level of consensus as to the overarching goals of justice. Instead, the ICC exists as a solitary institution in which multiple facets of criminal justice, including investigation, adjudication, and punishment, are amalgamated—which has raised questions over the Court's legitimacy and authority (Takemura 2012). The ICC's position as a solitary institution does not mean that it avoids the pitfalls of the collection of agencies that constitute domestic justice systems. Instead, the ICC is internally divided and fragmented, as is explored below.

One element that contributes to the ICC's fragmentation is the fact that it combines the adversarial approach of common law traditions with the inquisitorial approach of civil law traditions (Schabas 2004), mirroring the trends of the ad hoc tribunals (Burke-White 2004; Mundis 2001). This merging of legal cultures helped to create unity between different countries and, in particular, helped form a new 'global legal culture' during negotiations surrounding the Rome Statute (Burke-White 2004, p. 975). However, the blending of legal traditions creates tensions in the work of the Court (Schiff 2008) and poses unique challenges for the ICC (Tochilovsky 2003). A primary example is the clash between the roles of the Office of the Prosecutor (OTP) and the Pre-Trial Chamber (PTC). The OTP drives the system of prosecutions by initiating proceedings and bringing cases before the PTC for formal approval. This system gives the prosecutor powers similar to those of an adversarial system. At the same time the PTC is also afforded significant power to influence the direction of cases and trials, giving judges powers similar to those offered by the inquisitorial system (Schiff 2008). This has created inevitable clashes between the OTP and the PTC, as was evidenced in the case of both Uganda and the Democratic Republic of Congo (Schiff 2008). The merging of civil and common law traditions has impacted upon the structure of the Court by creating a Pre-Trial Division that is actively involved in the organization and supervision of each case during the pre-trial phrase (Sadat and Carden 2000), as well as an independent prosecutor with considerable power and prosecutorial discretion (Schabas 2008).

The OTP and PTC fit within the wider structure of the ICC. The Court is composed of four main organs: the Presidency, the Judiciary, the Office of the Prosecutor, and the Registry (Rome Statute 1998, Article 34). The Presidency is responsible for the overall administration of the Court, with the exception of the Office of the Prosecutor, and is composed of three judges who are elected by their fellow judges from the Judicial Division (Rome Statute 1998, Article 38). The Judicial Division is composed of 18 judges (Rome Statute 1998, Article 36(1)) and is separated into three distinct divisions: the Pre-Trial Division, the Trial Division, and the Appeals Division (Rome Statute 1998, Article 39).

The Office of the Prosecutor is an independent and separate organ of the Court. The OTP is responsible for receiving referrals and any substantiated information on crimes within the jurisdiction of the Court, for examining them, and for conducting investigations and prosecutions before the Court (Rome Statute 1998, Article 42). As highlighted above, although the OTP has a large amount of power and prosecutorial discretion, this is balanced by the supervisory role of the Pre-Trial Chambers (Sadat and Caden 2000) who have often had a more ambitious view of their powers than the prosecutor (Schabas 2008, p. 756). The Registry acts as the administrative organ of the Court and is also responsible for the operation of the Victims and Witnesses Unit (Rome Statute 1998, Article 43). There are several other semi-autonomous bodies that also contribute to the work of the Court but sit external to the Court's main structure, including the Office of Public Counsel for Victims, the Office of Public Counsel for Defence, and the Trust Fund for Victims.

To provide an oversight function for the Court, the Rome Statute created the Assembly of States Parties (ASP), which provides management, considers budgetary issues, and elects the judges, prosecutor and deputy prosecutor, among other tasks (Rome Statute 1998, Article 112). The ASP is composed of one representative from each member state. The ICC was established by multilateral treaty rather than as an organ of the United Nations, which means that the ASP is the body responsible for financing the Court and determining the bureaucratic structure (Sadat and Caden 2000). The ICC's relationship with the United Nations is therefore limited, particularly in comparison to the ad hoc tribunals (Cassese 1998); however, as the following chapters will highlight, the United Nations still has the ability to significantly influence the ICC, its jurisdiction, and the situations that come before it.

The ICC is divided and heavily influenced by a wide range of external actors, yet it is only one court focused on conducting symbolic trials. In domestic justice systems the trial stage represents only one part of the criminal justice process. For this reason, Duff et al. (2004b, p. 11) explain that the trial can only be theorized within a wider framework of justice and cannot be analysed in isolation. For the ICC, the trial is the primary part of the justice process as the ICC is not sitting within a formal system of justice. In addition, domestic justice systems have different tiers of courts to deal with different aspects of crime and therefore limit clashes between competing aims of justice. For example, lower courts can deal with minor offences in a manner more attuned to the crime control model of justice, whereas higher courts can deal with serious offences along the lines of the due process model. The ICC does not exist within such a court hierarchy, meaning it is expected to achieve much more than domestic courts while dealing with conflicting aims and models of justice. This is one of the reasons the ICC adopts the principle of complementarity, which means that in theory it will only prosecute the most serious international crimes while domestic jurisdictions are tasked with responding to the bulk of crimes.

As this brief overview demonstrates, the ICC is a fragmented institution comprised of several different agencies and influenced by numerous external actors. Each of these agencies has different aims and interests, and seeks to assert these interests in their work with the ICC. The ambivalent and contradictory nature of the ICC comes, in part, from internal conflicts that arise as one institution seeks to perform numerous roles and is pulled in many different directions by its multiple identities as a criminal justice 'system' in and of itself.

3.2 Tensions in international law

In addition to the structural tensions described in the previous section, the ICC is further defined by the tensions that are inherent in international law. Whereas domestic justice systems are embedded within established legal traditions, creating a comparatively coherent arrangement, the ICC builds on the developing field of international criminal law, which brings with it several structural tensions. The Court has developed incrementally and often in response to unfolding conflicts. This development mirrors Charlesworth's (2002) description of international law as a 'discipline of crisis' that is shaped by responses to contingent and urgent events. Further to this, Koskenniemi and Leino (2002) explore how international law is fragmented due to its evolution through the development of different judicial institutions in a post-modern environment. Many of the ICC's tensions and inconsistencies are grounded in the contradictions of international criminal law.

Human rights and international law frameworks

One of the major contributors to the structural tensions in international criminal justice is the way international criminal law has emerged through the assimilation of human rights and criminal law frameworks. Robinson (2008) highlights that international criminal law suffers an identity crisis, stemming from the amalgamation of the liberal principles of national criminal law with the normative assumptions of human rights. Teitel (2002, p. 362) further outlines the tensions resulting from the blending of human rights and international law, stating:

> the merger between humanitarian law and human rights law gives rise to a complicated and somewhat contradictory legal regime that challenges the very basis of longstanding notions of international rule of law. Whereas international rule of law was defined in terms relating to state sovereignty and self-determination, there is now a shift to a juridical definition of the state and an alternative discourse framed in the universalizing language of human rights.

Human rights significantly influenced the development of the ICC by constructing the need for a judicial institution to enforce standards in the wake of war, conflict, and violence (Glasius 2006; Teitel 2002). The coupling of human rights norms with the framework of criminal justice invokes punishment as a preventative mechanism to reinforce the legitimacy of human rights standards (Basssouni 1982). Schabas (2006, p. 424) explains this link between international criminal law and human rights:

> it is now well understood that the protection of such core human rights as the right to life and to dignity, . . . imposes positive obligations upon states. Not only must they refrain from such practices in a direct sense, they must also ensure that individuals who perpetrate such atrocities are brought to justice.

Through the merging of principles of criminal law and human rights, the prosecution of human rights violations becomes imperative and international criminal justice is validated.

The victim-oriented field of human rights is founded on idealistic standards that have moral resonance (Nussbaum 1997). Contrastingly, international law is focused on judicial processes whereby individual actors are prosecuted and punished for proscribed crimes (Ainley 2011). International law adds a practical element to idealistic human rights assumptions. The merging of the fields of human rights and international law thus produces highly idealistic aims that are reinforced through the practical constructions of international criminal justice, associated with international law. The Court is perceived as apolitical and criminal justice processes are justified as fair, impartial substitutes for political processes (this is explored further in Chapter 5).

However, despite the positive rhetoric, the strong influence of human rights assumptions sees international criminal law departing from the core principles of liberal criminal justice; for example, the principle of personal culpability is undermined by the development of joint criminal enterprise (Robinson 2008). Additionally, the victim-oriented focus of human rights (Schabas 2006) skews the focus of the ICC and contradicts the principles of equality that underpin liberal notions of criminal justice (Robinson 2008). The fusion of the fields of international law and human rights means that processes of international criminal justice and the individualistic framework of international law are used to achieve broader, idealistic social aims, such as setting standards, preventing international crimes, and bringing justice to victims. However, the individual-centred framework of international law cannot practically achieve these broader goals (Ainley 2011; Drumbl 2005; Oisel 2000, 2009; Simpson 2007). This causes contradictions—for example, the ICC seeks to have broad social effect through its adoption of the principle of general deterrence and the goal of setting international standards of criminal justice (aims of prevention and persuasion as examined in Chapter 2). It achieves these goals by selectively prosecuting a few symbolic, individual cases. However, the broad social goals underpinning these prosecutions can hamper fair trial standards and deny proportionate justice for the defendant. Additionally, the individual focus inadequately accounts for the widespread harm caused by mass atrocities (Robinson 2008).

The search for legitimacy

Another tension inherent in the ICC's international law framework is its desire to transcend the sovereignty of states, while simultaneously relying heavily on states for its existence and operation (Chazal 2013). Many states have an ambivalent relationship with the ICC, wishing it to operate effectively, but only if that means that they will not be prosecuted themselves. Other states have rejected the ICC and several powerful countries such as the United States, Russia, and China have actively opposed the ICC and refused to accept its authority or jurisdiction (Goldsmith 2003; Jianping and Zhixiang 2005; Ralph 2007; Rothe and Mullins 2006b; Tuzmukhamedov 2005).

The ICC has faced much resistance and scepticism (Orentlicher 2003) and has been referred to as a 'self-defeating' institution (Goldsmith 2003). It has been criticized for undermining delicate peace processes (Astor 2008), for enacting and enhancing local political struggles, and for mirroring broader geopolitical issues (Nouwen and Werner 2011). There has also been critique of the Court's selection of cases, the prosecution strategies of the chief prosecutor of the ICC, and the Court's collection and use of evidence (Flint and De Waal 2009). Additionally, the ICC's displacement, in terms of the lack of a broader system of governance, raises questions over its legitimacy. This antagonistic environment has seen the ICC battle to assert its legitimacy and authority in a fragmented, and often hostile, political environment (Teitel 2002). Clark (2008, p. 37) encapsulates the situation well, describing the Court as 'a nascent global institution still defining its identity and purpose, endeavouring to secure the recognition and confidence of the States Parties that back it, and sometimes making inconsistent decisions that undermine its legitimacy'.

In the face of such criticisms, the ICC has needed to expend much energy to justify its existence and prove its legitimacy, relevance, and authority on the world stage (Clark 2008; Rothe and Schoultz 2013). As such, the ICC has relied on idealpolitik based on simplistic yet inspirational narratives, such as the 'collectivity of humanity', the idea of 'never again', and a plethora of broad yet inspirational aims to garner support, mobilize international sentiment, and defend its existence. The idealistic narratives and aims that surround the Court are, in part, a reaction to persistent criticisms of the Court and an attempt to garner the enthusiasm required to support the work of the ICC. The aims, outlined in Chapter 2, provide an axiomatic foundation for the ICC that appeals to international sentiment and conscience. After all, questioning the goal to stop mass atrocities and prevent the widespread victimization and destruction associated with international crimes invites much criticism and derision. Aims such as prevention and persuasion provide a convincing and appealing rationale for the Court, and this rationale counteracts antagonistic discourses, even if the ICC's ability to practically achieve such aims is limited.

The perpetuation of idealistic aims and narratives, however, does little to develop the Court, but rather creates polarized debates between the idealistic visions of ICC supporters and the practical and political objections of ardent opponents of the Court. As Chapter 2 highlighted, the ICC is simultaneously characterized as both a positive tool that can end impunity and enforce human rights standards (Bassiouni 2000; Moreno-Ocampo 2009) and as a negative weapon that can amplify political struggles, reinforce geopolitical divides, and undermine national sovereignty (Goldsmith 2003; Nouwen and Werner 2011; Rudolph 2001). Such polarized debates limit constructive critique and contribute to the underdeveloped theoretical foundations of the ICC and the series of contradictory and unachievable aims and rationales that underpin the Court (Drumbl 2005; Handmaker 2011).

The lack of discussion over the unique aims of international criminal justice has deepened the clash between pragmatic concerns and idealistic visions of global justice and creates a gap between the aims and the functioning of the ICC. The lofty ideals that sparked the initial enthusiasm required to introduce the ICC are, therefore, part of the problem, as the lack of a practical direction and pragmatic plan for the Court undermines these ideals and creates schisms and tensions in its work. These schisms create even more expectation and pressure for the Court while undermining support for the ICC. The Court requires support to secure funding. Funding limitations significantly constrain the work of the ICC, particularly considering the extent of the ICC's aims and the complexity of the cases it prosecutes. To give an idea of the budget the ICC works with, in 2013, the ICC spent €114.07 million against its approved budget of €115.12 million (ICC ASP 2014). Funding for the Court comes from contributions from States Parties and is managed through the Assembly of States Parties. If financial support for the

ICC wanes, based on a perceived lack of legitimacy, credibility, or effectiveness, the Court could risk creating further gaps between its idealistic aims and the reality of its operation.

3.3 Social construction, the juridical field, and the ICC

Section 3.1 explored how the existence of multiple actors and agencies within criminal justice systems can create tensions in the pursuit of justice at both an international and domestic level. It is, therefore, important to view actors as central to the construction of justice and the ICC, making a social constructivist approach (Berger and Luckmann 1966) useful for understanding the schisms in the work of the Court. Giddens (1984) argues that repeated social practice by individual actors constitutes society and gives society structural properties. He emphasizes the role of individuals in reproducing and transforming society, claiming that social transformation relies on the reflexive nature of human beings and their ability to use knowledge to reflect on and change their actions and practices (Giddens 1984). For Giddens (1984), reflexivity is the key to social change in late modernity, a point explored in more depth in Chapter 4. Accordingly, individual actors from a range of groups and organizations, including states, the United Nations, NGOs, and civil society organizations, have the ability to create and transform the ICC through their reflexive actions, interactions, and practices.

It is through reciprocal interactions with a range of groups that the identity and interests of the ICC are formed (Wendt 1992). At the same time, these interactions shape the identities and interests of actors who interact with the Court, as actors define their interests in the process of defining situations (Wendt 1992). This means that the ICC is produced through processes of social construction whereby interactions simultaneously form the identities and interests of the Court and the actors who interact with it. The following subsections explore how the ICC is socially constructed through actors' interactions with it, including how actors form groups, construct the ICC through ideas based on idealpolitik and realpolitik, and are constrained by the structures (or fields) within which they operate. This discussion demonstrates that these complex processes of social construction contribute to the tensions and gaps in the work of the ICC.

Actors, groups, and the negotiation of the Rome Statute

The international environment is complex and fragmented with multiple actors attempting to assert their interests through their association with institutions such as the ICC. From a social constructivist perspective, ideas and ideals play a large role in the process of identity formation within a complex environment (Finnemore and Sikkink 2001). Ideas, based on both idealpolitik and realpolitik (explored in the following subsection), provide unification in a world of multiple and fragmented perspectives, interests, and identities. Mobilization around common ideas constructs groups according to their interests, giving actors more power in interactions. The strategy of constructing common interests can unify diverse groups. This strategy is seen in social movements, which Stammers (1999, p. 984) describes as 'collective actors constituted by individuals who understand themselves to share some common interests and who also identify with one another, at least to some extent'. The formation of groups around collective interests and ideas was a key strategy during the Rome Statute Conference. The development of the ICC through processes of negotiation and interaction at the Rome Conference illustrates the reflexive ability of actors to affect change, and the additional power of these actors when they form groups and mobilize around ideas and common interests. During the Rome Conference negotiations three core groups formed. The first group, labelled P5, consisted of the five permanent members of the UN Security Council (China, the United Kingdom, France, Russia, and the United States) who shared the idea of an ICC that was closely monitored by the Security Council. The second group, including countries such as India, Egypt, and Mexico, mobilized around the inclusion of nuclear weapons in the Statute of the Court and opposed Security Council involvement in the Court. The third, the largest and the most influential group, was the Like-Minded Group of states (LMG), which included African states, Canada, most European states, and Latin American states.

The LMG aligned itself with NGOs in the lead-up to the conference and received sustained support from NGOs. The central ideas around which the LMG was based were: jurisdiction over core crimes (war crimes, genocide, crimes against humanity, and aggression); jurisdiction over both internal and international conflicts; and an independent and impartial court with an independent prosecutor who has the authority to initiate proceedings, while also maintaining a working relationship with the Security Council. The LMG focused on these mutual interests and achieved more power and presence through the articulation of their shared interests. The LMG provided benefits for states that had less power or no strong agenda of their own, and also provided a counterbalance to the negotiating and bargaining power of the United States. Much has been written about the Rome Conference and the development of the Rome Statute of the ICC (see, for example, Rowe, McGoldrick, and Donnelly 2004; Sadat 2002; Schabas 2007b; Schiff 2008), but what is important to note here is the processes of negotiation and interaction which highlight the social construction of the Court, the reflexivity and ability of actors to shape social structures, and the strategy of using ideas to create groups, construct interests, and gain bargaining power in interactions. The Rome Statute Conference provides one example of how ideas form the basis of interactions and thus shape the construction of identity and interests.

Today, the Rome Statute significantly shapes and constrains the Court. As explored in Chapter 2, the Rome Statute can be described as a 'package deal' due to the complex negotiations around its development (Kirsch and Holmes 1999). The ICC must adhere to the rules codified in the Rome Statue and, as those who work with the Court have highlighted (discussed in more depth in Chapter 5), the Rome Statute Preamble shapes the aims, vision, and direction of the Court.

Social construction: idealpolitik and realpolitik

The ideas that groups use to construct the ICC can take the form of both idealpolitik and realpolitik (Atkinson 2011). Idealpolitik refers to circumstances where 'behaviour is dictated by "principles of legitimacy" and conditions where normative principles are privileged over simple power politics' (Atkinson 2011, p. 101). The ideas that underpin idealpolitik are predominantly normative or ideal-based. Normative-based idealpolitik is illustrated by the LMG of states at the Rome Conference, whose negotiations were based on ideals about justice and fairness, as discussed in the previous section. Conversely, the ideas that constitute realpolitik focus on power politics and strategic political interests (Rudolph 2001). The ideas of the P5 group of states during the Rome Conference provide an illustration of realpolitik, as the notion of a Court controlled by the Security Council clearly aligns with the political interests of these countries and their privileged status within the United Nations, as permanent members of the Security Council. Of course, normative ideas can, and often do, coincide with political interests. An example of the confluence of normative ideas and political interests is the groups of states seeking coverage of nuclear weapons by the ICC. This position could represent an ideological standpoint against the use of nuclear weapons and the damage they cause, yet could equally represent the strategic interests of these countries in relation to the use of nuclear weapons.

Actors and groups use idealpolitik and realpolitik to shape their interactions with the ICC. A key example of the use of idealpolitik in the construction of the Court is the international NGOs that support the work of the Court and use ideals, based on human rights, to construct the Court as a positive institution that can end impunity, achieve peace, and bring justice to victims. The Coalition for the International Criminal Court (CICC) is an organization that represents 2,500 civil society organizations in 150 different countries and illustrates the unification of diverse groups through the construction of common ideas and principles. The CICC typifies the strategy of using ideas to form groups and gain greater influence in the construction of the ICC and their own identities and interests.

The CICC works on the common principle of strengthening international cooperation with the ICC and aims to 'ensure that the Court is fair, effective and independent; make justice both visible and universal; and advance stronger national laws that deliver justice to victims of war crimes, crimes against humanity and genocide' (CICC 2015, n.p.). These broad aims unify an otherwise diverse group. For example, the Coalition consists of a large number of victims' rights groups, but also represents groups who advocate for the rights of the defence. Through interactions with the ICC, the CICC constructs its own identities and interests, as well as those of its constituent groups and actors and, importantly, constructs the identity and interests of the ICC.

The Court is also constructed through indirect interactions with supportive actors and broader social movements around international justice and mass atrocities. An example of this is the recent use of idealpolitik in the Kony 2012 campaign. The Kony 2012 documentary and campaign was led by the US-based organization Invisible Children, and aimed to stop Joseph Kony, the leader of the Ugandan rebel group, the Lord's Resistance Army, who has been accused of using child soldiers in the Ugandan war. This documentary exemplifies the use of idealpolitik as it is underpinned by ideologies of justice, fairness, and equality, coupled with the mobilization of world citizens and their conceptions of right and wrong or good and bad. The Court was able to connect to such campaigns and construct itself through the idealpolitik of ending impunity, stopping criminals, and bringing justice to the world. Such campaigns powerfully construct ideas of international justice and the ICC is able to locate itself within this ideology. The Chief Prosecutor of the ICC, Luis Moreno-Ocampo, featured in the documentary and later supported the movement, claiming the documentary mobilized the world and that the viral strategy and campaign to make international criminals famous could assist in the fight for international justice (Holligan 2012). This example illustrates the power of idealpolitik and the construction of the ICC through such campaigns, in addition to the interactions of NGOs who work closely with the Court.

At the same time, the ICC interacts with groups whose ideas are based on realpolitik, such as the United States, and these interactions shape the Court while also constructing the identity and interests of the United States. A primary example of this reciprocal identity formation is the United States' negotiation of Bilateral Immunity Agreements (BIAs).[1] BIAs are agreements with states that shield US citizens from ICC prosecution, in the event that these citizens are implicated in serious crimes of states that are subject to ICC jurisdiction (HRW 2003a). Although these agreements are inconsistent with States Parties' obligations under the ICC Statute, numerous ICC States Parties have signed the agreement, including Uganda, who referred its own situation to the Court (ICC 2004; US Department of State 2003). The United States has taken similar measures against the Court. For example, in 2004 the United States introduced the American Service Members Act, which prohibited US cooperation with the ICC, authorized the president to use all means necessary to free US and allied personnel detained by the ICC, refused military aid to ICC States Parties (except major US allies), and prohibited US participation in peacekeeping, unless immunity from the ICC was granted for US personnel (Benzing 2004).

These interactions construct the ICC as an institution lacking power, authority, and legitimacy on the world stage. They also simultaneously shape the identity of the United States by confirming its status as a superpower that sits above international criminal justice. Throughout these interactions, the United States was also constructed as a detractor of human rights and international justice,

1 The negotiations of BIAs formed part of a wider series of interactions with the Court. Since the negotiation of the Rome Statute, the United States has opposed the ICC (Rothe and Mullins 2006b). The United States signed the Rome Statute treaty at the last moment of the Rome Conference and with a series of caveats that meant that US ratification of the treaty was unlikely (Ettari 2005). The United States later withdrew their signature from the Rome Statute.

particularly by major NGOs such as Human Rights Watch (HRW 2003a). The United States' strategic interactions with the Court, from the withdrawal of their signature on the Rome Statute treaty to the BIAs and the American Service Members Act, illustrate how realpolitik influences constructions of the Court in a complex international environment.

As these examples show, the ICC is constructed through its interactions with groups who both oppose it, such as the United States, and groups who support it, such as international NGOs and organizations, for example, the CICC. This makes tensions between idealpolitik and realpolitik inevitable; the two will always exist as the Court is constructed through its interactions with a range of actors. The construction of such clear boundaries between idealpolitik and realpolitik and the construction of groups, such as the CICC and the United States, are, of course, a simplification of the fragmentation and complexity of international society. There are NGOs who oppose the Court (e.g. ICC Watch) just as there are groups within the United States that support the Court (e.g. Coalition for the ICC, a US-based NGO). The categorization of clear groups and the binaries of idealpolitik and realpolitik are themselves constructions; however, they are useful as ideal types that illustrate the macro processes of social construction that shape the ICC. It is through these interactions that the ICC forms its identity and interests, and the Court can, therefore, be described as a 'looking-glass self', whereby the Court's identity is constituted through the reflection of others' perceptions of it. As the Court interacts with a diverse range of groups, whose interests, identities, and perceptions of it vary, the ICC's reflected identity will inevitably mirror the complexities, contradictions, and pluralities that define international society, making idealpolitik and realpolitik equal parts of the construction of the ICC.

Bourdieu and the role of fields

The previous sub-sections highlighted the transformative role of actors in constructing identities and interests based around idealpolitik and realpolitik. While actors have the ability to act reflexively to construct institutions such as the ICC, in doing so they are constrained by existing social structures (Giddens 1984; Wendt 1995). This means that, in acting reflexively, actors are constrained by existing values and understandings of the world and the social context in which they are operating and interacting.

One way to look at this is through Bourdieu's (1977) theory of social reproduction, which highlights that the iteration of acts is not random, but occurs within a 'field' of established traditions and values. A field is an area of structured, socially patterned activity or practice (e.g. the juridical field patterns legal behaviour), and is a site of struggle and competition for control (Bourdieu 1977). Bourdieu defines the concept of 'habitus', which refers to the 'habitual, patterned ways of understanding, judging, and acting which arise from our particular position as members of one or several social "fields", and for our particular trajectory in the social structure' (Terdiman 1987, p. 811). Accordingly, the social world is constructed through a series of interactions, contestations, and negotiations, which are rooted in social fields and habitus. The juridical field is a social space in which conflicts are translated into recognized forms, and in which actors accept (and thereby reproduce) the authority of legal expertise in resolving disputes (Bourdieu 1987). Thus, although the ICC is constructed through the actions and interactions of a variety of groups and actors who have a reflexive and transformative potential, these groups are acting within, and are constrained by, the juridical field.

The effect of the juridical field is that it narrowly constructs the Court through accepted judicial practices and asserts the superiority of particular types of actors and law in response to violence and conflict (Clarke 2009), which in the case of international criminal justice means liberal notions of criminal law (Robinson 2008), as explored earlier in this chapter. Therefore, in responding to mass atrocities, the ICC reproduces traditional understandings of liberal criminal justice, such as individual criminal responsibility (Robinson 2008). The unique nature of international crime is reconstructed through these existing structures despite inherent differences between traditional understandings of domestic crime and the collective and widespread nature of international crimes. New configurations of law and justice emerge as a response to the specificities of international crime, such as the establishment of joint criminal enterprise and command responsibility, to account for the widespread, complex nature of mass atrocities (Haveman and Smeulers 2008). This illustrates the transformative potential of reflexive actors and the evolution of justice through interactions, negotiations, and contestations (Hagan and Levi 2005).

However, these initiatives are constrained by existing structures and understandings of law and justice, namely the notion of personal culpability that underpins liberal conceptions of law and justice, and the perpetuation of this framework illustrates the ongoing influence of structure over agency and the privileged position of liberal notions of law. Clarke (2009, p. 3) considers the outcome of these processes:

> One consequence of the increasing power of international justice . . . is its ability to use statutes, codify laws, and establish new transnational procedures to set new terms of engagement within which defendants, lawyers and prosecutors reclassify evidence and articulate crime in legally relevant terms. This reclassification of responsibility has had the effect of sublimating root causes of violence, reassigning accountability to those few high-ranking leaders in sub-Saharan Africa who are seen as responsible for mass violations.

Thus, while actors have the ability to reclassify evidence and reconstruct notions of crime, they articulate or construct these ideas in legally relevant terms, illustrating the constraints of existing within the juridical field. The result is the denial of the root causes of international crimes and a series of contradictions that arise due to the mismatch between the unique nature of international crimes and the traditional structure of liberal criminal justice, which is reproduced by the legal actors who construct the ICC. The influence of fields on actors' constructions of the ICC is explored further in Chapter 5.

3.4 Concluding comments: sustaining legality's power

This chapter has explored the variety of factors that create tensions in the pursuit of justice at both the international and domestic level. It is well acknowledged that justice systems cannot meet all of their stated aims and that tensions are often an inevitable outcome of the variety of actors and agencies involved in the pursuit of justice, particularly when viewed through the framework of social construction. In studies of the gap between law on the books and law in action (or law in theory and in practice), scholars have highlighted the multiple shortcomings of formal justice systems as they attempt to pursue idealistic justice goals yet are constrained by practical realities and the structural (political and economic) conditions in which they operate (Galanter 1974).

While there are many issues associated with the gaps and tensions outlined in this chapter and in Chapter 2, the schisms in the work of the ICC can also be considered positive. In their work on the gap between law on the books and law in action, Ewick and Silbey (1999, p. 1037) propose that 'the multiple and contradictory meanings of legality protect it from—rather than expose it to—radical critique'. As they point out, 'rather than a flaw, or something that can be explained away, we need to think about how the apparent oppositions and contradictions—the so-called gap—might actually operate ideologically to define and sustain legality as a durable and powerful social institution' (Ewick and Silbey 1999, p. 1036).

The ICC's broad aims and its tensions allow many different actors, agencies, and groups to engage with the Court, meaning 'any particular experience or account can fit within the diversity of the whole' (Ewick and Silbey 1999, p. 1040). Accordingly, we must view the gaps between rhetoric and reality in the work of the ICC as 'a space, not a vacuum' (Ewick and Silbey 1999, p. 1040), a space in which the ICC's power can be created and maintained.

The following chapters explore the productive potential of the ICC's gaps in more depth. The processes of social construction and the structural realities of the ICC, outlined in this chapter, demonstrate the need for the ICC to be able to be simultaneously constructed in a variety of different ways. This creates tensions, but also opportunities, which are important in the complex environment of late modernity.

4 Late modernity, social control, and the ICC

The complexities and contradictions that define the International Criminal Court reflect the complex and fragmented international environment in which the Court is acting. This environment is anarchic and chaotic, with many competing interests, identities, issues, and events emerging and evolving to create an international society that is constantly in the process of transformation and is complex, unpredictable, fluid, and pluralistic (Urry 2003; Bauman 2000). These qualities are heightened in late modernity—an era that evokes uncertainty, reflexivity, and anxiety (Giddens 1990; Hier 2003). The ICC must negotiate these conditions, respond to unpredictable events as they arise, and interact with a range of both hostile and sympathetic groups in order to construct its aims and identity, and assert its relevance and legitimacy on the international stage. However, as discussed in Chapters 2 and 3, the plurality of voices and polarized interests that surround the Court often result in a series of broad aims that are contradictory and unachievable, constructing the Court as a schizophrenic institution, which is caught between idealpolitik and realpolitik.

This chapter develops a theoretical framework to explain the contradictions and complexities of the ICC by examining the international environment in which the Court is acting. In theorizing this environment, the chapter examines the complexity of international society in the late-modern era, explores why certain aims, such as prevention and persuasion, become more prominent than others, and highlights the utility of the Court's continued espousal of broad and contradictory aims. The chapter explores how the late-modern environment creates the control-based aims of prevention and persuasion, as well as many other broad and ambiguous aims that construct the ICC. The Court's simultaneous adoption of control and ambiguity ensures that the Court is flexible and always able to respond to new and unpredictable events as they emerge. Therefore, although the Court shifts schizophrenically between a variety of contradictory aims, these shifts can be productive as a strategic response to the complexity, fragmentation, and plurality of an ever-changing international society.

4.1 The complex, late-modern environment

The processes of social construction that shape the ICC occur in an international environment that is complex, fragmented, fast-paced, and uncontrollable. This environment can be theorized through the lens of late modernity and the theory of global complexity (Urry 2003). Late modernity defines contemporary society as an extension and universalization of the project of modernity and a reconfiguration of modernity's institutions and social, cultural, and political traditions (Giddens 1990). Modernity itself involves a focus on science, bureaucracy, and technology, underpinned by faith in reason and truth, and the privileging of human rationality and advancement. Modernity conceives history as having a single, progressive direction that is marked by rational progress grounded in reason and the desire for order and control (Elliot 2007).

Giddens (1990) highlights three core aspects of society that define modernity: a set of attitudes towards the world as open to transformation by human intervention; a complex array of economic institutions, industrial productions, and a market economy; and a range of political institutions, especially the nation state and mass democracy (Giddens and Pierson 1998). These modernist principles are institutionalized in the form of capitalism, industrialism, surveillance, and military power (Giddens and Pierson 1998). With its focus on evolution and progress, modernity is also inherently globalizing and more dynamic than any previous type of social order as it involves constant evolution and change (Beck 1994). The dynamism of modernity can be linked to three interconnected movements: the uncoupling of time and space; the disembedding of social institutions through the 'lifting out' of social interaction from particular locales through the media, expert systems, and symbolic tokens (such as money); and far-reaching reflexivity (Giddens 1990). These processes of modernity are extended and intensified in the late-modern environment, and this radicalization, combined with the advancement of globalization, produces a runaway world (Giddens 2002) that can be described as a 'juggernaut' (Giddens 1990, p. 139). The conceptualization of late modernity and globalization as a juggernaut highlights the fast-paced, uncontrollable, and unpredictable nature of contemporary society, which is defined by constant evolution and change, driven by principles and processes of modernity.

The constant change associated with the late-modern world is largely linked to the intensification of reflexivity (Giddens 1990). Reflexivity describes the use of knowledge to reflect on practices and improve the human condition, and can be evidenced by modernity's belief in rationality, knowledge, progress, and truth. In late modernity, the simple reflexivity that forms the basis of modernity's advancement and progress is radicalized, causing a heightened awareness of the changeability of knowledge: what we know today may be undermined tomorrow as we acquire new knowledge (Heaphy 2007). This situation creates a form of double reflexivity which causes doubt and distrust of knowledge, meaning that knowledge is considered variable and unpredictable and therefore relevant only until new knowledge is produced (Heaphy 2007). The intensification of reflexivity in conditions of late modernity causes reflection on the principles, institutions, and processes of modernity itself and an acknowledgement of the unintended consequences of modernity, causing late modernity to be defined as a process of reflexive modernization (Beck, Giddens, and Lash 1994).

The process of reflexive modernization makes the contemporary era chaotic (Amin 1992), full of complexities and contradictions; a world of 'ambivalent unfixation and refixation, of fragmentation and reconcentration, of decentring and recentring' (Lippens 1998, p. 318). Bauman (1991) explains these processes by examining the co-existence of elements of modernity and post-modernity in the late-modern environment. Contemporary society revolves around both 'a modernist impulse for creating order, boundaries and classifications as well as a post-modern tolerance for plurality, difference and uncertainty' (Elliot 2007, p. 8). Late modernity can therefore be defined as involving aspects of both modernity and post-modernity, a situation which creates constant evolution, change, and tensions between the binaries of order and disorder, unity and plurality.

This is reflected by Bauman's (2000) concept of liquid modernity, which captures the ever-changing and fluid nature of contemporary society. Urry's (2003) use of complexity theory mirrors these definitions of late modernity by focusing on the mobility and fluidity of current times and the chaotic processes of globalization. Seen through the complexity thesis, international society is 'a set of emergent systems, processing properties and patterns that are often far from equilibrium' (Urry 2003, p. 7). Complexity theory characterizes the international environment as consisting of global world systems that are complex and on the edge of chaos, where there is a balance between component parts that are neither fully locked into place (i.e. they are fluid) yet do not fully dissolve into anarchy (i.e. there is some sense of unity and continuity) (Urry 2003).

Complexity theory's emphasis on the constant process of change is useful as it highlights the unpredictable emergence and evolution of events, ideas, issues, and interactions on the world stage. A recent example of the emergence of unpredictable events is the 2010 Arab Spring movement, which saw citizens overthrow governments in Tunisia, Egypt, and Libya, causing massive violence in these countries and surrounding countries such as Syria (Roth 2012). This movement resulted from a complex combination of events, including widespread social media coverage, and a growing sense of anger against self-serving governments, yet the eruption of violence was unexpected and had unpredictable and far-reaching effects (Goldstein 2012). The ICC, and international society in general, did not predict this sudden and violent episode (Goldstein 2012), yet was called upon to respond to it. Following these events, the ICC only actually responded to the violence in Libya, as will be explored further in Chapter 7. Such events highlight the increasingly uncertain and unpredictable nature of the contemporary era, which is characterized by the emergence of events and unpredictable interactions that create a dynamic and chaotic international society and an 'era marked by profound uncertainties' (Lippens 1998, p. 320). As the example of the Arab Spring movement highlights, the ICC must negotiate and respond to these unexpected and constantly evolving events if it is to remain relevant on the world stage.

Complexity theory captures not only the complexity of international society and the chaotic nature of the contemporary era in which the ICC operates but also illustrates how particular understandings come to gain prominence and legitimacy in a complex and disorganized world (Urry 2003). Seen through the lens of complexity theory, the work of the International Criminal Court is performed through billions of iterations, negotiations, and interactions (Urry 2003). These processes of performativity correspond with international relations theories of social construction, which similarly explore the construction of international society and its constituent institutions through processes of interaction (Dunne 1995; Wendt 1995; Ruggie 1998). Social constructionist theories analyse how processes of interaction produce and reproduce actors' identities and interests (Wendt 1995), meaning that institutions and structures exist only in processes (Wendt 1995). Stammers (1999, p. 981) explains this perspective through his examination of human rights, stating, 'To say that human rights are socially constructed is to say that ideas and practices in respect of human rights are created, re-created, and instantiated by human actors in particular socio-historical settings and conditions.' From this perspective, the ICC is formed through its interactions with a variety of groups and it is only through these processes that the Court is constructed and can be understood.

4.2 Reflexivity, risk, and control

The complex, late-modern environment in which the Court is constructed shapes the aims and identity of the ICC. Late modernity involves an extension and intensification of modernist principles as well as the fragmentation, plurality, and ambivalence associated with post-modernism (Bauman 1991). The concept of late modernity is therefore distinguished by its simultaneous analysis of the peculiarities that define contemporary society and recognition of the continuity with what went before (Garland 2001). This section examines these dualistic characteristics of late modernity in terms of the desire for control that stems from the intensification of modernist principles, such as reflexivity, and the processes of fragmentation, flexibility, and adaptability that arise from post-modern discourses and the complexity of the international environment.

As late modernity involves a desire for both control and flexibility, the Court mirrors the ambivalence of the contemporary era and switches between the control-based aims of prevention and persuasion, and the multiple and fragmented aims within these categories. In this environment the inability of the ICC to achieve all of its stated aims becomes irrelevant as its multiple aims ensure it is flexible and resilient, enabling it to respond to the many different situations, events, and interactions that arise in a complex international society. As the Court is constructed through these interactions and events, its broad aims ensure that it can respond to emerging and changing situations as they occur. Thus, the structured ambivalence of the ICC and the strategic ambiguity of its aims become productive as they allow the Court to gain authority, relevance, and legitimacy on the international stage through its multiple interactions in a complex and ever-changing world.

As highlighted, late modernity involves intensification of modernist principles and institutions and, in particular, an extension of modernity's desire for control and order. The desire for control and order stems from an increase in reflexivity and the unpredictable, uncontrollable nature of the complex, late-modern world. The heightened reflexivity of late modernity means that society is increasingly constituted by information (Castells 2000) rather than pre-given models of conduct or tradition. Individuals are forced to reflect on the choices they make, bringing the potential for transformation and change (Giddens 1990). This potential for change can be positive, as it enables the agency and social construction explored in the previous section. However, the increased reflexivity and choice of the current era also creates a sense of anxiety and insecurity in contemporary society (Salecl 2004, 2010). The intensification of reflexivity results in an awareness of the contingency of knowledge and consequent recognition of the unpredictable and uncontrollable nature of contemporary society. This awareness undermines ontological security, defined as 'the confidence that most human beings have in the continuity of their self-identity and in the constancy of the surrounding social and material environment of action' (Giddens 1990, p. 92). In late modernity, the unpredictability generated by reflexivity erodes ontological security, resulting instead in a sense of ontological insecurity (Giddens 1990) and pervasive anxiety (Salecl 2004).

Within this environment, risk and uncertainty emerge as key aspects of contemporary society as the acknowledgement of the side-effects of modernity, through processes of reflexivity, emphasizes the unpredictability, instability, and changeability of the world. Beck (1999) examines the centrality of risk through his world risk society thesis, which explores the increasingly global nature of risks, such as nuclear disasters, terrorism, and financial crises, which have the potential to arbitrarily affect all of humanity (Beck 1999). This sense of risk is heightened by mega-events (Roche 2000) such as 9/11 which exhibit the global nature of risk and insecurity, the limited protective capacity of borders, and the mutual connectedness and vulnerability of the world (Aas 2007).

The idea of collective vulnerability, risk, and insecurity is evident in the Rome Statute Preamble of the ICC (1998), which constructs international crimes as a threat to the whole of humanity, for example, in the phrase 'recognizing that such grave crimes threaten the peace, security and well-being of the world'. This construction aligns with the risk society thesis, which characterizes the current era as driven by the increasingly pervasive logic of manufactured uncertainty (Adam, Beck, and Van Loon 2000) causing widespread politics of insecurity (Ericson 2007). Beck's (1999) risk society thesis often over-emphasizes the nature and role of risk in the contemporary era (Stenson 2001); his ideas do reflect a wider trend towards the examination of risk and uncertainty in the construction of contemporary society (Lash 2000; Mythen and Walklate 2006; O'Malley 2006). Recently, the concept of uncertainty has taken precedence over the risk society thesis (O'Malley 2010 and 2011). Here, risk becomes a permanent condition of late-modern life and uncertainty is embraced (Baker and Simon 2002) through neoliberal modes of governance (Dean 1999; O'Malley 2011; Rose 1999) in which politics can be conceived of as dealing with the 'contingent event' and living in a state of ambiguity (Hannien quoted in de Lint and Virta 2004, p. 473).

The characteristics of reflexivity, anxiety, risk, and uncertainty coincide with a culture of control that characterizes the contemporary era (Garland 2001). Modernity's drive for order, rationality, and linearity is extended and intensified in contemporary society, with an increased focus on control and classification underpinning late modernity. As Garland and Sparks (2000, pp. 17–18) explain:

> the mobile and insecure world of late modernity has given rise to new practices of control and exclusion that seek to make society less open and less mobile: to fix identities, immobilise individuals, quarantine whole sections of the population, erect boundaries, close off access.

This culture of control is often translated into crime and justice discourses, with crime control becoming a prominent response to the anxiety, insecurity, and risk associated with late modernity (Garland 2001). Thus, late modernity involves the development of criminal justice measures, such as actuarial justice (Feeley and Simon 1994), precautionary logics (Zedner 2007), extreme security strategies (Ericson 2007), and punitive crime control measures.

An example of the convergence of uncertainty and control is seen in responses to the events of 9/11 and the London bombings (de Goede 2008). These events typified the precarious, uncertain, and contingent nature of the current era and, consequently, provoked (or justified) strong criminal justice measures that blurred the borders between crime and national security (McCulloch and Pickering 2009). As a reaction to the terrorist threat, strong, punitive measures, such as preventative detention and control orders, were introduced (McCulloch and Pickering 2009). These measures constructed the Muslim as the 'other' (Poynting 2003) and justified violations of political freedoms, civil liberties, and constitutional rights (Head 2002) through the privileging of human security over human rights (McCulloch 2003). Reactions to terrorism provide an example of the classification and control associated with the risk, uncertainty, and insecurity of late modernity; its translation into punitive and precautionary criminal justice measures; the construction of dangerous others; and the classification of new crimes that create an exclusive society (Young 1999).

The control-based environment of late modernity influences the construction of the ICC and underpins the Court's aims and identity. The Court reflects ideas of order, classification, and 'othering', and aligns with the preventative and precautionary focus of crime control in late modernity, as is evidenced by its core aims of prevention and persuasion. The Court's preventative aims seek to achieve control over the future through notions of precaution and preemption, while the Court's persuasive aims seek to achieve a sense of order by creating and enforcing a normative and classificatory framework for international society. The prevalence of these aims, in the midst of a plethora of other aims, such as restorative and rehabilitative justice aims, illustrates the influence of the late-modern environment on constructions of the ICC.

4.3 Control through prevention and precaution

As the previous discussion of responses to terrorism highlights, late modernity involves efforts to preempt imagined sources of harm (Ericson 2007), manage risk, and eliminate uncertainty, by adopting future-oriented strategies of control that parallel the risk logic by attempting to 'foresee and control the future consequences of human action' (Beck 1999, p. 3). These strategies embody the concept of pre-crime, which shifts the temporal perspective of crime control from a reactive approach to an anticipatory approach, designed to forestall crime in the future (Zedner 2007). As Zedner (2007, p. 262) highlights, 'In a pre-crime society, there is calculation, risk and uncertainty, surveillance, precaution, prudentialism, moral hazard, prevention and, arching over all these, there is the pursuit of security.' The concept of pre-crime illustrates how the environment of risk, uncertainty, and reflexivity causes us to 'become active today in order to prevent, alleviate or take precautions against the problems and crises of tomorrow and the day after tomorrow' (Beck 1992, p. 34). Preemption and precaution are responses to uncertainty that reflect the culture of control that is late modernity (Garland 2001).

The ICC's heavy focus on the preventative aims of ending impunity and deterrence reflects this precautionary logic and the notion of pre-crime (Zedner 2007). As explored in Chapter 2, the narrative of ending impunity is woven throughout the discourses surrounding the ICC and this makes deterrence a core aim of the Court. The concept of ending impunity and the aim of deterrence stem from the overarching aim of preventing international crimes. The ICC's role is defined through the paradigm of prevention and this paradigm overrules many other competing aims. For example, retribution and restoration are viewed primarily through their ability to help deter or prevent future crimes, rather than being inherently valuable as core aims. This preventative focus dictates the functioning of the Court by constructing the need to use symbolic, exemplary prosecutions in order to achieve general deterrence and prevent future crimes in countries around the world. This focus constructs the Court as a future-orientated institution. Of course, crime will always exist and the ICC will always find violence and conflict to prosecute.

Here, the Court is depicted as an institution that surveys international society, highlights atrocities, and catalyses responses to these atrocities in order to prevent future crimes. The Court is assumed to effect deterrence by its very existence. Through its overarching preventative aims, the ICC is constructed as an upper-level, supranational institution that prevents future crimes by monitoring international society while also threatening prosecution and punishment. In a similar capacity, the Court attempts to prevent future crimes by issuing preemptive and precautionary early warnings to countries where violence threatens to escalate

(HRW 2011a). As highlighted in Chapter 2, precautionary early warnings have been issued in countries such as Libya, Côte d'Ivoire, and Kenya. Through these strategies of symbolic prosecution, supervision, and precautionary early warnings, the ICC reflects the future-oriented trends of control of late modernity.

The future-oriented aims of the Court ensure that it is continuously relevant as it can respond to a variety of situations and use local conflicts and cases to increase its prominence on the international stage. The aim of preventing international crimes is axiomatic and constructs the idealpolitik of the Court, because, despite the multiple perspectives on the Court, the aim of preventing international crimes is accepted as self-evident and positive. Thus, it is not so much that prevention becomes the underlying aim of the ICC due to a lack of rational alternatives, as Tallgren (2002) suggests, but rather prevention is the primary aim as it serves a unifying function that underpins idealpolitik and provides an antidote to the environment of risk, anxiety, and uncertainty in which the Court is operating. The Court's limited ability to end impunity and achieve deterrence on a practical scale becomes irrelevant, as the aim of prevention provides a symbolic response to the complexity and chaos of the international environment, and ensures that the Court remains prominent and relevant within this ever-changing environment. By adopting a preventative, future-oriented focus, the ICC displays a desire for control that stems from the reflexivity, anxiety, and uncertainty that is characteristic of the late-modern environment. By focusing on the preventative aims of ending impunity and deterrence, the ICC is constructed as a forward-looking institution that uses the prevention of crime to provide a semblance of control over the uncertain, chaotic, and complex international environment.

4.4 Control through classification and persuasion

In late modernity, control and order is sought not only through preventative and precautionary aims, but also through the classification and ordering of behaviour. In addition to preventing crime, the ICC structures and orders international society through its persuasive aims which involve the development of a normative framework and set of moral standards. This normative framework is constructed by the definition and classification of crimes and criminals at an international level. Crime plays a particularly prominent role in classification as it has the power to assert moral frameworks, structure normative understandings, and order society through inclusion and exclusion—processes that respond to the pervasive anxiety and uncertainty associated with late modernity. Young (1999, p. 15) describes this process, stating:

> because of ontological insecurity there are repeated attempts to create a secure base. That is, to reassert one's values as moral absolutes, to declare other groups as lacking in value, to draw distinct lines of virtue and vice, to be rigid rather than flexible in one's judgements, to be punitive and excluding rather than permeable and assimilative.

Through the definition of international crimes as crimes against humanity, genocide, war crimes, and aggression, the ICC orders international society by creating a moral framework in which these acts are criminalized over other acts, such as drug trafficking or the use of nuclear weapons. The ICC's prosecutions reinforce these classifications and construct certain crimes as more dangerous and criminal than others. For example, the ICC's focus on child soldiers has constructed this practice as a particularly heinous war crime and worse than other war crimes, such as the systematic use of rape (Chaikel 2011; Davis 2001; Inder 2011). The difficulties defining and prosecuting aggression illustrate how the label of crime can mirror and reinforce existing power differentials. The construction of aggression as an international crime could be used to classify the realpolitik and strategic use of violence by more powerful states as crimes—for example, aggression could construct the US invasion of Iraq as an international crime (Kramer and Michalowski 2005; Kramer, Michalowski, and Rothe 2005). This illustrates the inherently political nature of constructing definitions of crime and ordering international society through these definitions. As Quinney (1970, pp. 15–16) highlights, 'crime is a definition of human conduct created by authorised actors in a politically organised society'.

Therefore, in late modernity, the definition of international crime is important for its ordering and structuring properties (Cohen 1985) that facilitate social control by making the world more knowable, creating an 'other', and consequently dividing the world into an understandable and predictable set of binaries, such as insiders and outsiders (Becker 1963). The ICC's prosecutions construct evil others who are labelled as international criminals or warlords. As Michalowski (2009, p. 305) states, 'it is likely that for the foreseeable future the docks of international human rights courts will be filled by dictators or warlords from peripheral or semi-peripheral nations who fit popular images of the "monstrous other"'. The Court's labelling of others mirrors the geological divides and existing power structures highlighted in Section 4.1. The current situations before the Court involve African countries, such as Sudan, the DRC, and Uganda. The prosecution of these countries reinforces the idea of the native savage and explains evil as something outside Western geographical and cultural borders. The labelling function of crime orders international society through moral judgements, the justification of some behaviour, and the demonization of other behaviour. The ICC's persuasive aims involve the construction of this normative framework and the labelling of certain acts as crimes. The ICC acts in a persuasive manner by adopting the principle of complementarity and attempting to catalyse and encourage national prosecutions that align with the principles and definitions of crime in the Rome Statute. This framework provides a sense of order and control in response to the anxiety and insecurity of late modernity.

The ICC's core aims of prevention and persuasion facilitate control and order at an international level. The Court's focus on prevention seeks to control the future and eliminate the uncertainty of late modernity, aligning with the preventative crime-control focus at national levels. The ICC's aims of persuasion seek to establish a normative framework for international society that provides order, control, and structure through the classification and labelling of crime. The ICC switches between these aims of prevention and persuasion as it attempts to achieve control by acting as a threatening weapon (prevention) and as a persuasive tool (persuasion). Despite the different focus of these two aims, they both seek to achieve the same outcome—the control and ordering of international society in response to the anxiety and uncertainty of late modernity.

4.5 Flexibility, strategic ambiguity, and resilience in late modernity

As previously highlighted, late modernity includes not only a modernist impulse for creating order, boundaries, and classifications, but also a post-modern tolerance of plurality, difference, and uncertainty (Elliot 2007). In late modernity the world becomes increasingly complex and plural, based on contingency and an awareness of the ephemeral nature of knowledge. Reflexivity and uncertainty drives a desire for control and order while also creating a simultaneous acknowledgement of the fast-paced (Virilio 2006), changeable, and fluid (Bauman 2000) aspects of contemporary society and the ephemeral nature of information and knowledge. Post-modern discourses on plurality, fragmentation, and the limits of grand narratives, truth, and linearity (Lyotard 1984) have shaped the contours of contemporary society, alongside the extension of modernist principles. This means that late modernity involves fluidity and movement between the desire for control and order on one hand, and plurality and flexibility on the other. The ICC is thus shaped by the desire for control, which constructs the core, control-based aims of prevention and persuasion and, simultaneously, by fragmentation and plurality, which results in multiple and broad aims.

The dialectic processes of late modernity (Beilharz 2000) are highlighted by Bauman's (2000) metaphor of liquid modernity, which explains the duality and flow of these two poles of late modernity and illustrates the tensions between control and flexibility, and order and ambiguity, that become an inevitable part of the complex, late-modern environment. Central to Bauman's conceptualization of this duality is the role of ambiguity and ambivalence. Bauman (1991) differentiates between the two concepts of ambiguity and ambivalence, describing ambiguity as a linguistic problem in which the meaning of a word or classification is unclear or vague, while defining ambivalence as a split in which contradictory feelings, values, or ideas coexist. Ambivalence is both a psychological and sociological concept. In the psychological sense, the coexistence of conflicting feelings—for example, love/hate (Yair 2007)—can create confusion and contradiction, as people experience aspects of opposite ends of binaries at the same time (Yair 2007). In the sociological sense, as is evidenced in Bauman's work, the concept of ambivalence describes more structural conflicts within social systems and institutions (Yair 2007).

Modernity and post-modernity can both be defined by their relationship to ambivalence: while modernity attempts to rid society of ambivalence and thus produce order and control through classification, post-modernity embraces ambivalence and accepts the ambiguous and uncontrollable aspects of society

(Bauman 1991). Thus, while post-modernity celebrates ambivalence, modernity abhors ambivalence, and in a late-modern world both of these aspects are present at the same time creating contradictions and confusions. This situation creates an ambivalence towards ambiguity and ambivalence itself, as, although in late modernity ambivalence and ambiguity is abhorred, it is also recognized as inevitable and, in some part, necessary in order to respond to the rapidly changing and complex world. Ambiguity and ambivalence provide an opportunity for flexibility and change that enables adaption to the constantly evolving, chaotic, and complex world that is constructed by interactions, processes, and practices, as explored in Section 4.1.

Flexibility is embodied in the idea of embracing uncertainty (Baker and Simon 2002), which constructs subjects as resilient in order to enable them to respond to the ever-changing and uncontrollable world (O'Malley 2011). Flexibility is also evidenced in ambiguous classifications, which satiate the desire for order while also remaining adaptable to the complex environment. Accordingly, ambiguous classifications and definitions of crime allow for more events or individuals to be captured by the law as situations change and evolve in unpredictable ways. As Ericson (2007, p. 211) states, 'governance through vague terms allows the net to be cast widely for signs of suspicion that are criminalised'. Ericson (2007) gives the example of criminal possession as a catch-all, residual or 'kicker' charge, used by police to control undesirables who cannot be controlled in other ways.

The International Criminal Court similarly adopts ambiguous classifications of crime. One example is the broad, catch-all classification of crimes against humanity. The broad definition of 'crimes against humanity' covers a list of several different acts which are required to meet the threshold of being 'committed as part of a widespread or systematic attack directed against any civilian population' (Rome Statute 1998, Article 7) in order to constitute a crime against humanity. This leaves interpretation open and flexible to respond to the changing nature of international society, allowing for many different situations and crimes to be brought under this umbrella charge. The ICC has used the crimes against humanity charge in a variety of different situations—for example, the civil war in Sudan, rebel attacks in Uganda and the DRC, election violence in Kenya, and violence surrounding the uprising in Libya. As these examples illustrate, the concept of crimes against humanity is a vague classification that can be used to capture numerous events in a capricious manner. The broad classifications of the ICC therefore create order and control, yet are also flexible enough to be used differentially in a range of situations and thus respond to the complexity that is international society in late modernity.

The fragmentation and plurality of late modernity is also evidenced by the Court's continued espousal of a range of different aims and by the often contradictory nature of these aims. Despite the prominence of the control-based aims of prevention and persuasion, the ICC continues to construct a variety of aims that include, achieving peace, bringing justice to victims, and playing a restorative role in victim communities (UN 1999). Often, these wider aims will be used to support the preventative and persuasive functioning of the Court as highlighted in the previous sections. However, the continued espousal of multiple aims allows the Court to be flexible in response to the plurality and fragmentation of international society in late modernity. Tensions and contradictions in the aims and work of the Court arise as the Court attempts to control and order international society through the control-based aims of prevention and persuasion, yet also tries to remain flexible and ambiguous through the espousal of broad and multiple aims in order to respond to the fluid and ever-changing nature of late modernity. In this approach, the ICC reflects the ambivalence of late modernity through its constant switching between control and fluidity. Although the Court is driven to control, it is also driven to flexibility in order to allow it to adapt to the complexity of late modernity.

4.6 Concluding comments

The complexity of the late-modern world means that international society is always changing, and events and interactions arise unpredictably and cause fragmentation and plurality, and a simultaneous desire for control and order. The ICC reflects these tensions between idealpolitik and realpolitik, and control and flexibility, by adopting the control-based aims of prevention and persuasion, as well as a series of other broad and ambiguous aims that reflect the plurality of international society.

The ICC is caught between a desire for control and a desire for flexibility as an outcome of the unpredictable processes of reflexivity and social construction that define late modernity. This causes the Court to switch schizophrenically between different aims and have limited success in achieving any of its stated aims. However, the ability of the Court to achieve its aims is of limited relevance for the processes of social construction that create the Court. As the ICC is constructed through its interactions with a range of actors, and its practices and processes in response to unpredictable events, the more interactions and events that the ICC can participate in, the greater prominence and relevance the Court will have through increased processes of social construction. The ICC gains prominence through its social interactions and, in order to maximize these interactions, the Court must remain flexible and resilient in the face of an ever-changing and unpredictable world. The ICC's aims of prevention and persuasion provide a semblance of control as a response to the anxiety and insecurity of this unpredictable world, thus justifying its existence. However, the Court can switch to more flexible aims, and interpret and apply ambiguous classifications of crime, to enable it to respond to a variety of different situations as they emerge—for example, the situation in Libya. In this sense, the tensions and contradictions of the ICC can be redefined as structured ambivalence and strategic ambiguity, which allow the Court to respond productively to the processes of social construction, making it constantly relevant in an unpredictable, ever-changing world.

5 The role of actors

Many different actors and groups interact with the International Criminal Court. In their interactions, actors reflexively construct and transform the aims of the Court (Giddens 1984), yet in doing so they are also influenced by the fields (Bourdieu 1977) in which they are located and the habitus, or the groups, of which they are a part. Considering the theoretical and conceptual framework outlined in the previous chapter, it is important to understand how those associated with the Court conceptualize and perceive the Court's aims, and to explore how these actors engage with both realpolitik and idealpolitik to articulate their interests. Accordingly, this chapter analyses interview data collected from actors associated with the ICC, to explore their constructions of the aims of the Court. The chapter examines how common, idealistic, and vague aims are created, and explores how differential and contested understandings and applications of these aims reflect the fractured environment of the Court and international society.

5.1 Structuring the use of idealpolitik and realpolitik

As explored in previous chapters, actors are reflexive and have the ability to construct and transform the Court and its aims through their discourse and interactions. Giddens (1984) emphasizes the important role that individuals play in reproducing and transforming social institutions and structures, such as the ICC, claiming that social transformation relies on the reflexive nature of human beings and their ability to use knowledge to reflect on and change their actions and practices. This means that the manner in which individuals perceive and convey the aims of the Court is important in constructing the Court itself.

Actors' constructions are not, however, created in a void but are significantly influenced by the structures within which these actors are located and in the wider environment of late modernity, as discussed in Chapter 4. In particular, actors' constructions of the ICC are shaped by the fields of international law and human rights (Robinson 2008). By way of example, Bourdieu (1977) highlights the influence of the juridical field on construction of crime and justice, noting that although actors have the ability to reclassify evidence and reconstruct notions of crime, they articulate or construct these ideas in legally relevant terms, illustrating the constraints existing within the juridical field.

In addition to the influence of the overarching fields of international law and human rights, actors' constructions of the Court are also shaped by the groups or agencies with which they are associated. Both the external environment within which the Court is acting and the internal environment from which the Court is constructed are fragmented and divided. The divisions of the external environment were explored in Chapters 3 and 4. In this chapter, the internal fragmentation of the Court is explored through the lens of the habitus and an examination of the groups, agencies, and offices within which actors are located.

Actors engage differentially with the commonly constructed aims of the Court according to the agencies they represent. This results in contradictory constructions of common aims of the Court and an ambivalent use of both realpolitik and idealpolitik. Here, actors espouse idealistic aims of prevention and persuasion while articulating their interests and identities through their differential engagement with, and use of, these aims.

The idealism of human rights and international law

The fields of human rights and international law underpin the International Criminal Court, as explored in Chapter 3. Most actors who work closely with the ICC are associated with human rights or international law frameworks. This means that actors' constructions of the aims of the Court are structured by the assumptions and principles of these two fields. The influence of the field of human rights on the ICC is reflected by the large number of human rights organizations associated with the Court (Glasius 2006). These organizations are focused overwhelmingly on victims, resulting in a victim-oriented Court (Schabas 2006).

> The Court is very much driven by NGOs, and the NGOs are of course mostly victim-oriented . . . so it makes also the Court victim-oriented.
>
> (Participant O)[1]

Actors who are directly associated with the Court by their human rights and victims focus, understandably construct the ICC through a victim-oriented perspective.

> The ICC's aim is bringing a sense of justice to victims.
>
> (Participant H, victim-oriented NGO)

> The ICC is definitely there to serve victim populations and to bring redress to those who were affected.
>
> (Participant F, victim-oriented NGO)

Often these victim narratives are linked to notions of prevention and deterrence which all participants referred to as an aim of the Court.

1 A guide to the interview participants can be found in the Appendix.

> When you talk about delivering justice . . . there is an idea of deterrence for the crimes being committed and an idea of reparation and redress for those who are victims of the crime.
>
> (Participant F)

Victim-oriented and human rights discourses also construct the Court as a persuasive institution that can be useful in affecting change at a local level by setting standards and assisting in the development of human rights.

> You couldn't do much human rights or transitional justice work if you wouldn't have the international law obligation behind you.
>
> (Participant C)

> Some gender groups are trying to get some of the principles from the Rome Statute on rape and sexual violence [to] be reflected in their own local systems so for some of them it's more a tool to have more power at home to change the system from inside. It has a role to play in the democratization of their own systems so they see it more as a part of a development process.
>
> (Participant E)

These comments illustrate how NGOs strategically use the common aims of the ICC to achieve their own goals and interests.

By their very nature, human rights are idealistic and ambitious; they are aspirations rather than guarantees, or, as Donnelly (2003, p. 12) frames them, 'demands for change'. The field of human rights thus constructs the Court in an idealistic and aspirational manner. Many interview participants reflected on the use of ideals in the work of the Court.

> The concept of international justice can be quite vague at times, quite idealistic, the Court has very idealistic goals . . . the aims of the Preamble of the Statute are very idealistic.
>
> (Participant G)

> The ICC has a very important but clearly restricted and limited role, but it can also have then a sort of symbolic and aspirational role.
>
> (Participant A)

In this context, the espousal of idealistic aims is unproblematic. Even if the ICC cannot realistically meet the ideals it sets for itself, these actors portray the communication of ideals as a valuable aspect of the Court. Idealistic aims are useful as they provide the enthusiasm to develop the ICC and set the tone of international justice.

> Human rights law is highly driven by idealistic concepts at times and I think that some of the human rights standards that are alluded to in the Rome

> Statute are an ideal, in the sense that they are difficult to apply in practice, but nevertheless they set the tone of international justice.
>
> (Participant A)

> The ICC is an ideal in the sense of being a bit detached, being more of an idea and detached from reality. I still find value in that. I mean, ideal to me does not mean that it is not something to work on or something to aim at. I mean, I think we can meet those ideals—it is just that they are detached from reality at times.
>
> (Participant G)

> International justice is an ambition and a standard that we all strive to [achieve] . . . it's the concept of justice being able to come at an upper level, or a higher level. In practice it might not really be working on the issues . . . but I think it's more an ambition; it's almost a dream in many ways.
>
> (Participant J)

As these comments illustrate, the ambitious aims of the ICC mirror the idealistic rhetoric of human rights and the ideals are valuable in and of themselves.

In the work of the ICC, these idealistic foundations of human rights assumptions are combined with the practical focus of international law to construct the ICC as an enforcement mechanism for human rights principles.

> The ICC represents the ultimate enforcement of human rights.
>
> (Participant A)

The field of international law thus structures actors' constructions of the Court alongside human rights assumptions. International criminal justice is often constructed as a neutral, apolitical process, which is evidenced in participants' discussions of the supposedly value-free aims of the Court.

> The primary aim of the ICC is to thoroughly and credibly investigate and prosecute those who are alleged to be responsible for the crimes within the Court's jurisdiction; so currently, genocide, crimes against humanity, and war crimes. I think that is at the core of the Court's mandate, it's really a judicial institution delivering justice.
>
> (Participant T)

Such statements make the complex ideas of international crime and justice self-evident and unproblematic and present the ICC as an impartial institution. Here, the Court is constructed as merely a judicial institution; the wider and more idealistic aims appear in the merging of international law and human rights, as two NGO interview participants explained:

> Initially there was the sense that this is a criminal court and it's going to be doing judicial proceedings and criminal proceedings and that's it, and then there was a big, big pressure coming from civil society and the Court got to understand that it was there also to prevent other crimes.
>
> (Participant F)

> The aim of the ICC is prosecuting the gravest crimes, crimes against humanity, genocide, war crimes—they are primary aims. Then to have the impact—the second set of aims is bringing justice back to the communities, explaining justice to them, providing reparations, making justice meaningful.
>
> (Participant E)

As this discussion highlights, the uncritical and procedure-focused nature of international law (Charlesworth 2002) makes deeper reflection on the broader aims and values of the ICC subordinate to the focus on processes and practices. The field of human rights then becomes valuable in providing ideals and the broader framework for the Court.

Another example of legalistic constructions of the ICC comes from two actors who work for the Court. These actors construct the aims of the Court through the narrow framework of the Rome Statute Preamble, relying on the idealistic narratives of the Rome Statute, grounded in human rights assumptions, for broader meaning.

> The goals are the ones of the Rome Statute; the goals are in the Preamble of the Rome Statute—so this is putting an end to impunity and punishing those responsible for the crimes and contributing to prevention of the crimes.
>
> (Participant T)

> When it comes to the aims of the Court, there is not much room for improvisation, and we actually look to the Preamble of the Rome Statute. That's really a source that we quote regularly and we try to remain very true to the text of the Preamble—that's really the guiding text for the aims of the Court.
>
> (Participant U)

Such comments are reflective of many interview participants' initial resistance to discussing the aims of the ICC, in broader terms, during the interviews. For many participants, the discussion of the wider aims of the Court and the idea of international justice seemed trivial or unnecessary. This is illustrated in the automatic referral to the Rome Statute described above. The field of international law is often preoccupied with procedural issues and therefore uses idealistic human rights discourses, merged with criminal law structures, to construct the aims of the Court. The neutral stance of international law, which relies on axiomatic and unquestioned notions of law and justice, therefore reinforces the idealistic notions of dominant human rights paradigms.

Fragmentation and the use of idealpolitik and realpolitik

In addition to being influenced by the fields of international law and human rights, actors are also significantly influenced by the groups and agencies that they represent. One way of looking at this is through Bourdieu's (1987) concept of the 'habitus' which can be described as 'the habitual, patterned ways of understanding, judging, and acting which arise from our particular position as members of one of several social "fields", and from our particular trajectory in the social structure' (Terdiman in Bourdieu 1987, p. 811). From this perspective, several different 'habitus' can be identified within the fields of human rights and international law, and these sets of practices are ordered by the different groups and agencies that comprise the ICC, as described below.

The ICC is constituted by several independent offices including the Office of the Prosecutor, the Presidency and Judiciary, the Office of Public Counsel for Defence, and the Office of Public Counsel for Victims. Many different NGOs and media organizations also interact with the ICC. Each of these groups has their own interests, practices, and aims, which actors articulate through their interactions and their constructions of the aims of the ICC. For example, the previous section alluded to how groups representing victims construct the Court through the prism of victims' rights and needs. These narratives feed into the overarching aims of prevention and persuasion; however, they also represent a differential construction of these aims when compared with, for example, the Office of the Public Counsel for Defence, which focuses on the importance of fair and effective trials.

> The ICC provides clarity in the law . . . it can help domestic courts to implement their legislation, it helps to know what is a war crime, what is a crime against humanity, to have that clearly set out so that you don't have problems with the principle of legality . . . it's also good for the fair trial standards because it's quite high standards . . . domestic courts can take from this example. It shows that if you are going to prosecute someone you have to prosecute them to a certain standard for [a] fair trial.
>
> (Participant N)

Considering the variety of groups and offices that interact with the ICC, the ICC is a fragmented system rather than a consolidated institution. Reflecting this fragmentation, the ICC's strategic plan outlines the 'one court' principle for the ICC to ensure that each of the agencies of the Court work towards common, collective goals (ICC Assembly of States Parties (ASP) 2006). The one court policy explains the independent nature of offices of the ICC; the Office of the Prosecutor is an independent and separate organ of the Court, while the Office of Public Counsel for Victims and the Office of Public Counsel for Defence also operate as independent offices, despite their inclusion under the Registry of the ICC for administrative purposes (ICC ASP 2006). The one court policy was designed to provide unity across the Court's independent offices, following fragmentation and differences between various sections of the Court.

> There is division in the Court, but now the Court has this one court policy that sets certain standard aims.
>
> (Participant E)

The common aims expressed by the one court strategy document are to contribute to 'an end to impunity for perpetrators of the most serious international crimes, the prevention of such crimes, and lasting respect for, and the enforcement of, international justice' (ICC ASP 2006, p. 2). These common principles reflect the idealistic aims of prevention and persuasion commonly constructed by actors working closely with the Court.

Despite this policy, and interview participants' communication of the common aims outlined above, the fragmentation between different sections of the Court and its surrounding agencies was evident in participants' constructions of the ICC's aims. Within the commonly expressed aims of prevention and persuasion, actors constructed aims differentially using idealpolitik and realpolitik to reflect their own interests and identities. As the previous examples from victims' groups and the defence illustrate, both of these agencies construct the ICC as persuasive, with the goal of defining crimes and setting standards. Despite these common constructions, each of these agencies interprets the persuasive aim of the Court differently; for the defence, the value lies in the assertion of fair trial standards and protecting the rights of the defence, while for victim-oriented human rights groups the value is the potential to use the Court to develop laws and protect victims at a national level. Thus, the commonly constructed aims of the Court are contradictory and often conflict due to actors' different interpretations of the idealistic aims of prevention and persuasion.

In this context, idealpolitik and realpolitik are used to assert particular aims and counteract the interests of other offices of the Court. The division can be seen primarily between those individuals working for the prosecution, defence, and victims' agencies, reflecting the strong influence of the adversarial model in the functioning of the Court (Ambos 2003; Kress 2003). NGOs and media also presented conflicting accounts of the ICC depending on their alignments and interests.

In these constructions, certain groups have more influence in their articulations of their aims and interests than others. The Office of the Prosecutor has a particularly strong voice due to its ability to lead prosecutions. Many of the wider discourses on the Court consequently reflect the prosecutor's interpretation of the ICC's aims.

> I think that the strategies taken by the prosecutor really affect what happens to the Court and how it's perceived and what it's trying to achieve.
>
> (Participant N)

> The prosecutor is very powerful internally but very weak externally.
>
> (Participant O)

As these quotations highlight, the Office of the Prosecutor drives the Court through its prosecutorial strategy and this gives the prosecution more symbolic capital (Bourdieu 1991) to assert the aims of the Court. Contrastingly, the defence has limited social capital, particularly as offenders are often depicted as heinous others (Michalowski 2009) who elicit little sympathy and have limited currency. The defence therefore has less opportunity to assert their interests and interpretations of the aims of the Court. One participant from the Office of Public Counsel for Defence reflects on this issue:

> The Office of the Prosecutor is completely independent—they have their own budget, they have their own services for things, so ultimately they can do what they want . . . there is no incentive to harmonize budgets or to share resources or to work in a collegial manner. So we don't have common standards throughout the Court because the prosecution like to do it differently.
>
> (Participant N)

This discussion illustrates the fragmenting influence of different habitus on constructions of the aims of the Court, as well as the unifying influences of the idealism perpetuated by the merging of the fields of human rights and international law.

5.2 Casting a wide shadow: the preventative role of the ICC

Preventing international crimes is one of the core aims of the ICC, as explored in Chapter 2. Prevention is cited by all actors when they construct the aims of the Court. However, the interpretation of prevention, and the ICC's ability to achieve this aim, varies according to actors' habitus. Many actors referred to prevention as one of the key aims of the International Criminal Court—for example:

> The aim of the Court is making sure that certain types of crimes do not occur in the future.
>
> (Participant G)

> It's obviously for contributing towards the prevention of crimes by prosecuting those who are the most responsible.
>
> (Participant L)

> The essential aim is to prevent, it's preventative, to prevent these things from ever happening again.
>
> (Participant N)

In actors' constructions of the Court, the idea of preventing international crimes is often synonymous with the notion of ending impunity, which featured prominently in many actors' discussions of the aims of the ICC.

> The aim of the ICC, as the founders would say, is to put an end to the culture of impunity.
>
> (Participant M)

> The Court's aim is really participating in the fight against impunity.
>
> (Participant N)

> In relation to justice, what is important is impunity, the fight against impunity.
>
> (Participant L)

The heavy focus on ending impunity mirrors wider discourses on the International Criminal Court, with the notion of ending impunity prevalent in discussions of the Court's aims (see Chapter 3) and enshrined in the Rome Statute Preamble (1998) which states, 'Determined to put an end to impunity for the perpetrators of these crimes and thus to contribute to the prevention of such crimes.' The concept of ending impunity infers the aim of deterrence through the threat of prosecution and punishment. Indeed, references to the aim of deterrence featured in many actors' constructions of the Court.

> We hope that this [the ICC] would help deter future crimes, that it has a role to play in deterrence in the long term and that it would impact communities in a positive way . . . deterrence is always at the back of our mind.
>
> (Participant E)

> It's really a judicial institution delivering justice. I do think that in creating the Court the international community also aspires to have a deterrent effect on future crimes.
>
> (Participant G)

Thus, prevention and ending impunity are used in the context of deterrence, and these aims are a common thread in all actors' discussions of the ICC. However, within the overarching aim of preventing international crimes through ending impunity and achieving deterrence, actors constructed the notion of prevention differently.

For participants from the Office of the Prosecutor, ending impunity is linked to achieving general deterrence through symbolic prosecutions.

> It is self-evident that removing these dangerous elements in society will potentially benefit those that would otherwise be victims of crime as well as

> having a potentially dissuasive effect on others who may be encouraged to mirror such crimes.
>
> (Participant S)

In this comment, the notion of achieving specific deterrence through incapacitation of dangerous offenders is portrayed as axiomatic or self-evident and the interview participant does not elaborate on the impact of prosecuting specific offenders and removing them from victim communities. Contrastingly, the participant goes on to describe in some detail the functioning of general deterrence and the impact of ICC prosecutions in other countries.

> In Columbia or in Nepal we hear information that the fact that we prosecuted Thomas Lubanga, a rebel leader in the DRC, for child soldier offences, had a ripple effect in a number of different countries, who then issued orders to demobilize children under the age of 15 because they were aware that the ICC could potentially exercise jurisdiction. . . . So there may be some evidence or anecdotal suggestion that there is some kind of persuasive or dissuasive effect or preventative or deterrent effect in relation to the Court.
>
> (Participant S)

Several other participants from NGO groups working closely with the Court also mirrored this notion of general deterrence.

> Our groups do mention the 'Lubanga effect'. After the issuance of the arrest of Lubanga, they heard some groups and some military leaders in Congo in Ituri talking about Lubanga and [saying] 'I don't want to be sent to The Hague'.
>
> (Participant E)

> When Lubanga was arrested on the accusation of child soldiering a lot of child soldiers were released from armoured groups, sometimes later on they were integrated again, but at least it is clear today for everybody that recruiting child soldiers is not something that you should do.
>
> (Participant R)

For the Office of the Prosecutor, the aim of general deterrence is implemented by prosecuting a small number of individuals who bear the greatest responsibility for international crimes (ICC OTP 2010). This strategy is explained by two representatives from the OTP.

> We choose to go after those who have the greatest responsibility . . . to have some very important symbolic cases and then to develop, heavily, communication around these cases to use them as examples. For example, to use the Lubanga case to show that recruiting children is a crime and to explain this.
>
> (Participant T)

> A phrase that the prosecutor often uses is 'how to maximize our impact' because one Court sitting in The Hague prosecuting, like, two or three cases a year is not going to achieve anything unless it can basically cast a very wide shadow. So this is the image or the symbols we are using in the discourse to show it's about what is the impact of these cases on the broader processes at the national level.
>
> (Participant S)

These discourses mirror prosecutorial strategy documents that describe maximizing the impact of prosecutions as a guiding principle of the Office of the Prosecutor (ICC OTP 2006b, 2010). The metaphor of casting a wide shadow presents the ICC as a threatening institution, reinforcing the notion of general deterrence that lies at the heart of understandings of prevention. As the OTP has a strong voice, these constructions of the Court are dominant in wider discourses (as explored in Chapter 2).

Despite agreeing with the notion of ending impunity and prevention, other actors interpreted these aims differently to these constructions by the OTP. For example, interview participants from the Office of Public Counsel for the Defence highlighted the problematic nature of using symbolic cases to achieve general deterrence.

> There has been so many human rights reports saying that the DRC government's forces have been implicated in the atrocities and yet nothing. So it's a sense of unfairness . . . that can sometimes make it difficult for local communities to accept the justice because in their heads they think, 'well OK, maybe I'm a part of Lubanga's ethnic group, maybe we committed atrocities, but what I can't understand is why we are being targeted by the Court when people who committed worse atrocities aren't'.
>
> (Participant N)

The sense of unfairness was also described by representatives from human rights organizations.

> I think one of the aspirations is certainly deterrence and preventing violence, but I would say that the fundamental aim is really . . . to communicate that justice to those that suffer from it, because they are often at such a remove from the Court itself.
>
> (Participant B)

> Only three, four, five people are going to be accused or prosecuted for the crimes in the country . . . victims of the crimes committed who still live in the communities tell you that, 'well I still have to run into this or that person who has committed crimes when I go to the market and no, I don't have a feeling of justice because he's not going to reach the ICC' . . . so there is still a sense of impunity.
>
> (Participant F)

While these actors engage with the idealpolitik of prevention, they simultaneously use realpolitik to counter prosecutorial constructions of general deterrence. In doing so, these actors assert their own aims and interests; for the defence, the focus is on unfair prosecutions and the impact of selective prosecutions on alleged offenders and criminalized groups, while for the victim-oriented human rights representatives, the focus is on a sense of unfairness for victims.

Journalists also engage with the preventative paradigm while highlighting the limitations of prosecutorial constructions of deterrence through selective prosecutions.

> I don't think there has ever been a direct discussion at the ICC of why certain people [are arrested] and not others. The other thing is they also say that they can't arrest everyone . . . they are just arresting a few to make an example out of them.
>
> (Participant K)

This participant emphasizes the lack of clarity in the Office of the Prosecutor's idealistic discussions, which can result in conflicting messages.

> The message that the ICC wants to send is that if you commit atrocities we are going to come after you, but the message they are actually sending is that if you commit atrocities, just make sure you are successful, make sure it actually leads to something, make sure you actually get into power, otherwise we will come after you.
>
> (Participant K)

As these discussions illustrate, although all actors highlight the importance of prevention, deterrence, and ending impunity, they engage with this goal differently. For the prosecutor, the notion of general deterrence is used to legitimate selective prosecutions. For the defence, preventing international crimes is important, but the strategy of symbolic prosecutions is problematic and presents unfair outcomes for certain groups. For NGOs, general deterrence is a key aim; however, it is equally important to communicate prosecutorial strategies so as to minimize expectation gaps and provide justice to victims. For journalists, the selective prosecutions of the Court need to be communicated effectively to achieve prevention and even-handed justice. This highlights how actors use idealpolitik and realpolitik to assert their own aims and interests within the overarching common aim of prevention.

The future-oriented nature of the Court

The focus on general deterrence constructs the Court as a future-oriented institution that seeks to project its power past individuals and specific situations and towards other situations around the world, using a few, selective cases as exemplars of the potential for prosecution and punishment. The future-oriented nature of the Court is expressed by a representative of the presidency, who explains:

> We are not looking at the past, the ICC is a forward looking institution. . . . It's dealing with current events and it has a potentially huge role with respect to the future. I think that's really crucial to explain.
>
> (Participant U)

The Office of the Prosecutor constructs its strategies based on the future-orientation. This is exemplified in the use of early warnings from the Court to prevent crime from escalating in countries currently experiencing conflict.

> Every time we have information about crimes that may be under our jurisdiction we try to be very public about it to contribute immediately and to immediately push local states to react. . . . The objective of this is that we contribute to prevention and that it will contribute to calm the atmosphere and to reduce the risk of crimes being committed.
>
> (Participant T)

> In Kenya we're hoping that our intervention there will help to dissuade [them] that in the next election cycle they will again gain power through violence, by showing that actually violence may well be a ticket to the prison cell rather than a ticket to the cabinet.
>
> (Participant S)

These comments mirror prosecutorial strategies around prevention and deterrence. The recent 2010 strategy paper from the OTP states that the 'mere announcement of ICC activities can have a preventive impact on this process. The monitoring of a situation can deter future crimes. It increases the risk of punishment even before trials begin. This effect is not limited to the situation under investigation but extends to all States Parties and reverberates worldwide' (ICC OTP 2010, p. 7). Other participants also referred to the system of early warnings and the ICC's capacity to prevent violence from escalating as a positive aspect of the Court.

> The Court can play a good role in preventing conflict. . . . It was actually quite good what the prosecutor did in Côte d'Ivoire—issuing a statement saying OK, I have jurisdiction over your country, be careful, if you commit an offence I will investigate. That is preventative; to try and put an end to the commission of crimes, and it can be quite a positive aspect of the Court.
>
> (Participant N)

Within these idealpolitik constructions of the Court's future-oriented prevention strategies, many interview participants highlighted the limitations of the Court. For example, a participant from an NGO agrees with preventative messages but raises the problems inherent in such messages.

> That has to be done very cautiously because when the ICC prosecutor says the situation is under analysis by his office, it raises a lot of expectation among those who are the victim of these crimes that there will in fact be an investigation, and given that the prosecutor is already looking at nine situations under analysis, that there are already five investigations, now six, even from a resource point of view it is unlikely that there will be investigations in all nine that the prosecutor is currently looking at.
>
> (Participant B)

Again, this message is constructed in terms of the victim-oriented focus of the group this individual represents.

Other participants also discussed the limitations of the Court in achieving deterrence through a future-oriented focus. These discussions highlighted the ICC's reliance on state support to achieve prosecutions.

> The ICC is powerful but at the same time it has limits and it's only in the hands of the states. Those limits are in the hands of the states so they can put the limits pretty much wherever they want.
>
> (Participant F)

> The Court is very much dependent on external power, for everything. For arrest, for investigations, to bring witnesses, everything, so it's a weakness for sure.
>
> (Participant O)

From here, participants discussed the political influences on the Court and how this determines who the ICC prosecutes, or issues symbolic warnings to.

> If the prosecutor knows that he needs the help from the government, he doesn't really have a strong incentive to go against the government, so most of our cases are political opponents. So, for example, in Congo it's all political opponents of Kabila. In Uganda it's the LRA, it's not the Ugandan army, even though the ICJ held that Uganda was involved in Congo committing atrocities.
>
> (Participant O)

> It is more difficult to prosecute people from Western countries or even in South America. Prosecuting Russians for what happened in Georgia, it's not easy, or for what happened in Afghanistan. . . . It is politically much more difficult to confront powerful countries . . . and even in Africa it's difficult to confront, for instance, the Sudanese president. . . . There's still no general feeling that such a form of justice is normal and to be respected and international justice is very close to politics and power.
>
> (Participant D)

This is not to say that representatives from the OTP do not acknowledge limitations. For example, one participant stated:

> We have acknowledged that obviously from the outset that the ICC is not a panacea for all prosecutions. Obviously it can't respond to justice as a whole.
> (Participant S)

Another participant from the OTP made reference to the notion of politics in the work of the Court.

> We are playing in a political world, we need to be aware of that fact that people will consider us as a political actor in some instances, but we need to maintain our non-political position. We are a judicial body, we go after, we prosecute, and we arrest people for crimes. This has a political impact.
> (Participant T)

Despite engaging in these wider and differential constructions, these participants often externalized limitations to reconstruct or minimize the role of politics in the selection of cases and to assert the authority and power of the ICC.

5.3 Acting as a catalyst: the persuasive capacity of the Court

Acting as a persuasive institution is the second commonly constructed aim of the ICC. The ICC is constructed as persuasive in several ways, from setting standards and acting as a model of international law and justice, to its capacity to 'catalyse' and encourage national proceedings using exemplar cases and the principle of complementarity. Many of these persuasive aims are underpinned by the preventative foundations discussed above, and they also build on wider discourses of the Court, as explored in Chapter 2. Similarly, the persuasive aim of the Court is constructed differentially according to actors' own aims and interests.

Reflecting broader discourses on the ICC, several interview participants described the Court as a standard setter—for example:

> It is perceived as a standard setting body . . . a standard setting body and an opportunity is a good way to present the International Criminal Court.
> (Participant G)

> The ICC is important in that the Rome Statute does set standards.
> (Participant U)

The notion of setting standards is associated with the ICC's recognition and codification of particular crimes at an international level. In this context, the value of the Court is its symbolic reinforcement of the types of acts and situations that constitute international crimes. The recognition of such crimes is achieved through the codification of crimes in the Rome Statute and the threat of punishment associated with symbolic prosecutions. In this construction, the ICC represents a strong symbolic reaction from the international community, which many interview participants viewed as a positive aspect of the Court.

> I think success for the Court in the short term is . . . really giving a sense that these crimes are not acceptable, that the international community won't accept them and that this is how we go about this. . . . I think in the longer term, success could be defined by the broader recognition of these crimes—that these acts are crimes, that the people that commit them will face consequences, and that there is a reduction in the kind of crimes.
>
> (Participant B)

Persuasion through setting standards and codifying international crimes is closely linked to the preventative imperatives of the Court. Such descriptions construct the Court as persuasive due to the threat that it poses by its very existence. The persuasive capacity of the Court is thus inherently linked to the concept of prevention and ending impunity, a link which is further evidenced by the following quotations:

> It has codified these crimes, even though they are only codified for the purpose of the ICC; still they are now in black and white and it's also enshrined the principle that these crimes must be punished, there must be accountability for these crimes, that perpetrators must be held responsible.
>
> (Participant A)

> The strength of the Court is that it exists. That's its main strength, that something like the Court can exist and be permanent and not be something that will arrive after the fact but be something that is available and that people can see somewhere as a possible threat to those that commit crimes and a credible threat so that these crimes will not be committed.
>
> (Participant T)

The relationship between prevention and persuasion in this discourse illustrates the merging of human rights assumptions and criminal law paradigms in the foundations of the Court. Human rights have traditionally created symbolic norms, which can have a persuasive capacity in international society due to their ability to create collective identity by defining deeply held norms (Hawkins 2004; Risse 1999; von Bernstorff 2008). International criminal justice brings an enforcement mechanism to these norms by providing the threat of sanction or punishment. The ICC is, thus, simultaneously conceived as an institution that can define norms, and also enforce these norms through punishment. The fusion of these principles makes the ICC a persuasive body that projects the dualistic aims of norm creation and norm enforcement; the ICC must simultaneously define and denounce acts as international crimes, thus creating stronger international norms, and also achieving deterrence as a means of enforcing these collective norms.

This norm-building, persuasive capacity of the Court was elaborated upon by many interview participants. While some used the terminology of standard setting and codifying crimes, others used the notion of the ICC as a model which can be instructive and persuasive in the sense of affecting laws at a national level.

> I really hope that [the ICC] [will] be just showing a good model of how it can work. . . . It's the model; it is the Court's potential as a model that is the most important.
>
> (Participant A)

> The ICC has to be a model, it has to go for the cases when the state cannot do it and go after those most responsible, but that needs to be complemented by local means.
>
> (Participant F)

Here, the ICC is constructed as a persuasive institution, due to its ability to define the parameters of legitimate justice processes and in doing so persuade countries to adopt particular laws and practices.

> I think we're only looking at it [justice] within the context of criminal justice and hoping that the process of accountability that we are trying to promote, both at our level and at a domestic level, will contribute towards a more rule-of-law orientated society . . . that the international level will have a trickledown effect at the domestic level.
>
> (Participant S)

The notions of the ICC as a standard setter and model of justice were commonly described by all actors. There were, however, differences in the way actors viewed the implementation of these aims and the relationship between the ICC and local jurisdictions. The notion of the ICC as a model envisages the Court as a wider system of international criminal justice.

> The system is not about the ICC isolated and alone, but it's a system of international criminal justice.
>
> (Participant F)

> It takes more than an international criminal court to make sure that war crimes are never committed again. . . . They often refer to the Court as the Rome Statute system, as opposed to the International Criminal Court.
>
> (Participant G)

References to the ICC as part of a wider system of justice take responsibility off the ICC for achieving comprehensive prosecutions, yet construct the Court as at the centre of the international justice system.

The centrality of the ICC to the system of international justice is implicit in constructions of the ICC as a model. Several interview participants also spoke more explicitly about the position of the Court in a system defined by the notion of complementarity.

> I think the ICC will play a key role . . . we see it already playing quite a preeminent role. We see other Courts and tribunals cite the ICC, so other courts and tribunals, such as the special tribunal for Lebanon or the Cambodia Courts, they actually refer to ICC jurisprudence.
>
> (Participant C)

> The ICC is a kind of safety net to catch anything that falls through the cracks in the domestic justice system. If the cracks are too big then the net will break. So it has a limited but very important role in that it's often called the centrepiece of the system of international justice. . . . It is the centrepiece that kind of holds the strings together.
>
> (Participant U)

Catalysing national prosecutions: the principle of complementarity

Constructions of the Court as a persuasive model and standard setter stem from the notion of complementarity, which dictates that the Court exists to complement rather than supersede national jurisdictions. Many interview participants discussed the role of complementarity as central to the work of the Court.

> Really the idea is to get justice for these horrific crimes and reparation for these crimes, if possible, at national level, and when it's not possible, in The Hague.
>
> (Participant E)

> The ultimate aims of the Rome Statute can only be achieved with the parallel and complementary roles of the ICC, states and international organizations, the UN, civil society . . . the Court alone has a limited role. . . . It's really the work of the domestic justice system that is more important in actually deterring crimes and punishing perpetrators.
>
> (Participant U)

The Office of the Prosecutor describes the principle of positive complementarity as central to the prosecutorial strategies of the Court (ICC OTP 2006b, 2010). Interview participants representing the OTP spoke at length about the conception and role of positive complementarity in prosecutorial strategies and processes.

> We are not looking at this as a negative, competitive model and we are positive about the notion of complementarity, we don't see it as a threat to the

> ICC. . . . The ideal scenario would be that the ICC would have no cases at all as a consequence of having well-functioning national cases because [of] the way that our system works, through complementarity.
>
> (Participant S)

> We are here as the ICC, but you are the first responsible as states to prosecute these crimes, and indeed if crimes are committed you need to do something so that it stops and so that it doesn't happen. And us [The ICC/OTP] we're saying if you don't do it, we will do it, and we hope that by saying this it will make the crime stop.
>
> (Participant T)

The principle of positive complementarity highlights the importance of national justice processes in supporting the work of the Court. This strategy allows the ICC to focus on prosecuting a handful of symbolic, exemplary cases to persuade local jurisdictions to undertake complementary prosecutions, thus supporting the ICC's focus on general deterrence and symbolic standard-setting or norm creation.

Within this system, then, the ICC's role is limited to encouraging national prosecutions through its own symbolic prosecutions, focused on general deterrence. Here, the ICC is constructed as a catalyst to achieve local prosecutions.

> There is a real potential for the Court to be catalysts.
>
> (Participant A)

> The ICC can be a source of inspiration, and a catalyst.
>
> (Participant U)

> Our goal is to put ourselves out of business . . . we hope that prosecutions will help to stimulate and catalyse and encourage complementary national prosecutions . . . which are the ultimate goal.
>
> (Participant S)

Following these constructions of the ICC as a catalyst, many interview participants described the role of the Court, in applying pressure to local communities and international society by drawing attention to particular conflicts through its prosecutions.

> The Court has the potential to shine a light on certain affected countries in the world, because most people have never heard of these regions which have been affected and the Court can draw attention.
>
> (Participant C)

The concept of applying pressure, and its link to general deterrence and complementarity, is encapsulated in the following quotation:

> Every time we have information about crimes that may be under our jurisdiction, we try to be very public about it to contribute immediately to push local states to react and to act on these crimes and to prosecute. For example, when we are in DRC, we hope that by prosecuting a few cases and being very vocal about all the crimes, this will push the DRC and donor states and the international community to support their national system to open cases against other people.
>
> (Participant T)

The various constructions of complementarity and the notion of persuasion by interview participants highlights the use of idealpolitik and realpolitik to construct the common aims of the ICC in terms that assert identity and interests of particular offices. For example, participants from the OTP used idealistic notions of complementarity to define and justify selective prosecutions.

> We believe that criminal prosecutions can have an influence on perpetrators and can potentially have an impact on the prevention of crimes and deterrence, but only to the extent the sanctions are predictable. . . . The prosecutor pointed out the need to have complementary national activities to complement the work of the Court, otherwise you would be left with an impunity gap—gap between those who are brought to trial, which may be a very select number, and the vast majority who may be less culpable to some extent. . . . The Court is now up and running, it is doing cases, it's fully functional, but the other half of the Rome Statute is still not fully functional, we still don't see numerous national trials complementing the work of the Court.
>
> (Participant S)

As this quotation highlights, the participant identifies the limitations associated with the ICC's aim of deterrence; however, a narrative is developed illustrating the responsibility of national jurisdictions to provide complementary prosecutions, thus limiting the responsibility of the OTP and reasserting the legitimacy of the preventative aims of the Court. This type of narrative is also evident in comments from another OTP representative.

> We are fully independent and we need to maintain this independence—at the same time we also rely on the cooperation of states to be able to operate. So that is the main limitation[, . . .] our capacity to do our work on the ground; it's our capacity to access territories, investigate and prosecute in good conditions.
>
> (Participant T)

Here the limitation of the Court's reliance on states is highlighted, but states are responsibilized, and the independence and authority of the OTP is maintained.

Contrastingly, interview participants from the Office of Public Counsel for the Defence highlighted the strategic use of the principle of complementarity by the Office of the Prosecutor and discussed the limitations and dangers associated with the selective nature of justice at the ICC.

> In a lot of the cases that the ICC has seized up at the moment, domestic courts are perfectly able, they just don't want to; it's more politically convenient for them for the ICC to have the case. So when that happens, the ICC isn't really reinforcing local justice . . . so rather than strengthening local judiciary and local institutions I think that sometimes we might be weakening them.
>
> (Participant N)

> If you think that the aim of the Court is to help the countries develop fair trial procedure and to implement in their own legislation then I think we are far from really achieving that. . . . Until now the ICC is very much encouraging the situation countries to send us their opponents. They have basically put the fight against impunity above the principle of complementarity and for this reason they just take all the people that are sent to us.
>
> (Participant O)

This can again be contrasted with the way that victims and NGOs construct the notion of complementarity and the persuasive capacity of the Court. For this group, complementarity provides the potential for influencing crime and justice systems at the national level, and this constructs the ICC as a potential capacity-building body.

> Complementarity means lots of things and the way the Court could contribute is by training local judiciary by passing on local information they collect when they do their investigations.
>
> (Participant F)

> The Court needs to be more closely connected to local communities. . . . The principle of complementarity could be used to help build local courts and develop proficiency at a local level.
>
> (Participant A)

This construction of the principle of complementarity as a means of building capacity in local jurisdictions is denied by those representing the OTP, and by other representatives of the Court, such as the Presidency.

> Different people have given different definitions [of positive complementarity] to the extent that the ICC should be engaging in capacity building and technical assistance with states and that should be its primary focus, which probably isn't possible because we're not a technical assistance body.

> The UN has numerous bodies for that, there are many others who do that, NGOs, but we are ultimately a judicial body.
>
> (Participant S)

> We are not a capacity-building organization, we are not a development agency, so it's up to other institutions to actually do the work and to actually finance and support national jurisdictions, [to] finance rehabilitation of the judicial system. What we do is show that something needs to be done.
>
> (Participant T)

> When it comes to the development of national capacities, what we keep stressing always is that the ICC is not a development agency; it's not a training academy. Others have to have the lead and bear the responsibility for strengthening positive complementarity . . . it's far better that one lets the ICC focus on its core mandate.
>
> (Participant U)

Thus, although constructions of the Court as a persuasive standard setter and model of justice are common, conceptualizations of the nature of complementarity and the role of local justice systems vary according to actors' positions and interests. For the OTP, complementarity legitimates selective prosecutions used as exemplars. The defence uses realpolitik to counter this construction of complementarity and reframes the notion in terms of achieving fair trial standards in national jurisdictions. Contrastingly, NGOs and victims' groups construct complementarity widely to try to build capacity and develop local justice systems. These wider constructions of complementarity are countered by the OTP, which confirms the ICC's narrow role as a catalyst for national prosecutions. As the OTP has the most power to define complementarity through its prosecutions, this version of complementarity is most evident in wider discourses surrounding the Court, as explored in Chapter 2.

5.4 Concluding comments

The analysis of interview data and actors' interpretation of the aims of the Court illustrates the use of the broad and overarching common aims of prevention and persuasion. The analysis also highlights the differences between the groups that construct the ICC and demonstrates how this fragmented environment creates contradictions in the work of the Court. Actors use both idealpolitik and realpolitik to translate the broad aims of prevention and persuasion according to their own aims and interests. Such interactions reinforce the identities of these actors while also creating contradictory interpretations of the aims of prevention and persuasion.

Actors' constructions of the aims of the Court mirror the wider contradictions explored in previous chapters. In this context, the sustained use of idealpolitik evidenced through the idealistic and vague aims of prevention and persuasion is strategic. These broad aims can be interpreted in numerous ways and this allows for the multiple, and often conflicting, constructions of the Court. The strategically vague aims of the Court provide a sense of unity between the disparate groups that make up the ICC. Idealpolitik and realpolitik are used simultaneously and ambivalently to allows actors to assert the primary aims of the Court, while also maintaining their own goals. The ICC's aims are therefore structurally ambivalent as they allow for both fragmentation and unity in a complex environment.

6 The trial as a site of contest: the DRC and Thomas Lubanga

The International Criminal Court is pulled in many directions by conflicting interpretations of its broad aims, making contradictions an inevitable part of the ICC. This chapter analyses the trial of Thomas Lubanga, using the trial as a case study to explore how the contradictions of the Court arise as idealpolitik and realpolitik are used during ICC cases. The trial of Thomas Lubanga demonstrates how different groups use common, idealistic aims, while interpreting these aims differently to further their own goals and interests. The aims of prevention and persuasion provide a sense of unity and momentum in the fragmented and antagonistic environment of late modernity, allowing different, and often conflicting, groups to engage with the Court. The chapter analyses transcripts, press releases, NGO documents, and media articles surrounding the Lubanga case. It also includes some relevant interview data where participants have referred to the Lubanga trial and situation in the Democratic Republic of the Congo. The chapter analyses the Lubanga trial from his arrest and transfer to the Court to his sentencing in 2012. Discussions of subsequent appeals and victim reparation lie outside the scope of this analysis.

The chapter begins by placing the Lubanga trial in context, providing a brief overview of the violence and conflict in the Democratic Republic of the Congo. From here, the chapter analyses how idealpolitik and realpolitik were used by a variety of actors during the Lubanga trial, considering how the aims of prevention and persuasion provided the momentum for the trial to continue through to a guilty verdict. The chapter concludes by examining the Lubanga trial in relation to other ICC trials and in the broader context of the ongoing violence in the DRC.

6.1 The situation in the Democratic Republic of the Congo

The DRC has suffered through two centuries of violence and conflict since its colonization in 1885 (Mullins and Rothe 2008a). After the brutality of its colonial period, the DRC underwent a turbulent transition to independence, which was followed by the harsh 32-year dictatorship of Mobutu Sese Seko. Since the fall of Mobutu's regime, the DRC has experienced two violent wars, perpetrated by numerous groups including rebel groups, armed forces, and government forces from both within the DRC and neighbouring countries, such as Rwanda and Uganda (HRW 2006a, 2010a). These wars have included sustained exploitation and plundering of the nation's vast mineral resources (Mullins and Rothe 2008b).

Historical overview: imperialism, colonialism, and dictatorship

Violence, brutality, and conflict in the Democratic Republic of the Congo can be traced back to 1885 when King Leopold II of Belgium acquired the country (Nzongola-Ntalaja 2002). Although King Leopold claimed altruistic motives for his colonization of the country, he did little to develop the DRC and instead exploited the Congo for personal profit (Hochschild 1999). King Leopold's reign of the DRC, then referred to as the Congo Free State, was characterized by brutality. The savage nature of the colonization was captured by Joseph Conrad's (1990) novel *The Heart of Darkness*, which was based on his experiences in the Congo, a situation he described as 'the vilest scramble for loot that has ever disfigured the human conscience' (Conrad 1934, p. 17). During his reign, King Leopold II plundered the country's rich mineral deposits and sold them internationally, pocketing the profits for himself rather than developing the country's infrastructure (Renton, Seddon, and Zeilig 2007).

In the early 1900s, these practices drew increasing international attention and condemnation, placing pressure on King Leopold and Belgium (Ascherson 1963), resulting in the Belgian parliament annexing King Leopold's ruling of Congo and taking control of the country in 1908 (Renton, Seddon, and Zeilig 2007). Although it assuaged international pressure, the takeover changed little for the people of the Congo with the brutal treatment and the plundering of natural resources continuing under Belgian rule (Nzongola-Ntalaja 2002).

In the late 1950s, nationalistic sentiments within the Congo were growing and there was increasing pressure for independence, including riots that were met with brutal repression (Nzongola-Ntalaja 2002, 2004). In 1960 the Mouvement National Congolais (MNC), led by Patrice Lumumba, won parliamentary elections and the Belgian government left the DRC shortly afterwards (Cole 2006). Despite the sentiments expressed during this handover, the Congo soon descended into chaos and violence as Lumumba inherited a country in need of national identity and social, political, and religious structures (Mullins and Rothe 2008a). In 1961 Lumumba was kidnapped and assassinated, allegedly with the assistance of the United States, who viewed Lumumba as a socialist and a Soviet ally (Weissman 2010). This coup d'état was led by Mobutu Sese Seko, who installed himself as president of the Congo, which he renamed Zaire. Mobutu's reign lasted 32 years, from 1964 to 1996, with support from international organizations and powerful countries such as the United States. Although relative peace ensued under his rule, Mobutu was a dictator and his regime was characterized by human rights abuses, corruption, and political repression (Nzongola-Ntalaja 2002). Mobutu continued the history of pillaging the DRC's natural resources for personal profit, with the proceeds of sales of the country's resources going to

Mobutu and his followers (Renton, Seddon, and Zeilig 2007). His practices continued the extreme poverty of the people of Congo and reproduced the repressive conditions of imperial and colonial rule.

The Congo wars and post-war violence

In 1996, Rwanda invaded Zaire with the support of Uganda and Burundi, triggering the First Congolese War (Turner 2007). The attack was led by the Alliance of Democratic Forces for the Liberation of Congo-Zaire (ADFL), a group that eventually toppled Mobutu and replaced him with Laurent Kabila, a leader who was seen as an ally to Rwanda and Uganda and their interests in Zaire (then renamed the Democratic Republic of the Congo).[1] Mobutu fled the country with his family, who had amassed an immense fortune through the exploitation of the Congo (Wong 2009). The fall of Mobutu's regime heralded 20 years of violence and chaos for the Congo (Mullins and Rothe 2008a).

The Second Congolese War, which occurred between 1998 and 2003, saw the destabilization of central Africa deepen considerably, with dozens of militia and armies from at least six different countries taking part in violence, fuelled by shifting alliances and competition for access to Congo's vast natural resources (Reyntjens 2001). The involvement of many groups, the large geographical area of the fighting, and the high level of death and destruction saw the war characterized as 'Africa's First World War' (Turner 2007).[2] The International Rescue Committee (2007) estimated that 3.9 million deaths were caused by the war between 1998 and 2004 alone, which saw the war likened to the Holocaust and a tsunami (Turner 2007).

In 1999 the Lusaka Ceasefire Agreement (UNSC 1999a) was signed by the major parties of the conflict. This agreement did not achieve peace as tensions escalated between Rwandan and Ugandan troops, and Kabila's forces continued to push forward towards Eastern Congo (Ngolet 2011). As part of the Lusaka Agreement, the United Nations Security Council established a peacekeeping

1 As the Cold War came to an end the US lost interest in the DRC and Mobutu consequently lost support from his most powerful allies (see Emizet 2000 for a discussion of the rise and fall of Mobutu's regime). This coincided with a growing desire for control of the Congo from neighbouring countries of Rwanda and Uganda (Prunier 2004). Following the genocide of 1994, Rwanda accused Mobutu and Zaire of harbouring Hutu combatants who fled Rwanda after the massacre of the Tutsi population (Prunier 2009). Both Rwanda and Uganda were keen to install a head of state in Zaire who would be sympathetic to their efforts against this population of refugees and the protection of their borders (Prunier 2004). Alongside these official motives, Rwanda and Uganda also sought to exploit the mineral-rich land and profit from mining the large deposits of coltan and cassiterite and selling the spoils to Western corporations for use in electronic products such as mobile phones and PlayStations (Hari 2006).

2 The violence in 1998 was sparked by Kabila's attempts to expel Rwandan staff and military from the DRC after he struggled to govern the country with a conspicuous Rwandan presence (Reyntjens 1999). In response, Rwanda, Uganda, and Burundi sent more troops into Eastern DRC and supported rebel groups such as the Rally for Congolese Democracy (RCD) while Kabila's government was supported by troops from Namibia, Zimbabwe, and Angola (BBC 2012c).

force known as the United Nations Mission in the Democratic Republic of the Congo (referred to as its French acronym MONUC and later MONUSCO) (see UNSC 1999b). This peacekeeping force was described by some as a failure, in the midst of continuing violence and a rising death toll (Dizolele 2004). The mission was also the subject of scandal, with accusations of peacekeepers sexually exploiting and abusing women and children and engaging in the survival sex trade (Notar 2006).

On 16 January 2001, Laurent Kabila was assassinated by one of his bodyguards (Reyntjens 2001). The next day his son, Joseph Kabila, was installed as the head of state, a position that he still holds. During 2002 and 2003 Kabila negotiated a series of peace deals which persuaded Rwanda and Uganda to withdraw from the DRC and created a power-sharing interim government, known as the Transitional Government of the Democratic Republic of the Congo (Zapata 2011). The DRC's first democratic elections since independence were held in 2006, in which Joseph Kabila was announced president over competitor Jean Pierre Bemba (IRIN 2006).[3]

Although the Second Congolese War ended in 2003, violence, conflict, and disorder have continued to plague the DRC (HRW 2012d). The majority of the post-war violence has occurred in the east of the country and in particular in the regions of Ituri and North and South Kivu. These areas are mineral-rich with large deposits of gold, coltan, and other precious metals. As such, many militia groups are struggling for control over the region. The militias are backed by the governments of Rwanda, Uganda, and the DRC. The conflict is also fuelled by ethnic tensions; however, the ongoing violence in these regions is more complex than ethnic rivalries—it is a national and international struggle for power with Rwanda, Uganda, and the DRC battling for control of the mineral-rich land (HRW 2003b). Although militia groups have been organized along ethnic lines, alliances are constantly shifting and militias have manipulated ethnic differences to incite violence, in the quest for control of the territory and its resources (Mullins and Rothe 2008a).[4] Human Rights Watch (HRW 2003b, p. 2) describes the conflict in Ituri as 'a complex web of local, national, and regional conflicts that developed after a local dispute between Hema and Lendu, . . . exacerbated by Ugandan actors and aggravated by the broader international war in the DRC'.[5]

3 Jean Pierre Bemba is currently being prosecuted for two counts of crimes against humanity and three counts of war crimes for murder and rape, allegedly committed in the Central African Republic between October 2002 and March 2003 (ICC 2008a).

4 The two traditional ethnic groups in the region are the Hema pastoralists and the Lendu agriculturalists. The division between these groups was reinforced by colonialization when the Belgian authorities created separate administrative systems and structures for each group, leading the Hema group to become the local 'elites' (Rothe and Mullins 2008a). As with other ethnic conflicts in Africa, such as Rwanda, the hostility between ethnic groups was fuelled by divisive colonial practices (see Mamdani 2001 for a discussion).

5 During the Second Congolese War, Uganda occupied Ituri from 1998 to May 2003 and provided arms and military training to different ethnic groups, fuelling a limited dispute between Hema and Lundu (HRW 2003b). When Uganda and Rwanda withdrew troops at the formal end of the war, they left behind several factional militias which they continue to support. Uganda supports

Similar patterns of violence occur in the Kivus where numerous militias battle for control of the land.

There are widespread reports of savage attacks, torture, brutal rape, extreme sexual violence, forced labour, harsh conditions in artisanal mines, and the widespread use of children as soldiers and sex slaves (UN Human Rights Council 2010). In 2008, it was estimated that 45,000 people were dying every month from the violence in the DRC (McGreal 2008). The ongoing conflict has caused severe death, destruction, and damage. The International Rescue Committee (2007) estimates that between August 1998 and April 2007 there have been 5.4 million war-related deaths in the DRC,[6] making the situation the deadliest conflict since World War II. An estimated 2.1 million of these deaths occurred since the formal end of the war in 2003 (International Rescue Committee 2007). The United Nations Human Rights Council (2010, 2012) documented widespread war crimes and crimes against humanity, including torture, violence, and sustained human rights abuses throughout the country. The conflict has included extreme sexual violence, with tens of thousands of women and girls suffering horrific rape and abuse (HRW 2009a). Children have also been particularly vulnerable in the conflict, with the use of children as soldiers and slaves a common practice in the war (Rakisits 2008). In 2010, Human Rights Watch (HRW 2010b) estimated that at least 1.8 million people had been displaced by the violence, making them vulnerable to abuse, hunger, and disease (HRW 2010b).

The International Criminal Court and the Democratic Republic of the Congo

As this brief overview highlights, the DRC has faced over a century of brutal conflict. Even after the formal end of the Second Congolese War, violence has continued to plague the east of the country (Carpenter 2012). Consequently, shortly after the establishment of the ICC, the chief prosecutor began closely analysing the situation. In September 2003, the prosecutor informed ICC States Parties that he was ready to request authorization from the pre-trial chamber to use his *proprio motu* powers to start an investigation, but that a referral and active support from the DRC would assist his work (ICC OTP 2004b). In March 2004, the DRC referred the situation in the country to the Court (ICC OTP 2004a). In June 2004, Prosecutor Moreno-Ocampo formally opened an investigation into DRC stating, 'The opening of the first investigation of the ICC is a major

the Front des nationalistes et intégrationnistes (FNI), a Lendu-based ethnic armed force, and the Party for the Unity and Safeguard of Integrity in Congo (PUSIC) and the Forces armées du peuple congolais (FAPC). Rwanda backs the RCD-Goma, a movement split from the RCD-ML, which provides aid to the Union of Patriotic Congolese (UPC), a Hema militia group. The DRC government now arms the Congolese Rally for Democracy-Liberation Movement (RCD-ML) which often joins in combat with militias from the Lendu groups (HRW 2003b).

6 The International Rescue Committee (2007) terms these 'excess deaths', as the number refers to the higher mortality rate in the DRC. These war-related deaths are attributable to violence as well as effects of conflicts including disease, famine, and easily preventable and treatable conditions, such as malaria, diarrhoea, pneumonia, and malnutrition.

step forward for international justice, against impunity, and for the protection of victims' (ICC OTP 2004b, n.p.).

To date, there have been six warrants of arrest issued by the ICC relating to the situation in the DRC, focusing on the east of the country and the regions of Ituri and the Kivus. As highlighted, and as will be discussed further in Section 6.2, Thomas Lubanga was the first case brought before the Court. The second case involved suspects Germain Katanga and Mathieu Ngudjolo Chui, who were alleged to have committed war crimes and crimes against humanity including murder, rape, inhumane acts, pillaging, and destruction of property (ICC 2008f).[7] On 18 December 2012, Mathieu Ngudjolo Chui was acquitted by the Court, with the judges ruling that it had not been proved beyond reasonable doubt that he had been the commander of the Lendu combatants during the attacks (ICC 2012d). On 7 March 2014, Katanga was convicted by the ICC on five counts of war crimes and crimes against humanity, marking the second conviction for the ICC following that of Lubanga.

The ICC has also issued a warrant of arrest for Bosco Ntaganda (ICC 2006b), who is the former alleged deputy chief of the general staff of the Forces patriotiques pour la libération du Congo (FPLC) and alleged chief of staff of the Congrès national pour la défense du peuple (CNDP), a group that is active in the North Kivu region of the DRC. On 18 March 2013, amidst continuing violence in the Congo, Ntaganda handed himself into the US Embassy in Rwanda and asked to be transferred to the ICC. On 22 March, he was taken into custody by the ICC.

The ICC also issued a warrant of arrest for Callixte Mbarushimana, the alleged executive secretary of the Forces démocratiques de libération du Rwanda (FDLR). Mbarushimana was charged with five counts of crimes against humanity and eight counts of war crimes; however, on 16 December 2011, Pre-Trial Chamber I of the ICC declined to confirm the charges due to a lack of evidence. Mbarushimana was released from custody and returned to France where he has refugee status (BBC 2011c). The final arrest warrant is for Sylvestre Mudacumura, the alleged supreme commander of the FDLR, who is accused of committing nine counts of war crimes in the Kivu regions, including attacking civilians, murder, mutilation, cruel treatment, rape, torture, and pillaging. Mudacumura remains at large.

6.2 Common and conflicting aims: ambivalent engagements with the Lubanga trial

The ICC's first arrest warrant was issued by Pre-Trial Chamber I on 10 February 2006 (ICC 2006a). The arrest warrant sought Thomas Lubanga, president of

7 Germain Katanga is the alleged commander of the Force de résistance patriotique en Ituri (FRPI). Mathieu Ngudjolo Chui is the alleged former leader of the FNI. The trial of these two suspects was brought together as the prosecutor alleged that they jointly committed war crimes and crimes against humanity during attacks in the Ituri region in 2003. In November 2012, the trial was separated into two cases.

the militia group the UPC and commander-in chief of the FPLC, for conscripting and using child soldiers in active hostilities during the conflict in Ituri in July 2002 and July 2003 (ICC 2006a). On 17 March, the arrest warrant for Lubanga was publicly announced and unsealed and, with the cooperation of DRC authorities, the French government, and MONUC, Lubanga was transferred to The Hague (BBC 2006). At the time of this transfer, Lubanga was already in detention in Kinshasa, after being arrested on the 19 March 2005 in connection with the killing of nine Bangladeshi UN peacekeepers in Ituri (IRIN 2005).

At a press conference held to announce the surrender of Lubanga to the International Criminal Court, the Chief Prosecutor of the ICC, Luis Moreno-Ocampo declared, 'This arrest is a step forward in realizing the Rome Statute vision—to end impunity and atrocities all over the world. For 100 years, a permanent international criminal court was a dream—this dream is becoming a reality' (ICC OTP 2006a, p. 3). The prosecutor's words exemplify how one solitary trial, the trial of Thomas Lubanga, can be used as a symbolic example of the ICC's authority, despite numerous practical limitations.

Those most responsible for the most serious crimes: Lubanga and the use of child soldiers

Lubanga appeared before ICC Pre-Trial Chamber I on 20 March 2006. Later that year, in November 2006, a three-week confirmation of charges hearing was held by the Pre-Trial Chamber. In January 2007, the Pre-Trial Chamber confirmed the charges, finding sufficient evidence to establish grounds to believe that Lubanga was criminally responsible for war crimes, namely: enlisting children under the age of 15, conscripting children under the age of 15, and using children under the age of 15 to participate actively in hostilities (ICC 2007).

From the start, the Lubanga trial received mixed reactions. Much of the early criticism of the trial concerned the prosecutor's sole focus on Lubanga's use of child soldiers to the exclusion of other serious crimes, such as the use of rape, which Human Rights Watch (HRW 2002) had termed the 'war within the war' in the DRC. Despite the sustained criticism of the limited and narrow charges, the prosecutor defended his choice to proceed with child soldier indictments. The use of idealpolitik and the common aims were central to this debate.

The Office of the Prosecutor (OTP) publicized the trial as an important case in a sequence of investigations and constructed the crime of child soldiers as particularly heinous, stating:

> The defendant stole the childhood of the victims by forcing them to kill and rape. Lubanga victimized children before they ever had the chance to grow up into full human beings who could make their own decisions. . . . Lubanga affected not just one child. Lubanga affected an entire generation.
>
> (ICC 2009c, p. 34)

The prosecutor later described the realpolitik considerations that influenced his decision to proceed with the Lubanga case with the limited charges:

> I knew to arrest Lubanga I had to move my case fast. So, I had strong evidence about child soldiers. I was not ready to prove the connection between Lubanga and some of the killings and rapes. And then I decided to move just with the case I had proofs [sic].
>
> (Interview with Moreno-Ocampo in *The Reckoning*, see Yates 2009, n.p.)

This argument is questionable as, at the time of the prosecutor's investigation, Lubanga was already in custody in the DRC (International Centre for Transitional Justice 2008). Although there may have been some speculation that Lubanga was going to be released from DRC custody, the prosecutor's fast action appears to have been driven by the need for a case to be brought before the ICC, to demonstrate the legitimacy and authority of the Court. While the prosecutor conceded that his decision on the Lubanga trial was driven by logistical considerations, he continued to use the idealpolitik of prevention to justify the focus on Lubanga's use of child soldiers. For example: 'Child conscription destroys the lives and futures of thousands of children around the world. This case will contribute to exposing the problem and stopping these criminal practices' (ICC OTP 2006c, n.p.); 'Thomas Lubanga has to learn that the Rome Statute cannot be circumvented. Children are not soldiers. If convicted, Thomas Lubanga's sentence will send a clear message: The era of impunity is ending' (ICC OTP 2009b, p. 30).

Despite this rhetoric, many human rights groups and NGOs continued to argue that the prosecutor's exclusive focus on the use of child soldiers did not accurately represent the nature and extent of the crimes in the DRC. In a joint letter to the prosecutor, human rights groups, such as Avocats Sans Frontières, Human Rights Watch, FIDH, and the International Centre for Transitional Justice, implored the prosecutor to widen the scope of the crimes stating, 'We are disappointed that two years of investigation by your office in the DRC has not yielded a broader range of charges against Mr. Lubanga' (ASF et al. 2006, n.p.). Many human rights groups also issued separate statements to express the inadequacy of the charges: 'Forcing young children to participate in warfare is a serious crime, but the ICC prosecutor must also press additional charges against militia leaders for massacres, torture, and rape' (HRW 2006b, n.p.).

> Lubanga is said to be responsible for widespread killings and countless incidents of sexual violence. Yet, Lubanga has only been charged with recruiting and using child soldiers. . . . The charges against Lubanga are so narrow in comparison to the others accused that there is a perception of imbalance on the ground.
>
> (REDRESS 2008, p. 1)

As these groups work in the field of human rights and have a strong victim-oriented focus, their objections were often framed through the lens of victims' needs and victims' rights: 'The narrow scope of the current charges may result in severely limiting victims' participation in the first proceedings before the ICC. This could negatively impact on the right of victims to reparations' (ASF et al. 2006, n.p.). While articulating their own interests and goals, and aligning themselves in terms of victims' needs, these groups also used familiar narratives and the common aims of prevention and persuasion, similar to the OTP: 'Charging those responsible . . . with representative crimes for which there is a strong evidentiary basis is crucial for the victims of these crimes and for ending the culture of impunity in the DRC' (ASF et al. 2006, n.p.).

> The ICC must send a strong signal that these crimes will be punished. . . . It is long past time to end the culture of impunity, and the ICC has taken its first step towards that goal. . . . The crimes committed in Ituri are part of a broader conflict in the Great Lakes region, and the court should finally pierce the veil of impunity that stretches beyond Congo's borders.
>
> (HRW 2006b, n.p.)

Thus, although there was division over the types of crimes that Lubanga should be charged with, both the prosecutor and human rights groups used the common aims of prevention and persuasion to provide a point of unity in their discourses.

Despite the idealpolitik, the division and contestation of the charges in the Lubanga case continued throughout the trial. During the early stages of the trial, the participating victims applied to have the facts of the case recharacterized to include charges of sexual slavery (ICC 2009a). Both the prosecutor and defence contested this application, with the prosecutor arguing that the 'appearance of impartiality will be affected if the same judges both define the charges and take a final decision on these same charges' (ICC 2009d, p. 9). The Trial Chamber later commented on the issue of charges when sentencing Lubanga, stating:

> The Chamber strongly deprecates the attitude of the former Prosecutor in relation to the issue of sexual violence. . . . Not only did the former Prosecutor fail to apply to include sexual violence or sexual slavery at any stage during these proceedings, including in the original charges, but he actively opposed taking this step during the trial when he submitted that it would cause unfairness to the accused if he was convicted on this basis.
>
> (ICC 2012b, p. 24)

While debates over the narrow focus on the use of child soldiers continued throughout the trial, the trial proceeded through to a guilty verdict. The idealpolitik enabled all parties to agree that the Lubanga case was necessary to help end impunity and act as an example to send a message to other militias. The trial thus proceeded with support despite the underlying disaccord and division over the types of crimes included.

The contested and protracted Lubanga trial and the fragmentation of the Court

As the previous discussion highlights, the Lubanga trial was characterized by tensions between the different parties. These parties struggled to come to terms with their roles and powers in the ICC's first ever trial. The trial was long and complex with several delays, which illustrated the fragmented nature of the Court and the difficulties associated with the fusion of civil and common law principles (as discussed in Chapter 3). Throughout the trial, contests between different actors, including the prosecutor, the defence, the Trial Chamber, and the Appeals Chamber, ensued.

In particular, the two stays in proceedings illustrated the contested nature of the trial. The first stay in proceedings occurred at the start of the trial. The trial was originally scheduled to commence on 23 June 2008 (ICC 2008b); however, ten days before the trial was due to start, the Trial Chamber stayed the proceedings stating that the prosecutor had failed to disclose potentially exculpatory evidence to the Court (ICC 2008c). The Trial Chamber consequently ordered the release of Lubanga on 2 July 2008 (ICC 2008d). The decision to stay the proceedings went to the Appeals Chamber, which confirmed the delay but ordered Lubanga to stay in custody (ICC 2008e). The issue arose after the prosecutor refused to produce documents that were restricted by confidentiality agreements under Article 54(3)(e) of the Rome Statute. Despite this, the clause conflicted with the duty of the prosecutor to provide exculpatory evidence to the defence and to the Trial Chamber to protect the rights of the defence (ICC 2008e). Many of the documents in question were provided to the prosecutor by the United Nations (ICC 2008e).

While the stay in proceedings represented a significant delay in the trial, many groups welcomed the judges' willingness to protect the rights of the defence. For example, the judges' insistence on protecting the rights of the defendant 'shows the ICC's commitment to fair trials' (HRW 2008, n.p.). This was particularly true of defence-oriented NGOs; for example, one interview participant representing an NGO focused on the rights of defence, explaining:

> Our position was that although we are conscious of the fact that it was hard to see the proceedings stop, we did applaud the fair approach that the judges took in making sure that the process, overall, would be fair to Mr Lubanga. . . . From our perspective we actually found it was an excellent example of the fairness of the proceedings of the ICC.
>
> (Participant G)

Others criticized the delay, particularly human rights groups who described the suspension as confusing and disappointing for victims. The FIDH (2009, n.p.), for example, expressed 'profound disappointment' at the delay, stating:

> Considering victims' strong expectations to see their cases heard at last before the International Criminal Court, we deeply hope that a judicial

> solution protecting both the right of the defence and the rights of victims to justice will be found permitting the organisation of Thomas Lubanga's trial.

As this illustrates, criticism was often expressed through the needs and rights of victims due to the victim-oriented focus of these groups. REDRESS's reaction (2009, p. 1) expressed similar sentiments:

> Survivors said that they in fact felt 're-victimised' by the consequences that the ICC's decision may now have on their security, hopes for peace and need for justice. The survivors now say they feel 'abandoned' by the international community.

Following the lengthy delay, the trial commenced on 26 January 2009 after the prosecutor disclosed all of his evidence, with the permission of the United Nations and other information suppliers (Kramer 2012). However, the trial did not proceed smoothly from here, with another stay in proceedings occurring on 8 July 2010 (ICC 2010c). This delay was again caused by the prosecutor's handling of evidence; this time the suspension of the trial related to the prosecutor's use of intermediaries who were used to source evidence and prepare witnesses for the trial (ICC 2010c).

The OTP had started using intermediaries, or individuals from local NGOs and activist groups, to gather evidence on the ground in situations where the presence of ICC staff could compromise the identity and safety of witnesses and informants. The practice of using intermediaries was designed to assist the OTP in gathering evidence in hostile situations of ongoing conflict (ICC 2010d). However, this practice came under scrutiny when it was revealed that some intermediaries were encouraging witnesses to provide false evidence. For example, one witness claimed:

> There was a story that they were telling to the witnesses. And I say that they're crooks. Why is it that I say that they're crooks and swindlers? Well instead of letting me tell the true story of what took place and instead of letting me describe all of the events that I lived through, they are inventing statements in order to manipulate the investigation.
>
> (ICC 2010b, p. 11)

Consequently, the Trial Chamber concluded:

> A series of witnesses have been called during this trial whose evidence, as a result of the essentially unsupervised actions of three of the principal intermediaries, cannot safely be relied upon. The Chamber spent a considerable period of time investigating the circumstances of a substantial number of individuals whose evidence was, at least in part, inaccurate or dishonest.
>
> (ICC 2012a, p. 219)

Following this controversy, the Trial Chamber ordered the prosecutor to disclose the identity of several intermediaries; however, the OTP refused, stating that the prosecution 'would rather face adverse consequences in its litigation than expose a person to risk on account of prior iteration with office' (ICC 2010e, p. 4). The Trial Chamber found that the refusal of the OTP to implement the chamber's orders constituted 'an abuse of the process of the Court' (ICC 2010c, p. 22) and created a situation in which the 'fair trial of the accused [was] no longer possible and justice [could not] be done, not least because the judges will have lost control of a significant aspect of the trial proceedings as provided under the Rome Statute framework' (ICC 2010c, pp. 22–23). Consequently the Trial Chamber suspended the trial and ordered the release of Lubanga (ICC 2010c).

This stay in proceedings illustrates the judges' commitment to upholding fair trial standards in the face of much public pressure to convict Lubanga (Associated Press 2011). It also illustrates the tensions between the prosecutor and the Trial Chamber as they competed for control throughout the Lubanga trial in an evolving, hybrid system of common and civil law (Schiff 2008). In their ruling, the judges maintained that 'no criminal court can operate on the basis that whenever it makes an order in a particular area, it is for the Prosecutor to elect whether or not to implement it, depending on his interpretation of his obligations' (ICC 2010e, p. 21); while the prosecutor insisted 'this is not a challenge to the Chamber; it is instead a reflection of the Prosecutor's own legal duty under the statute' (ICC 2010e, p. 4). As this demonstrates, both the judges and the prosecutors relied on interpretations of different aspects of the Rome Statute to broaden and assert their powers in the first case of the ICC.

For the defence, this stay in proceedings illustrated the inequality between the OTP and the defence and the longstanding issues with how the prosecutor collects evidence:

> We have been arguing for years now that this will create problems, because you're using people who aren't trained and it's problematic for these people as well because they don't know what the Court expects from them, the Court has no obligation to them, they give them no training on their ethical obligations and confidentiality obligations. We are now seeing these problems affect the cases, . . . while the defence have been arguing for years that it is affecting the quality of evidence.
>
> (Participant N)

Following the Trial Chamber's ruling that the trial be suspended and Lubanga released, the situation was sent to the Appeals Chamber. The Appeals Chamber found that the Trial Chamber resorted to a stay in proceedings too quickly, and subsequently overturned the suspension of the trial and ordered Lubanga to remain in custody. The situation was eventually resolved when the prosecutor offered to disclose the identity of the intermediary in question to the defence and the trial continued.

As the twists and turns of the Lubanga trial highlight, although it is often depicted as a coherent institution, the ICC is divided and fragmented. It is a collection of agencies and groups that are loosely held together by common idealistic aims. The Lubanga trial highlights how these different groups compete to achieve their goals and interests, while working under the broad rubric of ending impunity and creating a normative framework for fair trial standards at an international level. Throughout the trial, Lubanga was peripheral to the series of contests for power and control that played out between the various groups associated with the Court. Human rights groups and NGOs fought for wider charges and speedy prosecutions to ensure justice for victims. Conversely, the defence fought for a fair trial and for the ability to participate equally in a trial very much led by the OTP. The OTP held far greater and more extensive powers of investigation than the defence, which was often disadvantaged by the prosecutor's reluctance to disclose exculpatory evidence. With a far smaller budget and fewer resources, the defence was unable to collect as much evidence as the OTP. The prosecutor sought to use this as an advantage to expedite trials and achieve a fast and favourable verdict, in order to prove the legitimacy and relevance of the ICC.

The Trial Chamber and Appeals Chamber fought for due process, a fair trial, and the power to control and oversee many aspects of the case. They sought to broaden their powers to influence the direction of the trial by relying on the civil law oversight traditions included in the Rome Statute. Each party sought to establish their role in the trial and defend their goals and interests, leading to fragmentation and competition. However, unity was achieved through the common goals of prevention and persuasion.

A guilty verdict and the sentencing process

On 13 March 2012, after six years, the trial finally came to an end when the Trial Chamber convicted Lubanga of conscripting and using child soldiers (ICC 2012a). The guilty verdict reinvigorated the idealpolitik of the Court and the espousal of the aims of prevention and persuasion. In addition to a stream of positive media reports (Amnesty International 2012a; BBC 2012a; France 24 2012; Smith 2012b), numerous NGOs, human rights groups, and international organizations praised the guilty verdict for sending a strong message:

> The Lubanga trial has contributed to raising awareness about the plight of children forced to go to war. . . . Military commanders in Congo and elsewhere should take notice of the ICC's powerful message: using children as a weapon of war is a serious crime that can lead them to the dock.
>
> (HRW 2012f, n.p.)

> Today's decision sends a deterrent and unequivocal message to all those who still conscript, recruit or use children in armed conflict, or who are thinking of doing so.
>
> (No Peace Without Justice 2012, n.p.)

These proclamations were often combined with references to the aim of ending impunity: 'The conviction of Thomas Lubanga by the International Criminal Court sends a clear message to all armed groups that enslave and brutalize children: impunity will not be tolerated' (UNICEF executive director Anthony Lake quoted in Pruthi 2012, n.p.); 'The judgment is an important step forward in the worldwide struggle against impunity for grave crimes' (Open Society Justice Initiative 2012, n.p.); 'Today, impunity ends for Thomas Lubanga and those who recruit and use children in armed conflict. In this age of global media, today's verdict will reach warlords and commanders across the world and serve as a strong deterrent' (Secretary-General's Special Representative for Children and Armed Conflict, Radhika Coomaraswamy, quoted in UN 2012b, n.p.).

Despite the idealpolitik, many NGOs and human rights groups highlighted the problems and shortcomings of the trial and, in particular, the problems with the prosecutor's collection of evidence. For example, Human Rights Watch (HRW 2012f, n.p.) stated:

> The Lubanga case highlights at every phase the need for improved field investigations conducted directly by members of the Office of the Prosecutor. . . . The prosecutor and the court as a whole should draw important lessons from this first experience to improve the delivery of justice. Victims deserve nothing less.

In addition to emphasizing these problems, the guilty verdict was also used as a platform for groups to highlight their own interests and goals. Defence-based organizations emphasized the verdict as a victory for fair trial standards and protections for the accused. For example, Richard Goldstone, honorary president of the International Bar Association Human Rights Institute, declared:

> It is a tribute to their efforts, and the fortitude of the defence, that despite major setbacks, every effort was made to ensure that the trial was fair and justice done. Undoubtedly, future international trials will benefit from the jurisprudential foundations and the lessons learnt from the Lubanga case.
>
> (IBA 2012, n.p.)

Conversely, victims-oriented NGOs argued for reparations for victims, an intensification of communication and outreach to victim communities, and an increase in the number of trials brought before the ICC: 'Substantial efforts will be needed to reach out to victims on the ground. Some of the victims, living in the more remote locations, remain with little information, even on this important day' (REDRESS 2012, p. 2).

> Despite this important judgment on the use of child soldiers, victims of other atrocities at the hands of Lubanga's UPC troops have yet to see justice. . . . This verdict should not be an excuse to ignore other grave crimes committed

> by the UPC and other armed groups in Congo, and it underscores the importance of prosecuting others for a fuller range of serious crimes.
>
> (HRW 2012f, n.p.)

Shortly after the guilty verdict, on 10 July 2012, the Trial Chamber sentenced Thomas Lubanga to 14 years' imprisonment (ICC 2012b). As Lubanga had already been held in ICC detention for six years, he was only required to serve a further eight years in prison (ICC 2012b). In delivering their sentence the judges considered: the gravity of the crimes; the extent of the damage caused; the nature of the unlawful behaviour and the means employed to execute the crime; the degree of participation of the convicted person; the degree of intent; the circumstances of manner, time, and location; and the age, education, and social and economic condition of the convicted person (ICC 2012b). The judges also considered mitigating factors such as Lubanga's 'respectful and cooperative nature throughout the proceedings' (ICC 2012b, p. 34) and his motivations for the crime.

In delivering the sentence, the Trial Chamber reiterated criticisms of the prosecutor's investigation, including his extensive use of evidence restricted by confidentiality agreements, his failure to disclose exculpatory material, and his repeated failure to comply with the Chamber's disclosure orders (ICC 2012b). In addition, the Trial Chamber criticized the prosecutor's handling of the charges of sexual violence. The prosecutor responded to the sentence stating, 'By sentencing Thomas Lubanga Dyilo to 14 years in prison, . . . International Criminal Court judges have sent a clear message to perpetrators of crimes: you will not go unpunished' (ICC OTP 2012b, n.p.). However, he also highlighted the opportunity for an appeal against the 14-year sentence to seek a harsher penalty (ICC OTP 2012b). At the opening of the sentencing hearing the prosecutor recommended that Lubanga receive the maximum sentence of 30 years' imprisonment (ICC OTP 2012a). This reflects his opening statements: 'The Prosecution believes that the massive crimes litigated in this International Criminal Court, with hundreds or thousands of victims, with entire communities affected, warrant very high penalties' (ICC 2009c, p. 34).

The sentence of 14 years does not reflect the extensive harm caused by the conflict in the Democratic Republic of the Congo. Despite this, wider reactions to the sentence were quite positive, as the media, NGOs, and human rights groups used idealpolitik to praise the conclusion of the Court's first trial and to move on to urging the Court to pursue other cases:

> The International Criminal Court's sentencing . . . sends an important message about the gravity of this crime. The trial underscores the urgency of arresting Lubanga's co-accused, Bosco Ntaganda, and of prosecuting other crimes, including murder and rape, committed by his militia. . . . Lubanga's 14-year sentence demonstrates that recruiting and using child soldiers is a grave war crime that will be punished.
>
> (HRW 2012g, n.p.)

> Yesterday's sentencing decision signals an end to the accountability process for Thomas Lubanga, who was rightfully convicted of serious war crimes and will now serve almost 10 years in prison. It also importantly signals the start of a new era in prosecutions before the ICC.
>
> (Women's Initiative for Gender Justice 2012, p. 1)

Despite the continued use of idealpolitik and references to ending impunity, the sentence of 14 years appears inadequate in response to the widespread mass atrocities in the Congo. Lubanga's sentence is highly symbolic, yet disproportionate with the level of harm caused during the Congo conflict. This exemplifies the difficulty associated with prosecuting widespread mass atrocities through the individual-centred framework of international criminal law.

6.3 Justice in the Congo: the Lubanga trial in its wider context

As the start of this chapter illustrates, the recent history of the DRC has been defined by brutality, the outside influence of countries and companies, and the continued pillaging of the country's nature resources. The brutal pillaging of the Congo's resources, as established during colonial and Belgian rule, remains a driving factor for violence and conflict in the DRC, as does the continual interference by neighbouring countries who seek to exploit the mineral-rich land. The Lubanga trial is decontextualized from this conflict and it fails to represent the nature of the conflict and the crimes that have caused damage and destruction for the Congo. At the press conference announcing the surrender of Lubanga to the ICC the Chief Prosecutor proclaimed, 'We will investigate crimes committed by other militias and other persons—this is the first case, not the last. We are totally committed to staying in Congo—to make sure justice is done' (ICC 2006a, p. 3).

Despite these sentiments, there have been limited prosecutions in the DRC situation outside of the Lubanga trial. As the ICC has moved on to investigate further situations in Africa and the Middle East, the Court will not have the resources to continue wider investigations in the DRC. The trial of Thomas Lubanga was useful for the Court as its first successful prosecution, but it is questionable whether the trial has provided any sense of justice for the DRC.

A major criticism of the trial was the role that Lubanga had played in the wider conflict in the DRC. While the ICC expresses a policy of pursuing those most responsible for international crimes, or the 'big fish' (Takemura 2007), many considered Lubanga to be a minor actor in the broader Congo conflict. Hochschild (2009), for example, quotes a prominent social justice campaigner in the DRC who states, 'the ICC has taken the small fish . . . leaving the big fish because they're in positions of power' (Hochschild 2009, n.p.). Hochschild (2009, n.p.) continues by exploring the sentiments of Congo locals who attended an information session on the ICC and its Lubanga case:

> Why is Lubanga on trial, one asks, when 'others who did the same thing are working within the government?' 'Lubanga did not conscript forcibly,'

> another boy says. 'We went voluntarily. I myself went voluntarily. It was to defend my community. Why is he being judged for this?' A comrade adds: 'I also was not forced to enter [Lubanga's army]. All our houses were burned. We had nowhere to go—and Lubanga accepted me.'

These comments show the highly subjective nature of the conflict in the Congo and the decontextualization of Lubanga from the wider conflict through the ICC trial. Human rights groups mirrored these sentiments: 'Chief Prosecutor Ocampo should also investigate those who armed and supported militia groups operating in Ituri, including key players in power in Kinshasa, Kampala and Kigali' (HRW 2006b, n.p.). Interview participants representing NGOs and human rights groups from the Congo expressed similar arguments relating to the selective prosecution of Lubanga:

> Talking to people on the ground, some understand that the ICC cannot go after everybody and they say that they should at least go after those that are the most responsible but they are not doing it, for example, in Congo, how they could have gone after the ones that supported militias but not others.
>
> (Participant F)

One interview participant from the Democratic Republic of the Congo had experienced similar questions:

> In Congo, when you ask people questions about the ICC, they tell you that 'no, that is really something very politicized, it's not very important to speak about it', people often ask a lot of questions about the ICC. . . . Lots of Congolese or African people ask questions such as, 'Why is it only Congolese or African people that are appearing before the Court. . . . Why is it only Lubanga?'
>
> (Participant L)

Representatives of the defence also highlighted the sense of unfairness and confusion that has arisen from the limited prosecution of Lubanga in the DRC situation, while Lubanga himself voiced similar opinions in his remarks to the Court during his sentencing hearing:

> From 1999 to 2003 Ituri was struck by a tragedy that could not be given a name. I witnessed horrible massacres and killings. On several occasions, I saw hundreds of bodies savagely chopped up by machetes, bodies burnt alive in huts, villages completely destroyed, thousands of people fleeing in desperation, and sometimes I fled with them in circumstances where often what mattered was only one's life, and I have been deeply hurt by this situation; yet unfortunately no political or military official genuinely undertook to attend to the security of the people. Their lone concern was money and

> power. . . . Those who are responsible for those massacres are still in power in Kinshasa. Why have they not been prosecuted by this Court?
>
> (ICC 2012c, p. 67)

Hochschild (2009) suggests that the big fish in the DRC conflict would include generals and cabinet ministers from Uganda and Rwanda, who have supported the militias and sought to prolong and intensify the fighting in order to continue plundering the DRC's resources. These countries illegally exploit Congolese resources and benefit from having their financial status and economic health indicators upgraded by the IMF and World Bank (Mullins and Rothe 2008a). As a result of their improved financial status, and through the profit generated through the sale of their illegally gained resources, Rwanda and Uganda have funded further military operations that perpetuate crimes against humanity and make future resource theft possible (Mullins and Rothe 2008a). It is for this reason that some criminologists have labelled international institutions, such as the World Bank, as criminogenic (Friedrichs and Friedrichs 2002).

In addition to the illegal exploitation by bordering countries, Congolese resources are also controlled by an elite network of government officials and private business people who transfer publicly owned mineral assets through secret contracts and joint ventures controlled by private companies (Graff 2004). These exchanges amount to multi-billion-dollar corporate theft of the DRC's public assets and benefit the Congolese government, who use revenue from sales of resources to purchase arms and fund the mass atrocities being committed (Graff 2004). As Graff (2004, p. 25) argues, 'corporations could thus be implicated in, and found criminally liable for, a number of violations of international criminal law committed in the DRC'. These violations include crimes such as:

> subjecting local populations, including children, to forced labour in the extraction of natural resource; the torture, rape, and murder of thousands of civilians during military operations to secure mineral-rich land; and the destruction of agricultural infrastructure to force peasant farmers to participate in extractive work, resulting in reduced food supplies and slave-like conditions in the Colton mines.
>
> (Graff 2004, p. 25)

A UN panel report describes the vicious circle of the war in Congo, which is a product of both foreign powers, politics, and interests, and the mineral rich nature of the country, with all sides taking advantage of the anarchy to profit from the mineral wealth (UNSC 2003). In 2005, the International Court of Justice issued a judgment for Uganda's role in the DRC, finding it guilty of illegally exploiting the country's natural resources (Moffett 2009). Even the ICC prosecutor has acknowledged the involvement of other countries and companies in the DRC conflict, stating:

> The investigation of the financial aspects of the atrocities allegedly committed in Ituri will be crucial to prevent future crimes and for the prosecution of crimes already committed. If the alleged illegal business practices continue to fuel atrocities, these will not be stopped, even if material perpetrators are arrested and prosecuted. The Prosecutor of the ICC hopes that the prosecution of these cases will contribute to the ongoing peace process and ultimately yield stability for the DRC, fostering not just political stability but also healthy markets.
>
> (ICC OTP 2003b)

Despite this promising statement, there have not been any sustained investigations into the wider scope of the crimes in the DRC, with the Court relying on the symbolic trial of Thomas Lubanga and the narrow prosecution of the use of child soldiers. Yet the trial of Lubanga cannot cover the complex nature of the conflict in the Democratic Republic of the Congo. The Court is far removed from the reality of the situation and far removed from the people of the Congo, as the words of Thomas Lubanga illustrate:

> I have been portrayed as a warlord, pitilessly, taking hold of the children of the Ituri in order to feed his desire for power. . . . As far as I am concerned, the uncertainty is great. And I thought that it would even be greater in the minds of the Judges ten years after the events in a place so far removed from the Ituri. . . . Against the backdrop of what I have followed here over the last six years, and what I have again followed here today in this courtroom, all hinged on lies and completely disconnected from the reality that the people of the Ituri have experienced. I would have wished that those people of the Ituri who were concerned by these things that I am being accused of, I wish that they could have been listening to what we are saying and they would have been in a better position to judge me. It is unfortunate that these people in whose name this trial was brought have not been able to follow these proceedings.
>
> (ICC 2012c, p. 68)

As an example of this removal of the ICC from the local site of conflict, Kambale (2012, n.p.) describes how the news in the DRC on the day of the Lubanga judgment was dominated by reports 'glorifying the military prowess of a fugitive wanted by the Court [Bosco Ntaganda] but now working as a respectable army general for the same government that turned Lubanga over to the Court', rather than reports of the landmark Lubanga decision. As this illustrates, the local landscape in the DRC continues to be defined by realpolitik, while the ICC remains removed and distanced from the conflict and its victim communities.

6.4 Concluding comments

The Lubanga trial, the first trial before the ICC, began with much hope and expectation. It heralded the promise of universal justice and an end to impunity.

As the trial unfolded, the realpolitik of the international environment became apparent in the difficulties of investigating and prosecuting war crimes. The trial represented a series of contests and negotiations between the various groups associated with the Court, from the prosecutor, to the judges, the defence, victims' groups, and NGOs. These groups all competed for power and control and fought to have their interests heard and their goals realized. The trial illustrated the highly fragmented nature of international criminal justice.

Despite this fragmentation, a level of unity was reached and Lubanga was finally found guilty and sentenced to 14 years in prison. The continual use of idealpolitik and the common aims of prevention and persuasion provided the unity needed for the Court. This illustrates the utility of the Court's vague aims, as well as the Court's strategic ambiguity and structured ambivalence. Many groups could engage with, and support, the Court through the Lubanga trial; however, the ambiguity of the Court enabled them to still espouse their unique aims and pursue their own goals. Although the Lubanga trial was removed from the violence of the Congo, it was useful for the ICC as its first guilty verdict. The ICC was able to use the Lubanga trial to assert its relevance and legitimacy on the international stage, ten years after it came into existence.

7 The ICC as a tool

The ICC is an idealistic institution. Idealism and the simple soaring hope of universal justice (UN 1999) have helped the Court to navigate the rocky and uneven terrain and contested territory it has faced throughout its first decade of existence. Idealism is embodied in the rhetoric that surrounds the Court, in actors' constructions and engagements with the Court, and in the Court cases themselves. The broad and idealistic aims of prevention and persuasion enable a vast range of actors to engage with and support the Court. However, as the previous two chapters illustrate, these common, idealistic aims are often articulated according to actors' own interests, identities, and goals and can be mobilized differently as situations and circumstances change, in an unpredictable and fragmented international environment. This process constructs a series of contradictions, tensions, and schisms, which are not only an inherent part of the ICC, but are also useful and productive for the Court as they increase its flexibility and visibility in a late-modern environment.

This chapter brings together the analysis of the previous chapters and revisits the theoretical framework of late modernity and social construction, outlined in Chapters 3 and 4, to discuss the utility and dangers of the ICC's ambiguous aims and numerous contradictions. The chapter explores how the Court's identity and position in international society is constructed through vague aims, structured ambivalence, and a series of dichotomies and contradictions. Through these aims and contradictions, the ICC becomes prominent yet remote, visible yet inaccessible, flexible yet controlling, and unified yet fragmented. The Court is also constructed as a model of justice and a tool that can be used by many different actors in many different situations. These roles ensure that the ICC remains relevant and visible; however, they also construct the Court as a supranational institution of social control that has the potential to reinforce geopolitical divides and reproduce the unequal landscape of international society.

7.1 Visibility, adaptability, and the ICC as a model of justice

In a late-modern world, visibility and identity are important yet increasingly unstable and difficult to maintain due to the fragmented, fast-paced, and complex nature of the globalized world (Giddens 1990; Urry 2003). This world is in a constant state of flux, with events and institutions rising and falling unexpectedly and at great speed (Virilio 2006; Urry 2003). Bauman (2000, 2005) characterizes this late-modern environment as 'liquid' to capture its shifting nature, which means that social forms and institutions no longer have enough time to solidify (Bauman 2007a). The proliferation of information, the hyper-reflexivity of actors, and the associated displacement of tradition (Giddens 1990) have meant that institutions can no longer be static and must instead evolve to ensure their continued legitimacy. It is within this environment that the ICC has been required to develop its identity and credibility during its formative years. To ensure its continuing relevance in this complex environment of change and unpredictability, the ICC has needed to embrace uncertainty (Baker and Simon 2002) and remain flexible to respond to events as they unfold.

Visibility is, therefore, important to the International Criminal Court. If the Court is not visible, then it cannot establish and maintain a place in a fluid international society. Consequently, the ICC seeks to be involved in as many situations as possible and uses the vague and idealistic aims of prevention and persuasion to achieve this involvement and construct itself as a central actor in responses to conflict and violence. The desire for visibility explains the continued use of popular idealpolitik, which constructs the Court as a model of justice that sits as the centrepiece of an international system of justice. Paradoxically, behind the ICC's rhetoric of visibility, the Court remains remote and inaccessible, far removed from the local struggles that become its currency.

The ICC as a model of justice

The concept of the ICC as a model of justice was explored in Chapters 5 and 6. Many actors closely associated with the Court described the Court as a model (Chapter 5) and the use of the Lubanga trial also positioned the Court as a model of justice (Chapter 6). These constructions of the ICC stem from the aims of prevention and persuasion. As a preventative institution, the Court is constructed as a model, whose symbolic prosecutions act as examples to highlight the potential punishment for particular crimes. As a persuasive institution, the ICC's prosecutions act to catalyse, encourage, and guide local jurisdictions to respond to crimes in an appropriate manner.

Idealpolitik and the maintenance of a visible public facade are important for the Court and its construction as a model of justice. Brighenti (2007, p. 334) describes the connection between the concepts of models and visibility, stating:

> a model can be defined as something or someone who is endowed with visibility. For a model to exist, it has to be before everybody's eyes. Simultaneously, the model also tends to be defined in moral terms. It inspires behaviour and attitude. It is an example to follow.

Thus, visibility and transparency are central to the ICC's construction as a model of justice.

Despite the Court's symbolism of visibility, the ICC is far removed from the situations and conflicts that it prosecutes. The sense of removal of the Court was reflected by interview participants, as discussed in Chapter 5. For example, one participant states:

> To be the highest standard for justice, the ICC really wants to be seen as that, but I don't think that there is a wish from the Court or for people working at the Court to be seen as a Court which is close to the people that were affected.
>
> (Participant F)

Geographically and culturally, the ICC is distanced from the countries it prosecutes. The idealistic construction of the ICC as a visible model of justice can be contrasted against the location of the Court in Europe and the relative inaccessibility of the Court trials to the countries it is involved in. To date, all of the ICC's cases have involved African countries, yet the Court's location and procedures are far removed from the site of local conflicts.

The effect of the removal of the ICC from local situations is clearly illustrated in a 2008 population study of the eastern Democratic Republic of the Congo (Vinck et al. 2008), the situation that has the most advanced trials before the Court. Of 2,620 respondents, only a quarter (27 per cent) had heard of the ICC, and only 12 per cent knew how to access the ICC (Vicnk et al. 2008). Further to this, survey respondents from the DRC indicated a clear preference for national trials (45 per cent), followed by internationalized trials in the DRC (40 per cent). There was little support for no trials (8 per cent) and international trials abroad (7 per cent). In other words, 85 per cent of respondents preferred trials to be held in the DRC, whether national or internationalized trials (Vinck et al. 2008). This lack of knowledge and access to the Court was also highlighted by one interview participant from the Democratic Republic of the Congo:

> In the east of the DRC very few people know the ICC. They know the name 'The ICC', but they don't know really what they do. They are not very informed about everything that is happening with the Court and the trials. I found that a bit ridiculous because these are the trials for the people who committed crimes there and the people who were the victims of these crimes should normally be informed.
>
> (Participant U)

Eastern Congo has been the site of much violence and the region has been the focus of the ICC prosecutions. The lack of awareness of the Court in this region illustrates the ICC's geographic and cultural removal from the victims and communities who are affected by the crimes it prosecutes.

The spotlight of justice

As the above discussion highlights, although the ICC constructs itself as a visible model of justice, it is far removed from the situations it prosecutes and has limited capacity to achieve the aims of prevention and persuasion. The ability of the Court to prevent international crimes or influence the actions of regions and nations is of limited importance to the identity of the Court as a model. Instead, the ICC is positioned as an upper-level institution that sits above local jurisdictions and exists in a symbolic capacity, shining the spotlight of attention on to rogue states and belligerent warlords and dictators, and emphasizing the horrors of conflict in particular corners of the globe. By rendering conflicts and human rights abuses visible, the ICC becomes more visible itself. This is because the ICC's involvement in a wide variety of situations provides more opportunities for a range of actors to engage with the Court, while also increasing references to the ICC in discourses surrounding conflict and violence. Thus, the more conflicts the Court is engaged in, either directly or indirectly, the more visible the ICC becomes. The aims of prevention and persuasion enable the Court to be engaged in many different situations as these aims are sufficiently broad to be mobilized in a variety of contexts and are also idealistic enough to provide appealing justification for a range of interventions. However, the ICC has limited ability to achieve the aims of prevention and persuasion, as outlined in Chapter 2.

This predicament parallels the experience of domestic criminal justice systems in a late-modern environment. As Garland (2001) highlights, late-modern criminal justice systems are increasingly unable to respond to growing crime rates and heightened public awareness, fear, and expectation of crime. Despite this, it is increasingly important for justice systems to be seen as capable of responding to crime and projecting a facade of control to maintain their relevance and legitimacy in a changing late-modern world (Garland 2001). Similar to domestic justice systems, it is important for the ICC to visibly respond to an increasing and unpredictable stream of violence and conflict. Indeed, the ICC seeks to be involved in a wide range of events to amplify its visibility, relevance, and authority. However, the ICC cannot possibly respond to all instances of international crime and achieve the ambitious aims of preventing international crimes and establishing a normative framework in a contested society (Akhavan 2001; Damaška 2008; Tallgren 2002). The ICC thus adopts an adaptive approach to international crime and governs at a distance (Garland 2001) by making local jurisdictions responsible for responding to crime and violence. The ICC positions itself as the centrepiece of a system of international criminal justice, which encourages other actors and local jurisdictions to respond to international crimes, while the Court itself continues to espouse idealistic rhetoric in order to set standards and act as a model. This functioning is strengthened by the Court's use of the principle of complementarity, which pushes local jurisdictions to achieve the more practical elements of the Court's aims, as the Court itself maintains a position of omnipotent, adaptable authority.

The ICC achieves adaptability by espousing the broad aims of prevention and persuasion and by incrementally defining ambiguous categories of crimes, such as crimes against humanity, through its involvement in a range of situations. 'Crimes against humanity' is a broad term that includes many forms of violence. Robertson (2006) details how the concept has been used throughout recent history to respond to a range of human rights violations, from the Nuremberg Tribunals after World War II to attempts to prosecute Augusto Pinochet, and reactions to terrorism in the wake of 9/11. The ICC's definition of crimes against humanity has broadened previous definitions, such as that used by the United Nations (Bassiouni 1999a; Robinson 1999) and the Court has consequently initiated investigations and prosecutions of a wide range of different situations under the banner of crimes against humanity.[1] This includes election violence in Kenya, conflict during civil war in Uganda, and violence resulting from uprisings in Libya.

The broad nature of international crimes under the Rome Statute is coupled with the Court's broad aims, which endow the Court with adaptive potential to ensure its continued relevance and visibility in a late-modern world. The Court can intervene in numerous situations, and can also be linked to broader discourses and social movements concerning crime, violence, and justice. The ICC therefore 'consumes' violence (Bauman 2001, 2007b) as it seeks to be involved in, and use, as many situations as possible. As Bauman (2001, p. 13) explains, 'in the consumer society, consumption is its own purpose and so is self-propelling'. So too, the ICC's involvement in numerous and varied cases propels it forward and ensures its perpetual relevance in a fluid international environment. This is also reflected in the ICC's interactions with the situations it investigates and prosecutes. The ICC uses trials, and its engagements with situation countries, to increase its visibility and sphere of influence, while also acting as a model to influence norms in situation countries. This ambivalent relationship is facilitated through the dual aims of persuasion and prevention, which allows the ICC to project itself up into international society, using local conflicts as justification, and apply downwards pressure on to local jurisdictions, using concepts of international consensus and morality as justification.

In these ambivalent processes, actual conflicts are peripheral to the ICC. Although the image and symbolism of conflicts provides justification for the

1 Article 7 of the Rome Statute defines crimes against humanity as:

> any of the following acts when committed as part of a widespread or systematic attack directed against any civilian population, with knowledge of the attack: a) Murder; b) Extermination; c) Enslavement; d) Deportation or forcible transfer of population; e) Imprisonment or other severe deprivation of physical liberty in violation of fundamental rules of international law; f) Torture; g) Rape, sexual slavery, enforced prostitutions, forced pregnancy, enforced sterilization, or any other form of sexual violence of comparable gravity; h) Persecution against any identifiable group or collectivity on political, racial, national, ethnic, cultural, religious, gender . . . or other grounds . . . ; i) Enforced disappearance of persons; j) The crime of apartheid; k) Other inhumane acts of a similar character intentionally causing great suffering or serious injury to body or to mental or physical health.

Court's intervention, the aim of prevention through general deterrence means the ICC chooses a few symbolic and exemplary cases to prosecute, with the intention of increasing its international presence and potential effect. The many local events and instances of violence that make up the totality of the conflict are lost in the ICC's translation of violence into symbolic cases. As the Office of the Prosecutor highlights, it is important for these selective prosecutions to reverberate worldwide (ICC OTP 2010). The needs of local communities and broader notions of justice are then secondary to the aim of prevention and the ICC's international focus. Local conflicts are symbolically at the centre, but practically at the periphery, of the ICC's conception of the international justice system, thus illustrating the metaphor of consumption.

7.2 Flexibility, plurality, and the ICC as a tool

As the previous section highlights, the broad aims and contradictions of the ICC are useful for the Court as they provide the ICC with the flexibility to consume violence, thus achieving visibility and increasing its sphere of influence on the world stage.

The fragmentation and unity of the Court

The environment in which the ICC operates is fragmented and complex. As this book has explored, the ICC is constructed by a range of different groups and individuals through their many interactions with the Court. Numerous NGOs, civil society organizations, and human rights groups interact with the Court (Glasius 2006, 2009; Pace and Schense 2004), as do international organizations such as the United Nations (Jain 2005; Happold 2006; Stein 2006) and other international criminal justice mechanisms, such as the International Criminal Tribunal for the former Yugoslavia, as well as hybrid courts, such as those established in Kosovo (Dickinson 2003). The Court is also constructed through the plethora of media representations of it—representations which come from a great range of sources and actors.

The International Criminal Court is designed to be a representative institution constituted by the nation states that elect to be bound by it (Schiff 2008). These nations all hold different perspectives, ideas, values, realpolitik objectives, and traditions regarding the nature of crime and the shape that justice should take. The amalgamation of different judicial traditions is especially evident in the inclusion of both civil and common law practices in the construction of the Court (Schabas 2004), and in the process of negotiation that defined the Rome Statute (Arsanjani 1999; Bassiouni 1999b). The multitude of actors who engage with the ICC makes the external environment in which the Court is acting fragmented and contested.

The internal structure and environment of the ICC is equally fragmented and divided. The ICC is comprised of several offices including the Office of the Prosecutor, the Office of Public Counsel for the Defence, the Judiciary, the

Registry, and the Office of Public Counsel for Victims. The analysis of interview data in Chapter 5 illustrated that these groups are far from united and there is much division between the agencies that make up the ICC. This fragmentation was further evidenced in Chapter 6, which illustrated how both the internal and external divisions of the Court contributed to the complexities and contradictions of the protracted Lubanga trial. It is, therefore, not just the environment surrounding the Court that is fragmented, but the Court itself.

The divisions that define the ICC are inherent in its structure and its adversarial nature. The Court acts as a system of justice in and of itself as it does not exist within a framework of justice or separation of powers—concepts that are integral to national justice systems. It is consequently inevitable that the ICC consists of a range of groups with differing opinions and perspectives, stemming from their unique understandings of justice as well as their vastly different roles within the collection of agencies that is the ICC.

The fragmented nature of the Court is typical of criminal justice institutions in a late-modern setting. In domestic criminal justice settings, the pluralization, fragmentation, and contradictory nature of different aspects of the criminal justice system, from policing to punishment, is increasingly acknowledged (Loader 2000; Jones and Newburn 2002; O'Malley 1999; Simon 1995). Garland (1996, 2001) examines the fragmentation of crime control in late modernity, highlighting the variety of contradictory roles criminal justice actors must play, and how structural ambivalence helps them to deal with the need for both political (symbolic) and practical responses to crime. Similarly, the ICC displays incoherence in its contradictory aims and functioning, as it seeks to respond symbolically and practically to international crimes, in a fragmented and contested environment.

In this environment, the Court's broad aims are strategically ambiguous to provide a strong sense of unity and momentum for the Court. The Court's ambiguous and idealistic aims resonate with a diverse range of actors and allow these actors to interpret the aims of the Court in accordance with their own unique interests, goals, and values. Paris (2001, p. 88) explores the concept of unity through 'cultivated ambiguity' in relation to the field of human security, stating:

> As a unifying concept . . . human security is powerful precisely because it lacks precision and thereby encompasses the diverse perspectives and objectives of all members of the coalition. The term, in short, appears slippery by design. Cultivated ambiguity renders human security an effective campaign slogan.

The ICC's broad and idealistic aims of prevention and persuasion are similar 'campaign slogans' for the Court. These ambiguous aims are popular with the multiple groups and thus provide a sense of unity and direction for the Court. Chapter 5 illustrated how many actors representing different groups espoused the same aims of prevention and persuasion. Indeed, all actors interviewed mentioned prevention as the core aim of the Court. These actors often interpreted and applied the aim of prevention differently.

This wide range of interpretations was evidenced in the trial of Thomas Lubanga, as explored in Chapter 6. Different groups used this trial and the aims of prevention and persuasion according to their own interests. The ambiguity of the Court's aims is therefore useful as it provides unity, while also allowing for the fragmentation and plurality that defines the ICC.

The ambivalence between fragmentation and unity is characteristic of the late-modern environment in which the Court is operating, as explored in Chapter 4. Late modernity is fluid and complex (Bauman 2000; Urry 2003) and switches ambivalently between control and flexibility, plurality and unity (Bauman 1990, 1991). While the multiplicity of actors who interact with the Court is often acknowledged, there is a continuing desire for control and unity. The Court's broad and idealistic aims allow many actors to reach agreement on the aims of the ICC and therefore engage with the Court and its unifying idealpolitik. At the same time, actors can reflexively interpret these idealistic aims and use them accordingly to pursue their own goals.

The ICC as a tool

Seen in this light, the ICC shifts from being a consumer of violence to being a commodity that can be mobilized in many different situations by a range of actors. To use Bauman's (2007b) theory of consumer society as a metaphor for the functioning of the ICC is to view the Court as a consumer of violence that simultaneously uses this violence to promote itself as a commodity, which is a product capable of drawing attention. The Court must distinguish itself in a complex world full of multiple discourses and actors, as Bauman (2007b, p. 12) explains:

> the task of consumers, therefore, and the principal motive prompting them to engage in incessant consumer activity is the task of lifting themselves out of that grey and flat invisibility and insubstantiality, making themselves stand out from the mass of indistinguishable objects.

The Court makes itself a visible, attractive, and popular commodity through its idealpolitik and its consumption of particular types of violence. This ensures that it will be picked up and used by a range of individuals, thus allowing it to consume more violence and begin the ambivalent and unending cycle of acting as consumer/commodity again. Bauman (2001, p. 13) highlights that 'consumer society proclaims the impossibility of gratification and measures its progress by ever-rising demand', and indeed by acting as a consumer of violence (model of justice) and commodity (tool) the ICC is less interested in fulfilling its aims but rather ensuring its perpetual relevance and status as a commodity.

The flexibility of the ICC, as explored in this chapter, thus allows the ICC to become a tool that can be used by many different actors. As a flexible tool, the ICC can be used in a variety of situations and can be mobilized to serve a range of different purposes. It can be used as both a bottom-up tool and a top-down tool, as explored in the following sections.

A bottom-up tool

The Ugandan government has used the ICC as a tool in local political struggles to benefit at both a national and international level by referring the conflict in the country to the ICC in 2003 (Government of Uganda 2003). The conflict in Uganda is driven by a variety of groups and militias who have struggled for power.[2] Museveni and the Ugandan government have previously attempted to combat the militias, and in particular the LRA, which is allegedly supported by Sudan (Sudan Tribune 2012), through amnesties and military intervention (Moy 2006; Ssenyonjo 2005). When the International Criminal Court became operational, the Ugandan government referred the situation with the LRA to the Court, stating, 'Having exhausted every other means of bringing an end to this terrible suffering, the Republic of Uganda now turns to the newly established ICC and its promise of global justice' (Government of Uganda 2003).

Despite rhetoric espousing the desire for peace and global justice, Museveni and the Ugandan government strategically used the ICC in a bid to eliminate their political opponents, while increasing their international profile as allies of the West (Branch 2007; Nouwen and Werner 2011). The Ugandan government therefore used the Court as a tool and the ICC was happy to be mobilized in a situation with full government support, early after its creation. Akhavan (2005, p. 404), explains the mutual benefit of Uganda's self-referral to the ICC:

> For Uganda, the referral was an attempt to engage an otherwise aloof international community by transforming the prosecution of LRA leaders into a litmus test for the much celebrated promise of global justice. . . . The imprimatur of international criminal justice, sought through the referral to the ICC, was a means of thrusting this long-forgotten African war back onto the international stage. . . . For the ICC, the voluntary referral of a compelling case by a state party represented both an early expression of confidence in the nascent institution's mandate, and a welcome opportunity to demonstrate its viability.

Uganda's referral of the situation to the ICC focused exclusively on crimes committed by the LRA (Government of Uganda 2003). The International Criminal

2 Violence, political turmoil, war, and conflict have plagued Uganda since its independence in 1962 (Allen 2006). This violence has been caused by constant political coups and insurgencies from rebel groups struggling for political power over the past two decades (Mullins and Rothe 2008a, p. 129). In particular, rebel groups have operated from the north of the country since current president Yoweri Museveni, head of the National Resistance Army (NRA), took power in 1986 (Branch 2007, p. 180). The Lord's Resistance Army (LRA), allegedly led by Joseph Kony, is a particularly active rebel group that has committed significant violence including war crimes and crimes against humanity, in the struggle for political power in Uganda (HRW 2010a).

Court followed Uganda's lead by narrowly focusing its five Ugandan prosecutions on crimes committed by the LRA, despite calls for more balanced investigations and a consideration of crimes committed by Museveni's regime (Murumba 2012; Odora 2012). Museveni and his army have committed numerous war crimes and human rights abuses, including the use of child soldiers, murder, and rape, and have been criticized for their appalling treatment of internally displaced persons in what have been described as concentration camps (Burnett and Evenson 2012). By shining a spotlight of attention on the crimes of the LRA, the Ugandan government has effectively minimized political opposition and concealed their own crimes with a veneer of legitimacy, provided by the ICC's prosecution of the LRA. Further to this, Branch (2007, p. 185) argues that the Ugandan government 'called in the ICC against the LRA, not to help bring the war to an end but to entrench it', to continue benefiting from the effects of military intervention in northern Uganda.

In using the ICC as a tool in local political struggles, the Ugandan government has also benefited at an international level. Uganda has been constructed as a friend of the ICC and international criminal justice (Nouwen and Werner 2011). This resulted in Uganda hosting the Rome Statute Review Conference in 2010. This construction of Uganda conceals the government's ongoing complicity in the violence and conflict in its own country, and in neighbouring countries, particularly the Democratic Republic of the Congo. As explored in Chapter 6, Uganda continues to exploit natural resources from the DRC, including gold and diamonds, and benefits from political power and increased standing with the World Bank from this exploitation (Mullins and Rothe 2008b; Samset 2002). Uganda has also been accused of fuelling violence in the DRC (HRW 2001) and sustaining rebel attacks, in particular through its arming of the rebel group M23, which has committed numerous atrocities in eastern Congo (Charbonneau and Nichols 2012; Sawyer 2013; UNSC 2014).

Despite this, the Ugandan government continues to receive support from numerous Western sources, including military support from the United States (BBC 2011a) and financial assistance from the World Bank (Mullins and Rothe 2008b). Uganda has used the ICC as a tool to achieve legitimacy on the international stage while continuing to cause harm in the country and region. Branch (2007, p. 186) explains that the ICC's prosecutions provide 'support to Washington's partner in the war on terror and to the World Bank's neoliberal success story, while further demonizing the LRA'.

It appears contradictory to the aims of the Court to be used in such a way by one of the States Parties; however, such engagement is actually beneficial for the Court. Uganda was one of the first situations to be brought before the ICC in the Court's early years. The Court's engagement with the Ugandan situation and the LRA gave the Court the opportunity for more cases to pursue and therefore more visibility. Having a supportive African government was also important for the Court, as there has been much criticism and hostility towards the ICC from Africa (Clarke 2010; Mutua 2010; Reinold 2012). The Court needs States Parties and its relationship with Uganda, despite Uganda's rather problematic engagement with the Court, proved beneficial for the Court's visibility. The situation in Uganda, and its involvement with the ICC, illustrates how the Court may be mobilized as a tool by parties who use it to achieve their own interests. This instrumental use of the ICC is, nevertheless, beneficial for the Court as it increases engagement with the ICC and makes the Court more visible and relevant in particular regions and the world stage, giving the Court more violence to 'consume'.

A top-down tool

Another instance of different parties engaging the Court as a tool is the situation in Libya. Here, the ICC was mobilized by international actors to dispose of a problematic leader and achieve favourable political outcomes, while also justifying military intervention. Forming part of the Arab Spring movement, the violence in Libya was sparked by civilian uprisings against the Libyan regime and escalated as president Muammar Gaddafi struggled to maintain power.[3]

The international community quickly became involved as the situation in Libya unfolded. On 26 February 2011, the United Nations Security Council unanimously adopted resolution 1970 referring the unrest and violence in Libya to the International Criminal Court (UNSC 2011). The referral of the situation to the ICC for investigation was one of a range of measures taken by the Security Council in response to the violence. Other measures included travel bans and asset freezes for Gaddafi and his associates, and arms embargoes (du Plessis and Louw 2011). In response to the referral, the ICC prosecutor swiftly commenced an investigation of the situation in Libya on 3 March 2011 (ICC 2011f). Soon after, the prosecutor requested the Pre-Trial Chamber of the ICC to issue arrest warrants for Gaddafi, as well as his son Saif al-Islam Gaddafi, and de facto prime minister and head of the military intelligence, Abdualla al-Senussi (ICC 2011g). In announcing the request for the arrest warrants, the prosecutor declared:

> Most of the victims are Libyans, but the widespread and systematic attacks against them are affecting the international community as a whole. The crimes are crimes against humanity. . . . The execution of the warrants will have a deterrent impact for other leaders who are thinking of using violence to gain or retain power.
>
> (ICC 2011g)

3 The Arab Spring movement spread across numerous Middle Eastern countries, including Tunisia, Egypt, Libya, Syria, Yemen, and Bahrain, in 2011 (Goldstein 2012). In each country, mass protests were sparked by brutal acts of repression: in the case of Libya it was the arrest of Fathi Terbil, the lawyer for the victims of the 1996 Abu Salim prison massacre, that sparked the demonstrations (Roth 2012). In an attempt to control the uprisings in Libya, Gaddafi used excessive force against protesters and committed gross and systematic human rights violations, including indiscriminate armed attacks against civilians, extrajudicial killings, arbitrary arrests, and detention and torture of peaceful demonstrators (UN Human Rights Council 2011).

On 27 June 2011, the Pre-Trial Chamber of the ICC issued arrest warrants for all three suspects (ICC 2011h).

Closely following the initial referral of the situation to the ICC, the United Nations Security Council took further actions, outlined in Resolution 1973, ordering a ceasefire, authorizing a no-fly zone, and sanctioning the use of 'all means necessary', short of foreign occupation, to protect civilians in Libya (UNSC 2011). Military intervention in Libya began on 19 March with the French Air Force and a coalition of ten European and Middle-Eastern States, notably Qatar and the United Arab Emirates, participating in the intervention with US support (du Plessis and Louw 2011; Norton-Taylor 2011; Voice of America 2011). This was followed by sustained airstrikes by NATO and non-stop patrols by armed US drones and other surveillance missions, in an effort to curb violence and hamper Gaddafi loyalists (Borger 2011).

The NATO air-combat missions were criticized for causing unnecessary civilian deaths (Amnesty International 2012b; BBC 2012b), with Human Rights Watch (HRW 2012a) estimating that at least 72 civilians, one-third of them children under 18, were killed by the attacks. As Roth (2012) highlights, the decisive interventions in the Libyan crisis were disproportionate to the international responses in other countries experiencing similar violence, such as Tunisia and Egypt. The focused intervention in Libya can be explained by the West's desire to dispose of Gaddafi (Coughlin 2011). As Johnstone (2011) explains, the West has had a hostile relationship with Gaddafi over the past two decades, particularly since the Lockerbie bombings in 1988.

Viewed within this wider framework of international intervention, the ICC is constructed as just one tool in a range of measures taken by the international community in reaction to the violence in Libya. Through its association with UN-sanctioned measures, the ICC was constructed as the 'judicial arm' of the international responsibility to protect Libya (Stahn 2012).[4] The invocation of the responsibility to protect in the United Nations' referral of Libya to the ICC positions the Court as one of many existing tools, such as economic sanctions and military interventions, which are used by the United Nations in response to violence and conflict. The construction of the ICC as a tool in wider responses to violence was reinforced in a later debate in the Security Council which explored 'how the Court, as a tool of preventive diplomacy, can assist the council in carrying out its mandate to uphold the rule of law, maintain peace and security, and combat impunity while ensuring accountability for mass atrocities' (CICC 2015, n.p.).

The UN mobilization of the ICC, in early responses to the Libyan violence, established the ICC as a key actor in international interventions in unfolding

4 The preamble of Resolution 1970 invokes the responsibility to protect, stating, 'recalling the Libyan authorities' responsibility to protect its population'. Responsibility to protect (R2P) is a UN initiative established in 2005 to cover emerging norms, viewing sovereignty not as a right, but a responsibility. It seeks to prevent or stop international crimes by invoking a range of 'tools', including economic sanctions, military intervention, and mediation. For further discussion on the ICC and the responsibility to protect in the case of Libya, see Stahn 2011.

violence. However, the United Nations' referral was problematic for several reasons, primarily because Libya is not one of the States Parties to the ICC. As summarized in Chapter 1, although the ICC's jurisdiction is limited to states which have signed the Rome Statute, the UN Security Council has the power to refer situations to the Court for investigation. Despite these powers of referral, it is problematic to see many core actors using the Court, while simultaneously refusing to be bound by its jurisdiction. The United States, Russia, and China, three out of the five permanent members of the UN Security Council, are not parties to the ICC. Despite this, the UN referral was unanimous. This means that numerous actors, who are not parties to the Court, are either mobilizing the ICC or being investigated by the ICC. The African nations who were parties to the Security Council—Gabon, South Africa, and Nigeria—also supported the referral despite ongoing tensions between the ICC and African states (du Plessis and Louw 2011).

The ambivalent interactions with the Court, evidenced in the Libya situation, further construct the ICC as a tool to be used selectively to achieve broader realpolitik aims, such as getting rid of antagonistic leaders of particular countries. Smith (2012c, p. 2) emphasizes this use of the Court as a 'tool of coercive diplomacy'. By invoking the ICC in accordance with a range of other military measures, the ICC's selective prosecutions entrench the labels of enemies and friends (Nouwen and Werner 2011) on an international level. Despite the death and destruction caused by NATO airstrikes, there has been no attempt by the ICC to prosecute these crimes (HRW 2012a). Similarly, the ICC's prosecutions focus solely on crimes committed by Gaddafi's regime and ignore the violence perpetrated by rebel forces (Amnesty International 2011; HRW 2012c). Dicker (HRW 2012b, n.p.) highlights the selective use of the ICC as a tool, stating:

> when it comes to ICC referrals, the United States, Russia, and China seem more concerned about prosecuting their enemies and protecting their friends. . . . This checkered approach has left victims of abuses in Syria, Gaza, and Sri Lanka without recourse to justice.

For the ICC, its engagement as a tool in the Libyan situation provided it with much visibility and credibility. The inclusion of the ICC at the early stages of intervention was particularly beneficial for the ICC, as it reinforced the identity of the Court as a preventative and persuasive institution with a future-oriented focus and a desire to be involved in events as they unfold, as explored in Chapters 3 and 5. The Court capitalized on the United Nations' early engagement by promptly conducting investigations and issuing arrest warrants. However, this swift response was, in itself, problematic as the case was driven by political expediency rather than 'objective consideration of the situation or of whether the ICC may be in a position to successfully prosecute the cases' (Schaefer and Groves 2011, n.p.).

Indeed, as the situation has progressed, the ICC's involvement in prosecuting violence in Libya has been contested. After Gaddafi's murder, the ICC focused on its two other suspects, principally Gaddafi's son, Saif al-Islam Gaddafi. Saif al-Islam has been detained in Libya, and Libya's National Transitional Council is seeking to prosecute him themselves thus challenging the ICC's jurisdiction (Al Jazeera 2012). Saif al-Islam's defence lawyers are also fighting for him to be prosecuted by the ICC, as they argue he will not receive a fair trial in Libya (Escritt 2012; Walt 2012) and he will most likely face the death penalty if found guilty (ABC News 2012). This adds to earlier reports alleging that Saif al-Islam considered turning himself in to the ICC as 'he will feel safer in a European prison than in Libya—his and his father's enemies simply want to kill him' (RT 2011, n.p.). This is another example of the most unlikely actors using the ICC as a tool to achieve their own interests in a highly selective manner.

At the time of writing, the competition for the Gaddafi trial is being heard by the ICC Pre-Trial Chamber. This situation exemplifies the notion of conflicts as property (Christie 1977). The ICC seeks to 'consume' the conflict so that it can maintain its position as a commodity or a 'tool' to be used in international responses to violence in the future. The unfolding of the situation in Libya illustrates how many different actors can use the Court as a tool to achieve their realpolitik objectives. Even those who do not formally support the Court, or those who are opposed to it, can still use the ICC as a tool to further their own interests and goals. The Court's malleability enables these many engagements and mobilizations of the ICC. Although many of the ways in which the Court is used as a tool run counter to original intentions for the ICC—from supporting particular governments, who continue to cause harm, to being used by powerful sections of international society to legitimate their actions—these situations and mobilizations are still valuable for the Court. From its engagement in these many situations, the ICC gains prominence and visibility. The ICC is able to remain relevant on a continuously changing and shifting world stage, where events and situations rise and fall in the public eye. By acting in a variety of different manners, the ICC is able to maximize its visibility as it is engaged in these many different situations and contexts.

7.3 The ICC as a supranational institution of control

Through its idealpolitik of prevention and persuasion, the ICC is constructed as a model and a tool, roles which ensure the Court's visibility and relevance on the world stage. Section 7.2 provided several examples of how the ICC has been used as a tool by many different actors in the situations of Libya and Uganda. As these examples highlight, it is often powerful actors who can engage the ICC most effectively. In the situation in Uganda, the current government is able to mould the ICC to fulfil its realpolitik objectives of maintaining power and fighting political adversaries, while presenting the government as a friend of international criminal justice on the world stage (Nouwen and Werner 2011). In the situation in Libya, the United Nations Security Council, which has been described as the 'quintessential political body' (Arbour 2011, n.p.), was able to use the Court as one tool in a range of measures designed to fulfil their goals within this particular region. Within the Security Council, powerful actors such as the United States supported the move to legitimate military interventions with judicial justification, to fulfil the objective of disposing of the problematic Gaddafi regime. As Simpson (2011, n.p.) describes, this gives the perception that the Court is 'the judicial arm of NATO and that judicial interventions fall meekly into line with Western military interventions'.

The fusion of idealpolitik and realpolitik and the dark side of virtue

As powerful actors engage the Court as a tool more frequently and effectively, the Court reproduces existing power structures in a society of unequal sovereigns, consisting of great powers and outlaw states (Simpson 2004a). This is clearly exemplified in Libya, as a situation in an 'outlaw state' that is not party to the ICC is brought before the Court by a political body controlled by powerful countries—including the United States, the United Kingdom, China, Russia, and France—who themselves will not be brought before the ICC and have not been subjected to any international criminal court since 1945 (Simpson 2011). The reproduction of the inequalities of the international order is further exemplified by the prosecution history of the ICC, with all situations currently before the Court concerning African countries. Clarke (2010) highlights how this unequal focus arises from shifting definitions of criminality. The ICC criminalizes certain types of violence, while denying that the origins of this violence lie in the legacy of colonial policies and the exploitation of African resources in transnational neoliberal economies (Clarke 2010).

These examples illustrate the fusion of idealpolitik and realpolitik where ideals are used to conceal or legitimate realpolitik interests. Powerful narratives, such as preventing international crimes and enforcing human rights standards, provide popular justification for interventions and construct evil 'others' on the world stage. Although most actors associated with the Court consistently argue that the ICC is not a political institution, the fusion of idealpolitik and realpolitik exemplify how the ICC *is* an inherently political actor. This is because the act of defining criminal from non-criminal, bad from good, is intrinsically political (Becker 1963). Carl Schmitt's (1996) concept of the political is instructive here, as Von Bernstorff (2008, p. 922) explains:

> Schmitt saw a close connection between political violence and moral claims to universal justices. States attempt to wage wars in the name of humanity in order to justify political violence. By invoking terms such as 'humanity' the political opponent is rendered an outlaw, standing outside humanity and outside the law. Claims to universal values can be used to justify violence of a particularly extreme nature by drawing a moral boundary between oneself and the political 'enemy'.

Nouwen and Werner (2011, p. 962) build on Schmitt's concept of the political to examine the International Criminal Court as 'a powerful weapon in political struggles'. As Nouwen and Werner (2011) highlight, the ICC acts in a political capacity through its labelling of the enemies and friends of mankind. Schmitt (1996, p. 27) highlights that this distinction between good and evil lies at the very heart of the political, classifying the enemy as 'the other'—someone who is 'in a specially intense way, existentially something different and alien, so that in the extreme case conflicts with him are possible'. Schmitt's (1996) concept of the political describes how state unity is achieved by acting in opposition to this constructed other, enemy or stranger. In a similar manner, the act of defining 'outlaw states' provides a sense of unity or international community and legitimizes the morals of the great powers. Idealpolitik and realpolitik are, therefore, fused to constantly define the contours of international society by constructing 'others' through the terminology of law, crime, and justice. The flexibility of the Court allows it to adapt to the changes inherent in late modernity so that new 'others' can always be constructed, while the uneven landscape of international society and the legitimacy of existing powers is maintained.

However, the flexibility of the Court also provides opportunities for it to be used in different ways and in acts of resistance to dominant powers. The examples of Uganda and Libya both illustrate how less powerful actors can engage the Court as a form of resistance and to suit their own interests. For example, although the Museveni government is powerful within Uganda, Uganda lacks relative power on the international stage (Clarke 2010). Uganda is able to use the Court to increase its international standing and reputation while avoiding undertaking justice itself, and ensures its own legitimacy and power in Uganda. In the case of Libya, one of the accused, Saif al-Islam Gaddafi, is able to consider using the ICC to avoid political assassination, or to achieve a more favourable trial. These unconventional engagements with the ICC illustrate that, as a tool, the ICC is more complex than simply a form of unidirectional power and control to be used by powerful actors over other traditionally less-powerful actors. The flexibility of the Court means that the ICC can be used in multiple, ambivalent, and unexpected ways. This reflects the circular nature of power and the relationship between power and resistance (Foucault in Rabinow 1991) in a world that is complex, fragmented, and ever-changing.

The potential for ambivalent, complex, and contradictory engagements of the ICC is further evidenced by Africa's changing interactions with the Court. All of the ICC's prosecutions have taken place in African situations. Subsequently, there has been much criticism of the Court for its exclusively African focus (Clarke 2011; Jabre and Moni 2012). Ford (2012, n.p.), for example, describes the ICC as 'an injudicious, selective enforcer of imperial policy, rather than a global standard of criminal law'. Such criticisms have mobilized the African Union to act together in opposition to the Court's unequal focus on the continent (Nowlin 2012). The African Union has been critical of the Court's arrest warrant for Sudanese president Omar al-Bashir and has encouraged the United Nations Security Council to defer his prosecution (see Akande, du Plessis, and Jalloh 2010). The African Union also introduced a treaty that was signed by many African countries, declaring that 'AU Member States shall not co-operate pursuant to the provisions of Article 98 of the Rome Statute of the ICC relating to immunities, for the arrest and surrender of President Omar El Bashir of The Sudan' (African Union 2009, p. 2). Many of the countries that signed this treaty, such as Kenya and Chad, are members of the ICC (Van der Vyver 2011), thus illustrating the ambivalent interactions between African countries and the ICC.

Similar antagonistic sentiments were expressed by several African countries in the wake of Libya's referral to the Court. For example, even though South Africa supported the adoption of Resolution 1973 in the Security Council, it later criticized the international intervention in Libya, with the African National Congress calling the intervention imperialist and a lust for Libyan oil (Clarke 2011). Africa's contradictory engagement with the Court in the Libyan situation is also exemplified by the reactions of the president of Uganda who claimed, 'I am totally allergic to foreign, political and military involvement in sovereign countries, especially African countries' (Deccan Herald 2011, n.p.). President Museveni also accused the West of double standards by imposing a no-fly zone on Libya but taking no action against other Arab nations facing popular upheaval (Deccan Herald 2011). These statements contradict Museveni's referral of the situation in Uganda to the ICC, illustrating how the ambivalent nature of the Court facilitates contradictions that provide actors the opportunity to simultaneously support and oppose the Court according to their own interests.

Thus, the International Criminal Court is able to be used reflexively by many actors in forms of dynamic and ambivalent resistance to dominant powers, rather than simply maintaining the status quo and the uneven international landscape. In a further example, the ICC's African focus has mobilized the African Union to respond to situations of mass violence. For example, in response to the Libyan situation the African Court on Human and Peoples' Rights issued a unanimous Order for Provisional Measures in respect of Libya, which demanded that Libya 'immediately refrain from any action that would result in loss of life or violation of physical integrity of persons' (Sander 2012, n.p.). The mobilizations of the African Union and African Court illustrate that the ICC can be used by less powerful groups to empower action at a different level. However, it is questionable as to the level of power and autonomy these groups have, as the Court acts as a tool within wider political frameworks that often repress dissent. For example, countries such as Kenya and Chad have been referred to the UN Security Council for refusing to arrest al-Bashir, and the ICC prosecutor has called for aid cuts to any country that allows al-Bashir in (Thijssen 2012). Africa's moves against the ICC have also been framed as setbacks that need to be managed by the Court and associated organizations, such as the United Nations (Keppler 2011).

The construction of the ICC as a model also reinforces the superiority of the great powers. These constructions of the ICC position the Court's Western conceptions of justice as more legitimate than other forms of justice, as is evidenced by the contest over the Gaddafi case between Libya and the ICC. Narratives of the Court's superiority to local forms of justice are reinforced by the Court's practical interpretation of the principle of complementarity. The Democratic Republic of the Congo has established criminal justice mechanisms to respond to violence and conflict. Thomas Lubanga was in custody in the DRC when he was sent to The Hague for prosecution by the Court. The Court, thus, takes over conflicts to enhance its visibility, while reinforcing the narrative of Western or international superiority and its monopoly of justice, morality, and virtue.

This superiority constructs the ICC as a saviour (Mutua 2001). David Kennedy's (2004) book, *The Dark Sides of Virtue*, highlights that the saviour metaphor blinds those who adopt it, often in the guise of humanitarian assistance, to the potential damage of their interventions. Kennedy (2004) argues that human rights frameworks decontextualize problems through claims of universality and neutrality, and reassert the superiority of the Western liberal tradition of human rights, while negating other options for justice. In the case of the ICC, the moral superiority of international institutions and the competition for trials has been accused of actually weakening local justice systems. In situations such as the DRC, the ICC has been 'fundamentally motivated by self-interested pragmatic concerns . . . overlooking the capacity of domestic jurisdictions to address the atrocities concerned' (Clark 2008, p. 44). In the DRC, there has been no pressure for the country to undertake their own prosecutions when international trials are continuing (Burke-White 2005; Schabas 2007a). Similarly, there is no sustained assistance provided to local jurisdictions or an attempt to hand over trials to local courts, with NGOs providing most capacity-building assistance with some consultation (ASF 2010). Thus, through its desire to use situations to increase its visibility, the ICC undermines the notion of complementarity and does little to support the establishment of local and alternative measures of justice.

The narratives of Western superiority seek to implant international standards into local jurisdictions, thus further reinforcing symbolic divides between savage countries, often the global south, and saviour countries, the global north. These narratives erode the reflexivity and power of local jurisdictions and African countries whose cases are before the Court. As Hardt and Negri (2000) highlight, this mirrors narratives of colonization. The practices also mirror victor's justice, as more powerful nations are free from the threat of prosecution while less powerful nations are vulnerable to prosecution by the Court, which is clearly illustrated in the Court's track record. Zolo (2009) supports this thesis, viewing international law as a two-track system of made-to-measure law for the hegemonic states and their allies, and a punitive regime for losers or the disadvantaged. As Zolo (2009) illustrates, this asymmetrical and unequal international order sees justice used to legitimate some causes and acts, while demonizing others, thus reinforcing the uneven international landscape.

7.4 Concluding comments

The spectre of the International Criminal Court is invoked regularly in many different situations. The use of the Court as a visible tool is facilitated by the Court's ambiguities and ambivalences, illustrating that the contradictions of the Court have indeed been beneficial in establishing the ICC and maintaining it as a prominent actor on the international stage for the past ten years. The broad aims of prevention and persuasion provide axiomatic and popular justifications for engaging the ICC. As the ICC's actions evolve to be different to this idealpolitik, further contradictions occur. For example, as highlighted, the ICC is yet to actually prosecute anyone from Libya or Uganda. While the 'consumption' approach has been beneficial for the Court in its first decade, where visibility has been crucial, it is questionable how long the ICC can continue in this vein without achieving more successful prosecutions. There is a limit to the number of cases that the ICC can accumulate without closure, before the deeper legitimacy and effectiveness of the Court comes into question, due to increasingly wide gaps between idealpolitik and realpolitik. At this stage, however, it appears that the idealpolitik will continue as the ICC is driven forward on the juggernaut that is globalization and late modernity (Giddens 2002), increasing its power, visibility, and influence through its contradictions and vague aims and thus, constantly seeking to consume more violence.

8 Conclusion

At the start of its second decade, the International Criminal Court is engaged in many different situations around the world. The Court is prosecuting crimes in seven situations: the Côte d'Ivoire, Libya, the Central African Republic, Darfur, Sudan, the Democratic Republic of the Congo, Uganda, and Kenya. To date, there have been 18 cases within these situations (ICC 2015). In addition, the Court has recently opened a formal investigation into the situation in Mali concerning the violence and war crimes committed in conflicts between the government and armed forces.[1] The ICC is also conducting preliminary investigations into violence and conflict in several other countries, including Afghanistan, Georgia, Guinea, Colombia, Honduras, Korea, and Nigeria. Further to these investigations and prosecutions, there have been widespread calls for the ICC to act in Syria, with more than 50 nations calling for the United Nations Security Council to refer the Syrian crisis to the ICC (AAP 2013; Sands 2013).

Despite this increasing list of prominent investigations and prosecutions, the ICC has only completed two trials: one convicting Thomas Lubanga for war crimes in the DRC and sentencing him to 14 years' imprisonment (ICC 2012b; ICC 2012c), and the other acquitting Mathieu Ngudjolo Chui of war crimes and crimes against humanity in the DRC (ICC 2012d). The Pre-Trial Chamber of the Court has declined to confirm charges in four cases and at least nine suspects remain at large (ICC 2015). As this record shows, the gap between the ICC's threat of prosecution and the ICC's reality is becoming wider. Yet the ICC has never been as prominent or visible on the world stage. When the idealpolitik of the Court is contrasted against the functioning of its realpolitik, a large gap and a series of contradictions emerge. It is this gap between rhetoric and reality, and the associated series of contradictions that this book has explored.

1 The situation in Mali was referred to the ICC by the government of Mali on 13 July 2012. The Office of the Prosecutor opened an investigation into alleged crimes committed in Mali since January 2012. The situation in Mali is currently assigned to Pre-Trial Chamber II. See ICC OTP 2013a and b.

8.1 Producing resilience and negative externalities by consuming conflict

The contradictions of the Court are created by the fragmented nature of the ICC and by the different interpretations and applications of the Court's vague aims of prevention and persuasion, as explored in Chapters 5 and 6. These overarching aims construct the Court as a flexible model and adaptable tool of justice. By interchangeably acting in these roles, the ICC is defined by a bundle of paradoxes: it is prominent yet remote, visible yet inaccessible, flexible yet controlling, and unified yet fragmented. These contradictions cause harm, as the ICC fails to achieve its highly idealistic aims and aspirational promises, selectively criminalizing certain individuals and groups, reinforcing existing geopolitical divides, and ignoring (and thus reproducing) the inequalities that structure the international environment.

However, the ICC appears oblivious to the harm it can cause and unconcerned by its contradictions and paradoxes. This is because the Court's potential for harm arises from its adaptability and flexibility, which facilitates its use as a tool and a model of selective justice. The Court's adaptive qualities are important, as they ensure that the ICC remains resilient in a complex and late-modern environment. The Court's strength lies in its ability to adapt to unpredictable situations and to be picked up and used in many different circumstances by a range of different actors. By being consumed in such a manner the Court becomes a valuable commodity. It remains relevant, visible, and useful. It ensures its continued survival in an uncertain world and secures its place on an international stage that is occupied by numerous, and often conflicting, international actors, set against an ever-changing backdrop of unforeseen events. Through its flexibility, the ICC is a resilient institution.

The ICC needs to be resilient so that it can respond to the 'crises' that emerge in the unpredictable international environment of late modernity. As Charlesworth (2002) highlights, international law is a discipline that is defined by a series of crises. The field of international criminal justice has developed through iterative responses to urgent situations that have prompted the amalgamation of the field of human rights and law in an attempt to protect civilians from crimes that 'deeply shock the conscience of humanity' (ICC OTP 2013b, n.p.). Similarly, the ICC has itself been defined through its responses to a series of crises. For example, through the Security Council's mobilization of the Court in Libya, the ICC was defined as an institution that can be mobilized strategically by a range of actors, even if they have not formally joined the ICC. The Court was constructed as the judicial arm of international humanitarian intervention in conflict (Fitz 2011). The Court's flexibility enabled it to be used in this manner and it was through its use in the Libya crisis that the Court's identity and role was iteratively defined; the Court became a body to be used in conjunction with other real-time responses to unfolding violence.

The Court's mobilization in the Libya situation shaped subsequent engagements of the Court. For example, as highlighted in the introduction to this chapter, at the start of 2013 the ICC was used alongside military intervention early in the crisis in Mali, with the start of the ICC's investigation coinciding with a French military invasion to combat terrorism and al-Qaeda cells (Amnesty International 2013; Cole 2013; Henderson 2013). The ICC's adoption in Mali reinforces the construction of the ICC as a coercive tool that can be used as part of the international responsibility to protect, despite the Court's inability to produce timely and successful prosecutions. As this example shows, it is through its involvement in a series of unfolding crises that the ICC is developed. Its engagement in a variety of events ensures that it evolves and responds to the changing needs of international society, and remains constantly valuable, useful, and resilient. As Hills (2000, p. 109) highlights, 'resilience is displayed by an institution in response to external pressures or crises'. The Court must be able to change and adapt to the capricious nature of the international environment if it is to be continuously productive, relevant, and visible. This means that the aims of the Court must be sufficiently vague and ambiguous to allow it to capitalize on many different events or crises as they emerge and evolve.

Any harm that arises from the ICC's flexibility is external to its drive for resilience. The ICC's contradictions, paradoxes, and potential to produce harm are negative externalities for the Court. Adopted from the field of economics, the term 'negative externalities' describes the practice whereby corporations 'place some of the costs of their profit-seeking activity onto society' (Mackenzie 2010, p. 22). This means that the ICC produces negative outcomes as a product of its operation, that these negative outcomes are less detrimental to the Court than changing its current practices, and that the negative effects are absorbed by other organizations, groups, or individuals outside of the ICC. In other words, the ICC creates harms, the costs of which are then placed on to local jurisdictions, individual actors, or other organizations at the international level, in order to maintain the ICC's mode of 'consuming' violence to ensure its resilience.

The Court produces negative externalities in the form of contradictions, unachieved aims, selective criminalization, and the reproduction of power differentials and geopolitical divides. One example is the ICC's use by the Ugandan government. As explored in Chapter 7, the Ugandan government has used the ICC as a tool to enhance its power and legitimate its rule in Uganda, while also benefiting from increased prominence at an international level (Nouwen and Werner 2011). However, the use of the ICC by the Ugandan government perpetuates violence, conflict, and harm in Uganda, as the government continues to commit unchecked human rights abuses and contributes to the destabilization of surrounding countries, such as the DRC. This harm is a negative externality for the Court. For the ICC, its mobilization by Uganda is beneficial as it demonstrates cooperation by an African government and provides several high-profile cases, such as that of Joseph Kony, which helps increase the visibility and relevance of the ICC. Thus the ICC's desire for resilience overrides the harm that can be caused by selective prosecutions and the use of the Court as a tool.

Another similar example is the ICC's involvement in the DRC. The prosecution of Thomas Lubanga provided a beneficial landmark for the Court in the form of its first guilty verdict, which increased the Court's legitimacy and visibility. However, the narrowness of the charges and the selective nature of the prosecution left many victims and entire communities with little real justice (REDRESS 2008, 2012; Vinck et al. 2008). The conflict in the DRC also continued with the complicity of the local and regional actors who offered Lubanga to the Court (Kambale 2012) and the international organizations and corporations who plundered the country's vast natural resources (Mullins and Rothe 2008a). The ICC's prosecution thus caused harm, as it did little to address the underlying causes of the violence, criminalized particular individuals and groups in a complex, multi-actor conflict, and failed to deliver its promise of justice in the region. However, these harms were externalized, as the Court used the Lubanga trial to enhance its relevance, visibility, and legitimacy, in the form of a completed trial. In both Uganda and the DRC, the ICC gave responsibility to local jurisdictions and outside NGOs and encouraged them to complement its selective prosecutions. The Court thus externalized the social harms it produced through its interventions, so that it could continue to consume more violence and enhance its institutional resilience.

As these examples illustrate, the Court does not prevent international crime, but legitimizes particular types of violence and causes social harms through its superficial response to violence. The ICC's mode of consuming conflict is important for the Court as it ensures that the Court remains in business. Of course, as mentioned at the end of Chapter 7, the viability of this strategy is questionable in the long term as the Court will eventually be required to produce more prosecutions to legitimate its existence. However, for now, the Court can rely on a handful of symbolic prosecutions to maintain its consumption model. The unavoidable side effects of the Court's desire to consume violence are that the ICC becomes an inaccessible, remote, fragmented, and control-based institution. For the ICC, these outcomes are less important than its need to be relevant and resilient, meaning the social harms it produces become negative externalities.

As this highlights, the ICC is less concerned with effectiveness and achieving its idealistic aims than it is with its visibility and resilience, which is ensured through its involvement in many different situations. Indeed, effectiveness and resilience are two separate measures for the ICC. Effectiveness refers to the extent to which the Court achieves its objectives or purposes and fulfils its goals, while resilience refers to the staying power of the ICC in the face of external challenges (Hasenclever, Mayes, and Rittberger 1996). The Court's effectiveness could be measured by its ability to achieve its idealpolitik, while its resilience is measured by its adaptability to realpolitik. For the Court, achieving its highly idealistic aims is not a priority. It is difficult, if not impossible, for the ICC to achieve the aims of prevention and persuasion; however, these aims are important as they provide justification for the Court's existence. The Court, thus, uses these aims flexibly to focus on its resilience, rather than its effectiveness. The ICC does not need to be effective to be resilient.

This reading of the ICC's resilience matches Hills's (2000) argument that the most significant factor facilitating institutional resilience is not the skills and goals of participants, but rather the institution's fulfilment of a function or role considered useful by a government or regime. For the ICC to be resilient, it does not need to achieve the goals of all participating actors, but it must remain useful for powerful sectors of international society, and useful for states themselves, as these are the groups that will mobilize the ICC and thus ensure that it has a continuing role in international society. The ICC's flexibility ensures that it remains useful, as it can be mobilized to serve the needs of a variety of different groups, individuals, and governing organizations. While the ICC may not be effective in terms of achieving its idealistic goals of prevention and persuasion, it is effective in fulfilling the needs of a broad range of powerful groups, from nation states to international organizations, such as the United Nations and the general 'regime' of international law.

As 'resilience is displayed in reaction, rather than strategic vision' (Hills 2000, p. 117), the ICC must be able to react to unpredictable events and adapt its aims and functioning to suit the particular needs of different situations and groups, and in order to display its relevance and legitimacy. Thus, the ICC is a resilient institution as it can be characterized as 'evolutionary, reactive, and well positioned to accommodate unavoidable political change' (Hills 2000, p. 110). Through its desire to 'consume' violence and be used as a valuable commodity, the ICC becomes a resilient institution, as it is valuable to numerous groups in international society.

8.2 Future directions

As this discussion highlights, the ICC draws its power from its ability to be used as a tool or a model to, selectively and flexibly, criminalize particular acts and actors. In this ability, the Court can be considered a criminogenic institution as it causes harm by perpetuating division and inequality, classifying particular events as crime and confirming others as legitimate, and ignoring the root causes of complex conflicts and widespread violence. The ICC was designed to recognize and respond to the harm caused by state crime; however, the power politics that contribute to state crime also extend to the ICC. This means that the critical framework of state crime must be expanded to include international institutions, a project advanced by the study of 'crimes of globalization' (Friedrichs and Friedrichs 2002).

At a national level, it is well recognized that criminal justice systems can cause harm (Barak 2005; Pepinsky and Quinney 1991). As a justice 'system' in and of itself, the ICC also carries the potential to cause harm and must be considered accordingly. The idealistic rhetoric and laudable aspirations of the ICC often conceal its potential for harm, but criminology must not be seduced by the ICC's attractive idealpolitik and consequently blinded to its potential for harm. It must critically examine the Court as an institution of power that subsequently has the potential to cause harm and, thus, become criminogenic. As the ICC's criminalization of conduct is used to facilitate its resilience, and harms are framed as negative externalities, criminology must continue to recognize the 'artifice of the category of crime and its susceptibility to influence' (Mackenzie 2006, p. 163).

This does not mean that a future research agenda for the ICC must be intent only on critiquing the Court. Rather, future study must consider how to use the strengths of the Court to enhance its effectiveness as well as its resilience and to capitalize on the Court's flexibility to minimize its negative externalities. The Court's strength lies in the space between its vulnerability and its resilience. It is this space that criminology must occupy to use the strengths of the Court to counteract its weaknesses. The Court's flexibility and its identity as a tool and a model provide many opportunities for different engagements of the ICC—engagements which can counteract the negative externalities of the Court's current mode of operation.

The Court is adaptable in response to the hyper-reflexivity of late modernity (Giddens 1990) and the consequent trend for change and evolution. As Giddens (1990, pp. 36–37) suggests, 'the reflexivity of modern social life consists in the fact that social practices are constantly examined and reformed in the light of incoming information about those very practices, thus constitutively altering their character'. Reflexivity can therefore be used to construct the Court as a positive tool that can be used to balance the uneven landscape of international society.

As the flexibility of the Court facilitates reflexivity and change, the Court can be used as an instrument to shine a spotlight of international attention on to a range of different situations across the world. As illustrated in Chapter 7, many different groups can use the Court as a tool, and although the Court is more often used by the most powerful actors, the Court's flexibility also presents the opportunity for other, less powerful actors to assert their agency and use the Court to highlight their needs. Thus, a key field of future research is to consider how the Court can be mobilized by a wider range of actors to make the landscape of international criminal justice, and the contours of international society, more even. This agenda stems from an acceptance of the complexities and contradictions of the ICC and an acknowledgement of the limited, and potentially harmful, role the Court can play in international society as just one tool among many (Simpson 2008), used by different actors to contribute towards peace and justice.

A recent example of traditionally less powerful groups engaging with the ICC is the Palestine Authority. The Palestine Authority was granted non-Member Observer State status by the United Nations in November 2012 (UN News Centre 2013). This landmark decision followed a history of Palestinian efforts to engage with the ICC. In 2009, the Palestinian Authority lodged a declaration under Article 12 (3) of the Rome Statute, which allows a state that is not party to the Rome Statute to consent to retroactive jurisdiction of the Court (Kearney 2012). This declaration aimed to grant the ICC jurisdiction over war crimes and crimes against humanity committed in Gaza and the West Bank since July 2002 (see Kearney 2012 for a broader discussion). Surrounding the UN decision to grant observer status, commentators speculated that this development could see the Palestinian Authority seek to bring their situation before the ICC (Gross

2012; Middle East Monitor 2012). Since the vote, it has been indicated that the Palestine Authority plans to approach the ICC. While, in realpolitik terms, the Palestine Authority holds relatively little power, the ability for this group to engage the Court illustrates the potential for a range of different voices to be heard, and for many situations to be rendered visible on the world stage.

Of course, the mere fact that the Court now holds the potential to be able to investigate the Palestinian situation does not mean that this avenue would be successful or present any material change. Indeed, the ICC has been non-committal about pursuing the situation in Palestine and it is uncertain how the ICC will proceed (Fairlie 2013). Despite this, the engagement with the ICC brings attention to the situation, thus giving it visibility and prominence and framing it through crime and justice narratives, using the ICC as a tool to do so. This situation provides one example of more diverse engagements with the Court and an avenue for future research and practice.

Another recent example of alternative engagements with the ICC is attempts to use the Court to frame 'church abuse' as a crime against humanity and prosecute such crimes before the ICC. In 2010, Geoffrey Robertson called for church abuse to be prosecuted by the Court (Robertson 2010). In 2011, several groups representing victims of sexual abuse by Catholic priests, including the Centre for Constitutional Rights and the Survivors Network of those Abused by Priests, approached the Court and made formal complaints, accusing the Pope, the Cardinal Secretary of State, and two other high-ranking Holy See officials of crimes against humanity (McVeigh 2011; Goodstein 2011; Zwartz 2012). The groups' submissions accused the Church of failing to prevent or punish perpetrators of rape and sexual violence, and engaging in the systematic and widespread practice of concealing sexual crimes around the world (McVeigh 2011).

Pamela Spees, a lawyer with the Centre for Constitutional Rights, stated, 'prosecuting individual instances of child molestation or sexual assault has not gotten at the larger systemic problem here. Accountability is the goal, and the ICC makes the most sense, given that it's a global problem' (quoted in Goodstein 2011, n.p.). This example illustrates an engagement with the broad, overarching aims of the ICC in terms of establishing accountability and ending global impunity. Spees (quoted in Goodstein 2011, n.p.) highlights that the point of the claims is to look at church abuse from 'a higher altitude', illustrating how the ICC can be used to call attention to the power structures and broad social inequalities that facilitate crimes at a local level. While the case against the Church has not made much progress, and there are numerous political and practical barriers that hamper it (Landry 2012), it does illustrate the ability for different groups to engage with the Court. As Mark Ellis, director of the IBA (quoted in Goodstein 2011, n.p.), states, 'when you look at the concept of why and how the ICC was created, I just don't think this fits . . . but the filing does something that's important. It raises awareness.'

These two cases illustrate the ability of the Court to be used by a wider range of actors. The strategy of engaging with the Court to highlight human rights abuses and attempt to frame certain acts as international crimes takes advantage of the Court's flexibility and desire for resilience. These examples highlight the possibility of considering different voices when the ICC is accepted as a tool and a model that exists to shine a spotlight of attention on to crimes worldwide. Through wider engagements and interactions with the Court, a greater range of situations could gain visibility, making the landscape of justice slightly more even. The spectre of the ICC could thus be used as a tool for awareness and visibility while avoiding 'the dark sides of virtue', including the reproduction of existing power structures and geopolitical divides (Kennedy 2004).

However, if the ICC continues to exponentially increase the number of situations it is involved in, without increased funding and resources to enable it to materially execute its investigations and prosecutions, greater consideration must be given to the 'system' within which the ICC works. The ICC's potential to develop the capacity of local jurisdictions must be further explored so that instead of competing for trials that could be conducted at a national level, as was evidenced by the Lubanga trial explored in Chapter 6, the ICC could work with national jurisdictions to facilitate local trials. These local trials would prevent the current removal of the Court from the situations it prosecutes and would thus construct the Court as a positive model rather than a competitive institution, vying for attention, visibility, and legitimacy. Although the ICC claims to be the centrepiece of the system of international criminal justice, this system is underdeveloped and more support is needed to enhance domestic jurisdictions and facilitate local trials.

These two research agendas ask: if the ICC is a tool, how can it be used more effectively? And if the Court is a model, how can it operate within a stronger system of international criminal justice measures? By recognizing the International Criminal Court as a model of justice and a tool, and by acknowledging the harm inherent in these roles, the ICC could be used to combat the uneven international landscape. As the idealpolitik of the Court continues to obscure the use of the Court as an instrument for political objectives, this potential lies dormant. However, in late modernity, reflexivity provides the space for change as the ICC continues to 'consume violence' (Bauman 2007b), establishing itself as a resilient commodity in a contested, complex, and ever-changing global world.

Appendix: interview participants

Name	*Category*	*Organization*
Participant A	NGO	Amnesty International
Participant B	NGO	Human Rights Watch
Participant C	NGO	International Centre for Transitional Justice (ICTY)
Participant D	NGO	Advocats Sans Frontier (ASF)
Participant E	NGO	Coalition for the International Criminal Court
Participant F	NGO	International Federation of Human Rights (FIDH)
Participant G	NGO	International Bar Association (IBA)
Participant H	NGO	REDRESS
Participant I*	NGO	ICC Watch/ICJ Columnist
Participant J	Media	Radio National Worldwide/International Justice Tribune
Participant K	Media	International War and Peace Reporting
Participant L	Media	International War and Peace Reporting – DRC
Participant M	Media	AFP – International Trials Reporter
Participant N	ICC	Office of Public Counsel for the Defence
Participant O	ICC	Office of Public Counsel for the Defence
Participant P*	ICC	Office of Public Counsel for Victims
Participant Q*	ICC	Victim Participation & Reparations Section
Participant R	ICC	Representative of Victims (independent counsel)
Participant S	ICC	Office of the Prosecutor
Participant T	ICC	Office of the Prosecutor
Participant U	ICC	Presidency

*Participants are not quoted in the main text but were interviewed.

Bibliography

AAP 2013, 'Aust backs criminal court move on Syria', *Sydney Morning Herald*, 12 January, accessed 12 June 2015, http://news.smh.com.au/breaking-news-national/aust-backs-criminal-court-move-on-syria-20130112-2cm8w.html.

Aas, K. 2007, *Globalization and Crime*, Sage, London.

ABC News 2012, 'Gaddafi's son facing gallows in Libya: lawyer', *ABC News*, 11 October, accessed 12 June 2015, www.abc.net.au/news/2012-10-10/gaddafis-son-will-be-hanged-lawyer/4306462.

Adam, B., Beck, U., and Van Loon, J. 2000, 'Introduction: repositioning risk, the challenge for social theory', in B. Adam, U. Beck and J. Van Loon (eds), *The Risk Society and Beyond: Critical Issues for Social Theory*, Sage, London, pp. 1–32.

Afflitto, F. M. 2000, 'Victimization, survival and the impunity of forced exile: a case study from the Rwandan genocide', *Crime, Law and Social Change*, vol. 34, pp. 77–97.

African Union 2009, 'Decision on the report of the commission on the meeting of African states parties to the Rome Statute of the International Criminal Tribunal (ICC) (Assembly/ AU/ Dec.245(XIII) Rev.1)', *Assembly of the African Union Decisions and Declarations*, 3 July, accessed 10 August 2015, www.au.int/en/sites/default/files/ASSEMBLY_EN_1_3_JULY_2009_AUC_THIRTEENTH_ORDINARY_SESSION_DECISIONS_DECLARATIONS_%20MESSAGE_CONGRATULATIONS_MOTION_0.pdf, para. 10.

Ainley, K. 2011, 'Excesses of responsibility: the limits of law and the possibilities of politics', *Ethics and International Affairs*, vol. 25, no. 4, pp. 407–31.

Akande, D., du Plessis, M., and Jalloh, C. 2010, 'An African expert study on the African Union concerns about Article 16 of the Rome State of the ICC', *Institute for Security Studies Position Paper*, accessed 10 August 2015, www.elac.ox.ac.uk/downloads/AkandeDuPlessisJallohICCPositionPaper.pdf.

Akhavan, P. 2001, 'Beyond impunity: can international criminal justice prevent future atrocities?', *The American Journal of International Law*, vol. 95, no. 7, pp. 7–31.

Akhavan, P. 2005, 'The Lord's Resistance Army case: Uganda's submission of the first state referral to the International Criminal Court', *The American Journal of International Law*, vol. 99, no. 2, pp. 403–21.

Aljazeera 2012, 'Libya renews bid for trial of Gaddafi Son', *Aljazeera* online, 9 October, accessed 12 June 2015, www.aljazeera.com/video/africa/2012/10/201210954150265362.html.

Allen, T. 2006, *Trial Justice: the International Criminal Court and the Lord's Resistance Army*, Zed Books, London.

Ambos, K. 2003, 'International criminal procedure: "adversarial", "inquisitorial" or mixed?', *International Criminal Law Review*, vol. 3, pp. 1–37.

Amin, S. 1992, *Empire of Chaos,* Monthly Review Press, New York.

Amnesty International 2011, *The Battle for Libya: Killings, Disappearances and Torture,* accessed 26 August 2012, www.amnesty.ie/sites/default/files/2011%20-%20The%20Battle%20for%20Libya%20%28English%29.pdf.

Amnesty International 2012a, 'Landmark ICC verdict over use of child soldiers', Amnesty International website, 14 March, accessed 12 June 2015, www.amnesty.org/en/news/landmark-icc-verdict-over-use-child-soldiers-2012-03-14.

Amnesty International 2012b, 'Libya: civilian deaths from NATO airstrikes must be properly investigated', Amnesty International website, 19 March, accessed 12 June 2015, www.amnesty.org/en/news/libya-civilian-deaths-nato-airstrikes-must-be-properly-investigated-2012-03-19.

Amnesty International 2013, 'Mali: ICC investigation of conflict crimes a key step towards justice', Amnesty International website, 16 January, accessed 10 August 2015, www.africanchildinfo.net/index.php?option=com_content&view=article&id=1863%3Amali-icc-investigation-of-conflict-crimes-a-key-step-towards-justice&catid=34%3Anews&Itemid=84&lang=fr.

Anheier, H., Glasius, M., and Kaldor, M. 2001, 'Introducing global civil society', in H. Anheier, M. Glasius, and M. Kaldor (eds), *Global Civil Society*, Oxford University Press, Oxford, pp. 3–22.

Annan, K. 1999, 'Statement at the opening of the Preparatory Commission for the International Criminal Court', *Secretary-General's Address*, New York, 16 February, accessed 6 December 2009, www.ngos.net/un/icc.html.

Aradau, C. and Van Munster, R. 2009, 'Exceptionalism and the "war on terror": criminology meets international relations', *British Journal of Criminology*, vol. 49, no. 5, pp. 686–701.

Arbour, L. 2011, 'The rise and fall of international human rights', *Sir Joseph Hotung International Human Rights Lecture*, British Museum, 27 April, accessed 2 February 2012, www.crisisgroup.org/en/publication-type/speeches/2011/the-rise-and-fall-of-international-human-rights.aspx.

Arrighi, G., Silver, B., and Brewer, B. 2003, 'Industrial convergence, globalization, and the persistence of the north-south divide', *Studies in Comparative International Development*, vol. 38, no. 1, pp. 3–31.

Arsanjani, M. 1999, 'The Rome Statute of the International Criminal Court', *American Society of International Law*, vol. 93, no. 1, pp. 22–43.

Ascherson, N. 1963, *The King Incorporated, Leopold the Second and the Congo*, George Allen & Unwin, London.

Ashworth, A. and Redmayne, M. 2010, *The Criminal Process: An Evaluative Study*, 4th ed., Clarendon Press, Oxford.

Associated Press 2011, 'Judges urged to convict Congo warlord Thomas Lubanga', *The Guardian* online, 25 August, accessed 12 June 2015, www.guardian.co.uk/world/2011/aug/25/judges-urged-convict-thomas-lubanga.

Astor, M. 2008, 'Group urges caution in dealing with Sudan's leader', *Associated Press* newswires, 23 September.

Atkinson, L. 2011, 'Knights of the court: the state coalition behind the International Criminal Court', *Journal of International Law and International Relations*, vol. 7, pp. 66–103.

Avocats Sans Frontiers (ASF) et al. 2006, 'DR Congo: ICC Charges Raise Concern: Joint letter to the Chief Prosecutor of the International Criminal Court', accessed 1 July 2012, www.hrw.org/news/2006/07/31/dr-congo-icc-charges-raise-concern.

Avocats Sans Frontières (ASF) 2010, *Promoting complimentarity* [sic] *in the Democratic Republic of Congo,* accessed 12 June 2015, www.asf.be/wp-content/publications/ASF-Promoting_Complementarity_in_the_DRC.pdf.

Baker, T. and Simon, J. 2002, 'Embracing risk', in T. Baker and J. Simon (eds), *Embracing Risk*, University of Chicago Press, Chicago, pp. 1–26.

Barak, G. 2005, 'A reciprocal approach to peacemaking criminology: between adversarialism and mutualism', *Theoretical Criminology*, vol. 9, no. 2, pp. 131–52.

Barzak, I. and Teibel, A. 2012, 'Tensions rise on both sides of Gaza border', *The Sydney Morning Herald*, 15 November, accessed 12 June 2015, http://news.smh.com.au/breaking-news-world/tension-rises-on-both-sides-of-gaza-border-20121115-29emb.html.

Bassiouni, M. C. 1982, 'The proscribing function of international criminal law in the processes of international protection of human rights', *Yale Journal of World Public Order*, vol. 9, pp. 193–216.

Bassiouni, M. C. 1995, 'Establishing an International Criminal Court: historical survey', *Military Law Review*, vol. 149, pp. 49–63.

Bassiouni, M. C. 1997, 'From Versailles to Rwanda in seventy-five years: the need to establish a permanent international criminal court', *Harvard Human Rights Journal*, vol. 10, pp. 11–62.

Bassiouni, M. C. 1999a, *Crimes Against Humanity in International Law*, Kluwer Law International, The Hague.

Bassiouni, M. C. 1999b, 'Negotiating the Treaty of Rome on the establishment of an international criminal court', *Cornell International Law Journal*, vol. 32, pp. 443–70.

Bassiouni, M. C. 2000, 'Combating impunity for international crimes', *University of Colorado Law Review*, vol. 71, pp. 409–22.

Bauman, Z. 1989, *Modernity and the Holocaust,* Polity Press, Cambridge.

Bauman, Z. 1990, 'Modernity and ambivalence', in M. Featherstone (ed.), *Global Culture: Nationalism, Globalisation and Modernity*, Sage, London, pp. 143–70.

Bauman, Z. 1991, *Modernity and Ambivalence*, Polity Press, New York.

Bauman, Z. 2000, *Liquid Modernity*, Polity Press, Cambridge.

Bauman, Z. 2001, 'Consuming life', *Journal of Consumer Culture*, vol. 1, no. 1, pp. 9–29.

Bauman, Z. 2005, *Liquid Life*, Polity Press, Cambridge.

Bauman, Z. 2007a, *Liquid Times: Living in an Age of Uncertainty*, Polity Press, Cambridge.

Bauman, Z. 2007b, *Consuming Life*, Polity Press, Cambridge.

BBC 2006, 'DR Congo rebel faces Hague trial', *BBC News*, 17 March, accessed 18 June 2010, http://news.bbc.co.uk/2/hi/africa/4815966.stm.

BBC 2011a,'US to send troops to Uganda to help fight LRA rebels', *BBC News Africa*, 15 October, accessed 12 June 2015, www.bbc.co.uk/news/world-africa-15317684.

BBC 2011b, 'Sudan's Omar al-Bashir in Malawi: ICC wants answers', *BBC News Africa*, 20 October, accessed 2 February 2012, www.bbc.co.uk/news/world-africa-15384163.

BBC 2011c, 'ICC frees Rwandan rebel Callixte Mbarushimana', *BBC News Africa,* 23 December, accessed 12 June 2015, www.bbc.com/news/world-africa-16319059.

BBC 2012a, 'ICC delivers first ever verdict in Thomas Lubanga Trial', *BBC News*, 14 March, accessed 12 June 2015, www.bbc.com/news/world-africa-17356339.

BBC 2012b, 'Nato urged to investigate civilian deaths in Libya', *BBC News*, 14 May, accessed 12 June 2015, www.bbc.co.uk/news/world-africa-18053488.

BBC 2012c, 'Democratic Republic of Congo profile', *BBC News*, last updated 4 August 2015, accessed 10 August 2015, www.bbc.com/news/world-africa-13283212.

BBC 2015, 'Will ICC membership help or hinder the Palestinians' cause?', *BBC News*, accessed 12 June 2015, http://www.bbc.com/news/world-middle-east-30744701.

Beck, U. 1992, *Risk Society: Towards a New Modernity*, Sage, London.

Beck, U. 1994, 'The Reinvention of politics: towards a theory of reflexive modernization', in U. Beck, A. Giddens, and S. Lash (eds), *Reflexive Modernization: Politics, Tradition and Aesthetics in the Modern Social Order*, Stanford University Press, Stanford, California.

Beck, U. 1999, *World Risk Society*, Polity Press, Cambridge.

Beck, U, Giddens, A. and Lash, S. (eds) 1994, *Reflexive Modernization: Politics, Tradition and Aesthetics in the Modern Social Order*, Stanford University Press, Stanford, California.

Becker, H. 1963, *Outsiders: Studies in the Sociology of Deviance*, The Free Press, New York.

Beilharz, P. 2000, *Zygmunt Bauman: Dialectic of Modernity*, Sage, London.

Bekou, O. and Cryer, R. 2004, *The International Criminal Court*, Ahsgate/Dartmouth, Aldershot.

Benzing, M. 2004, 'U.S. Bilateral Non-Surrender Agreements and Article 98 of the Statute of the International Criminal Court: an exercise in the law of treaties', *Max Planck UNYB*, vol. 8, pp. 181–236.

Berger, P. and Luckmann, T. 1966, *The Social Construction of Reality*, Allen Lane, London.

von Bernstorff 2008, 'The changing fortunes of the Universal Declaration of Human Rights: genesis and symbolic dimensions of the turn to rights in international law', *European Journal of International Law*, vol. 19, no. 5, pp. 903–24.

Biernacki, P. and Waldford, D. 1981, 'Snowball sampling: problems and techniques of chain referral sampling', *Sociological Methods Research*, vol. 10, no. 2, pp. 141–63.

Bisset, A. 2009, 'Rethinking the powers of truth commissions in light of the ICC statute', *Journal of International Criminal Justice*, vol. 7, pp. 963–82.

Black, I. 2011, 'Muammar Gaddafi lashes out as power slips away', *The Guardian* online, 21 February, accessed 22 February 2011, www.guardian.co.uk/world/2011/feb/21/libya-protests-bloodiest-yet-gaddafi.

Blumenson, E. 2006, 'The challenge of a global standard of justice: peace, pluralism, and punishment at the International Criminal Court', *Suffolk University Law School Faculty Publications*, Paper 22, accessed 22 February 2010, http://lsr.nellco.org/suffolk-fp/22.

Borger, J. 2011, 'NATO may end Libya air strikes', *The Sydney Morning Herald*, 7 October, accessed 15 November 2012, www.smh.com.au/world/nato-may-end-libya-air-strikes-20111006-1lbnu.html.

Bourdieu, P. 1977, *Outline of a Theory of Practice*, Cambridge University Press, Cambridge.

Bourdieu, P. 1987, 'The force of law: toward a sociology of the juridical field', *Hastings Law Journal*, vol. 38, pp. 805–53.

Bourdieu, P. 1991, *Language and Symbolic Power*, Polity Press, US.

Branch, A. 2007, 'Uganda's civil war and the politics of ICC intervention', *Ethics and International Affairs*, vol. 21, no. 2, pp. 179–98.

Branch, A. 2012, 'Dangerous ignorance: the hysteria of Kony 2012', *Aljazeera*, 12 March, accessed 23 March 2012, www.aljazeera.com/indepth/opinion/2012/03/201231284336601364.html.

Brighenti, A. 2007, 'Visibility a category for the social sciences', *Current Sociology*, vol. 55, no. 3, pp. 323–42.

Broomhall, B. 2003, *International Justice and the International Criminal Court: Between Sovereignty and the Rule of Law*, Oxford University Press, Oxford.

Burgess, R. 1984, *In the Field: an Introduction to Field Research*, George Allen & Unwin, London.

Burke-White, W. 2004, 'International legal pluralism', *Michigan Journal of International Law*, vol. 25, pp. 963–80.

Burke-White, W. 2005, 'Complementarity in practice: the International Criminal Court as part of a system of multi-level global governance in the Democratic Republic of Congo', *Leiden Journal of International Law*, vol. 18, pp. 557–90.

Burnett, M. and Evenson, E. 2012, 'The other half of the Kony equation', *The Washington Times*, 4 April, accessed 10 April 2012, www.washingtontimes.com/news/2012/apr/4/other-half-of-the-kony-equation.

Campbell, D. T. and Stanley, J. C. 1966, *Experimental and Quasi-Experimental Designs for Research*, Rand McNally, Chicago.

CARE 2012, 'Democratic Republic of the Congo: sexual violence rising due to escalating conflict', *CARE Newsroom*, 7 August, accessed 8 November 2012, www.care.org/newsroom/articles/2012/08/care-drc-conflict-violence-rape-women.asp.

Carpenter, L. 2012, 'Conflict minerals in the Congo: blood minerals and Africa's under-reported first world war', *Suffolk University Working Paper*, 2 April, accessed 3 July 2012, http://web.mit.edu/12.000/www/m2016/pdf/Congo.pdf.

Casey, L. 2002, 'The case against the International Criminal Court', *Fordham International Law Journal*, vol. 25, pp. 840–72.

Cassese, A. 1998, 'Current trends towards criminal prosecution and punishment of breaches of international humanitarian law', *European Journal of International Law*, vol. 9, pp. 2–17.

Castells, M. 2000, *The Rise of the Network Society, the Information Age: Economy, Society and Culture*, vol. 1, Blackwell, Oxford.

Chabas, C. 2011, 'Ivory Coast violence continues after the fall of Laurent Gbagbo, says Amnesty', *The Guardian* online, 4 October, accessed 6 November 2012, www.guardian.co.uk/world/2011/oct/04/ivory-coast-africa-violence-continues.

Chaikel, D. 2011, 'Does gender matter at the International Criminal Court', *International Women's Day Speech*, 8 March, accessed 6 February 2012, www.haguejusticeportal.net/index.php?id=12400.

Charbonneau, L. and Nichols, M. 2012, 'Exclusive: Rwanda, Uganda arming Congo rebels, providing troops-U.N. Panel', *Reuters*, 17 October, accessed 9 November 2012, www.reuters.com/article/2012/10/17/us-congo-democratic-rwanda-uganda-idUSBRE89F1RQ20121017.

Charlesworth, H. 2002, 'International law: a discipline of crisis', *The Modern Law Review*, vol. 65, no. 3, pp. 377–92.

Charmaz, K. 2005, 'Grounded theory in the 21st century: applications for advancing social justice studies', in N. Denzin and Y. Lincoln (eds), *The Sage Handbook of Qualitative Research*, Sage, Thousand Oaks, pp. 507–35.

Charmaz, K. 2006, *Constructing Grounded Theory: A Practical Guide Through Qualitative Analysis*, Sage, London.

Chazal, N. 2013, 'Beyond Borders?: The International Criminal Court and the geopolitics of international criminal justice', *Griffith Law Review*, vol. 22, no. 3, pp. 707–28.

Chesterman, S. 1997, 'Never again . . . and again: Law, order, and the gender of war crimes in Bosnia and beyond', *Yale Journal of International Law*, vol. 22, pp. 299–344.

Chiomenti, C. 2006, 'Corporations and the International Criminal Court', in *Symposium—Transnational Corporations and Human Rights* (Global law working paper 01/05), NYU School of Law, New York.

Christie, N. 1986, 'The ideal victim', in E. Fattah (ed.), *From Crime Policy to Victim Policy*, The Macmillian Press Ltd, London, pp. 17–30.

Christie, N. 1997, 'Conflicts as property', *The British Journal of Criminology*, vol. 17, no. 1, pp. 1–15.

CICC 2015, Coalition for the International Criminal Court website, accessed 12 June 2015, www.iccnow.org.

Clark, P. 2008, 'Law, politics and pragmatism: the ICC and case selection in Uganda and the Democratic Republic of Congo', in N. Waddell and P. Clark (eds), *Courting Conflict? Justice, Peace and the ICC in Africa*, Royal African Society, London, pp. 37–46.

Clarke, K. 2009, *Fictions of Justice: the International Criminal Court and the Challenge of Legal Pluralism in Sub-Saharan Africa*, Cambridge University Press, New York.

Clarke, K. 2010, 'Rethinking Africa through its exclusions: the politics of naming criminal responsibility', *Anthropological Quarterly*, vol. 83, no. 3, pp. 625–51.

Clarke, W. 2011, 'Zuma voices unease on Libyan intervention', *Think Africa Press*, 5 May, accessed 2 November 2012, http://thinkafricapress.com/south-africa/zuma-voices-unease-libyan-intervention.

Cohen, S. 1985, *Visions of Social Control: Crime, Punishment, and Classification*, Polity Press, Cambridge.

Cohen, S. 2001, *States of Denial: Knowing about Atrocities and Suffering*, Polity Press, Cambridge.

Cole, A. 2013, 'Mali and the ICC: what lessons can be learned from previous investigations?', *The Guardian* online, 17 January, accessed 17 January 2013, www.guardian.co.uk/law/2013/jan/17/mali-icc-lessons-learned-investigations.

Cole, J. 2006,'The Congo question: conflicting visions of independence', *Emporia State Research Studies*, vol. 43, no. 1, pp. 26–37.

Comiteau, L. 2006, 'World court begins hearings against alleged Congo warlord', *VOA News*, 9 November, accessed 8 June 2011, www.voanews.com/content/a-13-2006-11-09-voa25/397791.html.

Conrad, J. 1934, *Last Essays*, edited by R. Curle, Dent, London.

Conrad, J. 1990, *The Heart of Darkness*, Hodder & Stoughton, London.

Coughlin, C. 2011, 'Libya: the west wants to get rid of Gaddafi, but doesn't know how', *The Telegraph*, 14 March, accessed 5 November 2012, www.telegraph.co.uk/comment/columnists/concoughlin/8381739/Libya-The-West-wants-to-get-rid-of-Gaddafi-but-doesnt-know-how.html.

Creswell, J. 2003, *Research Design: Qualitative, Quantitative, and Mixed Methods Approaches*, 2nd ed., Sage, Thousand Oaks.

Creswell, J. 2007, *Qualitative Inquiry and Research Design: Choosing Among Five Approaches*, 2nd ed., Sage, London.

Cruvellier, T. 2010, *Court of Remorse: Inside the International Criminal Tribunal for Rwanda*, University of Wisconsin Press, Madison.

Curtis, P. and McCarthy, T. 2012, 'Kony 2012: what's the real story?', *The Guardian* online, 8 March, accessed 2 April 2013, www.guardian.co.uk/politics/reality-check-with-polly-curtis/2012/mar/08/kony-2012-what-s-the-story.

Daly, K. 2012, 'Aims of the criminal justice system', in M. Marmo, W. de Lint, and D. Palmer (eds), *Crime and Justice: A Guide to Criminology*, 4th ed., Lawbook Co., Sydney, ch. 17.

Damaška, M. 2008, 'What is the point of international criminal justice', *Chicago-Kent Law Review*, vol. 83, pp. 329–65.

Damaška, M. 2009, 'The International Criminal Court between aspiration and achievement', *UCLA Journal of International Law and Foreign Affairs*, vol. 14, pp. 19–36.

Danner, A. 2003, 'Enhancing the legitimacy and accountability of prosecutorial discretion at the International Criminal Court', *American Journal of International Law*, vol. 97, pp. 510–53.

Davis, P. 2001, 'The politics of prosecuting rape as a war crime', *International Lawyers*, vol. 34, no. 4, pp. 1223–48.

Dealy, S. 2009a, 'Interview: Sudan's President Omar al-Bashir', *Public Broadcasting Service*, Transcript, 14 August, accessed 20 June 2010, www.pbs.org/newshour/bb/africa-july-dec09-bashir-full_08-13.

Dealy, S. 2009b, 'Omar al-Bashir: Sudan's wanted man', *Time World*, 13 June, accessed 20 June 2010, www.time.com/time/world/article/0,8599,1916107,00.html.

Dean, M. 1999, *Governmentality: Power and Rule in Modern Society*, Sage, Thousand Oaks.

Deccan Herald 2011, 'Uganda's Museveni criticises West's action on Libya', *Deccan Herald*, Kampala, 22 March, accessed 13 September 2011, www.deccanherald.com/content/147822/ugandas-museveni-criticises-wests-action.html.

Denzin, N. and Lincoln, Y. 2003, *The Landscape of Qualitative Research: Theories and Issues*, Sage, Thousand Oaks.

Denzin, N. and Lincoln, Y. 2005, 'Introduction: the discipline and practice of qualitative research' in N. Denzin and Y. Lincoln (eds), *The Sage Handbook of Qualitative Research*, Sage, Thousand Oaks, pp. 1–32.

Dickinson, L. 2003, 'The relationship between hybrid courts and international courts: the case of Kosovo', *New England Law Review*, vol. 37, no. 4, pp. 1059–72.

Dizolele, M. P. 2004, 'The UN in Congo: the failure of a peacekeeping mission', *The New York Times Opinion*, accessed 5 May 2012, www.nytimes.com/2004/05/10/opinion/10iht-eddizolele_ed3_.html.

Donnelly, J. 2003, *Universal Human Rights in Theory and Practice*, Cornell University Press, New York.

Downer, A. 1998, 'The International Criminal Court: our commitment to future generations', Speech by the Hon-Alexander Downer, MP to the Diplomatic Conference on the Establishment of an International Criminal Court, 15 July, accessed 16 August 2010, www.foreignminister.gov.au/speeches/1998/icc_150698.html.

Drumbl, M. 2005, 'Collective violence and individual punishment: the criminality of mass atrocity', *Northwestern University Law Review*, vol. 99, no. 2, pp. 539–610.

Drumbl, M. 2009, 'The push to criminalize aggression: something lost amid the gains?', *Case Western Reserve Journal of International Law*, vol. 41, pp. 291–320.

Duff, A., Farmer, L., Marshall, S., and Tadros, V. (eds) 2004a *The Trial on Trial: Volume 1: Truth and Due Process*, Hart, Oxford.

Duff, A., Farmer, L., Marshall, S., and Tadros, V. 2004b 'Introduction: Towards a normative theory of the criminal trial', in A. Duff, L. Farmer, S. Marshall, and V. Tadros (eds), *The Trial on Trial: Volume 1: Truth and Due Process*, Hart, Oxford, pp. 1–28.

Dunne, T. 1995, 'The social construction of international society', *European Journal of International Relations*, vol. 1, pp. 367–89.

Durkheim, É. 1960, *The Division of Labour in Society*, Free Press, Glencoe.

Durkheim, É. 1984, 'Two laws of penal evolution', in S. Lukes and A. Scull (eds), *Durkheim and the Law*, Blackwell, Oxford.

Economist 2011, 'Dim prospects: the International Criminal Court loses credibility and co-operation in Africa', *The Economist*, 17 February, accessed 20 February 2011, www.economist.com/node/18176088.

Elliot, A. 2002, 'Beck's sociology of risk: a critical assessment', *Sociology*, vol. 36, no. 2, pp. 293–315.

Elliot, A. (ed) 2007, *The Contemporary Bauman*, Routledge, Oxon.

Elliot, A. 2009, *Contemporary Social Theory: An Introduction*, Routledge, Oxon.
Ellis, E. 2012, 'Room for everyone at The Hague', Eric Ellis website, 8 February, accessed 10 August 2015, http://ericellis.com/room-for-everyone-at-the-hague.
El Zeidy, M. 2002, 'The principle of complementarity: a new machinery to implement international criminal law', *Michigan Journal of International Law*, vol. 23, pp. 869–976.
Emizet, K. 2000, 'Explaining the rise and fall of military regimes: civil-military relations in the Congo', *Armed Forces & Society*, vol. 26, pp. 203–27.
Enough 2009, *A comprehensive approach to Congo's conflict minerals—strategy paper*, accessed 1 May 2012, www.enoughproject.org/publications/comprehensive-approach-conflict-minerals-strategy-paper.
Ericson, R. 2007, *Crime in an Insecure World*, Polity Press, Cambridge.
Escritt, T. 2012, 'Libya promises ICC Gaddafi's son will get a fair trial', *Reuters*, 9 October, accessed 15 October 2012, www.reuters.com/article/2012/10/09/us-libya-icc-gaddafi-idUSBRE89812D20121009.
Ettari, S. 2005, 'Foundation of granite or sand: the International Criminal Court and United States bilateral immunity agreements, a note', *Brooklyn Journal of International Law*, vol. 30, pp. 205–56.
Ewans, M. 2002, *European Atrocity, African Catastrophe: Leopold II, the Congo Free State and its Aftermath*, Routledge, London.
Ewick, P. and Silbey, S. 1999, 'Common knowledge and ideological critique: the significance of knowing that the "Haves" come out ahead', *Law & Society Review*, vol. 33, no. 4, pp. 1025–41.
Fairlie, M. 2013, 'Palestine's upgraded status and the International Criminal Court', *Jurist*, 22 January, accessed 23 January 2013, http://jurist.org/forum/2013/01/megan-fairlie-palestine-icc.php.
Feeley, M. and Simon, J. 1994, 'Actuarial justice: the emerging new criminal law', in D. Nelken (ed.), *Futures of Criminology*, Sage, London, pp. 173–201.
FIDH (International Federation for Human Rights) 2009, 'Profound disappointment following the suspension of the Lubanga case', 12 January, accessed 13 July 2010, www.fidh.org/Profound-Disappointment-Following.
Finnemore, M. and Sikkink, K. 2001, 'Taking stock: the constructivist research program in international relations and comparative politics', *Annual Review of Political Science*, vol. 4, pp. 391–416.
Fitz, N. 2011, 'Security Council referral confirms ICC as critical institution', *Open Society Foundations*, 4 March, accessed 2 April 2011, www.opensocietyfoundations.org/voices/security-council-referral-confirms-icc-critical-institution.
Flint, J. and Waal, A. de, 2009, 'Case closed: a prosecutor without borders', *World Affairs*, Spring, accessed 3 March 2010, www.worldaffairsjournal.org/article/case-closed-prosecutor-without-borders.
Flyvberg, B. 2006, 'Five misunderstandings about case-study research', *Qualitative Inquiry*, vol. 12, no. 2, pp. 219–45.
Fontana, A. and Frey, J. H. 2005, 'The interview: from neutral stance to political involvement', in N. K. Denzin and Y. S. Lincoln (eds), *The Sage Handbook of Qualitative Research*, 3rd ed., Sage, Thousand Oaks, pp. 695–728.
Ford, G. 2012, 'The ICC: the empire's court', *Project Pan Africa*, 23 November, accessed 25 November 2012, www.projectpanafrica.org/28306/icc-the-empires-court/.
Fournet, C. 2007, *The Crime of Destruction and the Law of Genocide: Their Impact on Collective Memory*, Ashgate, Aldershot.

France 24 2012, 'ICC finds Congolese warlord Lubanga guilty of war crimes', *France 24*, 14 March, accessed 16 March 2012, www.france24.com/en/20120314-congo-thomas-lubanga-guilty-war-crimes-the-hague-international-criminal-court-child-soldiers.

Freeland, S. 2013, 'International criminal justice in the Asia-Pacific region: the role of the International Criminal Court treaty regime', *Journal of International Criminal Justice*, vol. 5, no. 11, pp. 1029–1057.

Friedrichs, D. O. and Friedrichs, J. 2002, 'The World Bank and crimes of globalization: a case study', *Social Justice*, vol. 29, no. 1/2, pp. 13–36.

Galanter, M. 1974, 'Why the "haves" come out ahead: speculations on the limits of legal change', *Law and Society Review*, vol. 9, no. 1, pp. 95–160.

Garland, D. 1990, *Punishment and Modern Society: A Study in Social Theory*, University of Chicago Press, Chicago.

Garland, D. 1996, 'The limits of the sovereign state: strategies of crime control in contemporary society', *The British Journal of Criminology*, vol. 36, no. 4, pp. 445–71.

Garland, D. 2001, *The Culture of Control*, Oxford University Press, Oxford.

Garland, D. and Sparks, R. 2000, 'Criminology, social theory, and the challenge of our times', in D. Garland and R. Sparks (eds), *Criminology and Social Theory*, Oxford University Press, New York, pp. 1–22.

Gerring, J. 2006, *Case Study Research: Principles and Practices*, Cambridge University Press, Cambridge.

Gibb, M. 2010, 'The ICC alone cannot end the era of impunity', *The Guardian* online, 12 June, accessed 16 July 2011, www.guardian.co.uk/commentisfree/libertycentral/2010/jun/12/icc-impunity-rwanda.

Giddens, A. 1984, *The Constitution of Society*, Polity Press, Cambridge.

Giddens, A. 1990, *The Consequences of Modernity*, Stanford University Press, Stanford.

Giddens, A. 2002, *Runaway World: How Globalisation is Reshaping our Lives*, Profile Books, London.

Giddens, A. and Pierson, C. 1998, *Conversations with Anthony Giddens: Making Sense of Modernity*, Polity Press, Cambridge.

Gillett, M. 2009, 'Victim participation at the International Criminal Court', *Australian Law Journal*, vol. 16, pp. 29–46.

Gioia, F. 2006, 'State sovereignty, jurisdiction, and "modern" international law: the principle of complementarity in the International Criminal Court', *Leiden Journal of International Law*, vol. 19, no. 4, pp. 1095–1123.

Glaser, B. G. 1978, *Theoretical Sensitivity*, The Sociology Press, Mill Valley.

Glaser, B. G. and Strauss, A. L. 1967, *The Discovery of Grounded Theory*, Aldine, Chicago.

Glasius, M. 2006, *The International Criminal Court: A Global Civil Society Achievement*, Routledge, New York.

Glasius, M. 2009, 'We ourselves, we are part of the functioning: the ICC, victims, and civil society in the Central African Republic', *African Affairs*, vol. 108, pp. 49–67.

Goede, M. de, 2008, 'Beyond risk: premeditation and post-9/11 security imagination', *Security Dialogue*, vol. 39, no. 2–3, pp. 155–76.

Goldsmith, J. 2003, 'The self-defeating International Criminal Court', *University of Chicago Law Review*, vol. 70, pp. 89–104.

Goldstein, E. 2012, 'Before the Arab Spring, the unseen thaw', *Human Rights Watch World Report 2012*, accessed 12 November 2012, www.hrw.org/world-report-2012/arab-spring-unseen-thaw .

Goldstein, K. 2002, 'Getting in the door: sampling and completing elite interviews', *PS, Political Science & Politics*, vol. 35, no. 4, pp. 669–74.

Goldstone, J. 2010, 'More candour about criteria: the exercise of discretion by the prosecutor of the International Criminal Court', *Journal of International Criminal Justice*, vol. 8, no. 2, pp. 383–406.

Goldstone, J. 2004, 'Response: reasoning about history, sociologically', *Sociological Methodology*, vol. 34, no. 1, pp. 35–61.

Goldstone, R. and Fritz, N. 2000, 'In the interests of justice and independent referral: the ICC prosecutor's unprecedented powers', *Leiden Journal of International Law*, vol. 13, no. 3, pp. 655–67.

Goldstone, R. and Simpson, J. 2003, 'Evaluating the role of the International Criminal Court as a legal response to terrorism', *Harvard Human Rights Journal*, vol. 16, pp. 13–26.

Goodman, D. and Cumming-Bruce, N. 2012, 'Diplomats warn Syria of consequences for violent crackdown', *The New York Times*, 28 February, accessed 19 March 2012, www.nytimes.com/2012/02/29/world/middleeast/government-troops-close-in-on-syrian-rebels-after-referendum.html.

Goodstein, L. 2011, 'Abuse victims ask court to prosecute the Vatican', *The New York Times*, 13 September, accessed 20 December 2011, www.nytimes.com/2011/09/14/world/europe/14vatican.html?_r=1&.

Government of Uganda 2003, *Referral of the situation concerning the Lord's Resistance Army*, 16 December, accessed 14 July 2010, www-rohan.sdsu.edu/~abranch/Current%20Projects/Uganda%20ICC%20Referral%202003.pdf.

Graff, J. 2004, 'Corporate war criminals and the International Criminal Court: blood and profits in the DRC', *Human Rights Brief*, vol. 11, pp. 23–26.

Green, J. and Thorogood, N. 2009, *Qualitative Methods for Health Research*, Sage, London.

Greenawalt, A. 2007, 'Justice without politics? Prosecutorial discretion and the International Criminal Court', *New York University Journal of International Law and Politics*, vol. 39, pp. 583–674.

Greenwood, F. 2012, 'Syria violence: the ceasefire that wasn't, *Global Post*, 29 October, accessed 8 November 2012, www.globalpost.com/dispatch/news/regions/middle-east/syria/121029/syria-violence-the-ceasefire-wasnt.

Gross, A. 2012, 'Following UN vote on Palestine, Israel may now find itself at The Hague', *Haaretz*, 2 December, accessed 3 December 2012, www.haaretz.com/opinion/following-un-vote-on-palestine-israel-may-now-find-itself-at-the-hague.premium-1.481919.

Guba, E. and Lincoln, Y. 2005, 'Paradigmatic controversies, contradictions, and emerging confluences', in N. Denzin and Y. Lincoln (eds), *The Sage Handbook of Qualitative Research*, Sage, Thousand Oaks, pp. 191–216.

Guest, G., Bunce, A., and Johnson, L. 2006, 'How many interviews are enough? An experiment with data saturation and variability', *Field Methods*, vol. 18, pp. 59–82.

Haas, P. and Haas, E. 2002, 'Pragmatic constructivism and the study of international institutions', *Millennium—Journal of International Studies*, vol. 31, pp. 573–601.

Hagan, J. and Levi, R. 2005, 'Crimes of war and the force of the law', *Social Forces*, vol. 83, no. 4, pp. 1499–534.

Handmaker, J. 2011, 'Facing up to the ICC's crisis of legitimacy: a critique of *The Reckoning* and its representation of international criminal justice', *Recht der Werkelijkheid*, vol. 32, no. 3, pp. 100–106.

Happold, M. 2006, 'Darfur, the Security Council, and the International Criminal Court', *International and Comparative Law Quarterly*, vol. 55, pp. 226–36.

Hardt, M. and Negri, A. 2000, *Empire*, Harvard University Press, Cambridge, MA.

Hari, J. 2006, 'Congo's tragedy: the war the world forgot', *The Independent*, May 2006, accessed 21 May 2011, www.independent.co.uk/news/world/africa/congos-tragedy-the-war-the-world-forgot-476929.html.

Hartung, W. D. and Moix, B. 2000, 'Deadly legacy: U.S. arms to Africa and the Congo War', *Arms Trade Resource Center, World Policy Institute*, accessed 22 May 2011, www.worldpolicy.org/projects/arms/reports/congo.htm.

Hasenclever, A., Mayer, P., and Rittberger, V. 1996, 'Interests, power, knowledge: the study of international regimes', *Mershon International Studies Review*, vol. 40, pp. 177–228.

Haveman, R. and Smeulers, A. 2008, 'Criminology in a state of denial—towards a criminology of international crimes: supranational criminology', in A. Smeulers and R. Haveman (eds), *Supranational Criminology: Towards a Criminology of International Crimes*, Intersentia, Oxford, pp. 3–26.

Hawkins, D. 2004, 'Explaining costly international institutions: persuasion and enforceable human rights norms', *International Studies Quarterly*, vol. 48, no. 4, pp. 779–804.

Head, M. 2002, '"Counter-terrorism" laws: a threat to political freedom, civil liberties and constitutional rights', *Melbourne University Law Review*, vol. 26, pp. 666–89.

Heaphy, B. 2007, *Late Modernity and Social Change: Reconstructing Social and Personal Life*, Routledge, Oxon.

Heinsch, R. 2010, 'The crime of aggression after Kampala: success or burden for the future?', *Goettingen Journal of International Law*, vol. 2, pp. 713–43.

Held, D. and Kaya, A. (eds) 2007, *Global Inequality: Patterns and Explanations*, Polity Press, Cambridge.

Henderson, G. 2013, 'War on terrorism needs a united front', *The Age*, 22 January, accessed 22 January 2014, www.theage.com.au/opinion/politics/war-on-terrorism-needs-a-united-front-20130121-2d2zg.html.

Henham, R. 2002, 'The internationalisation of sentencing: reality of myth?', *International Journal of the Sociology of Law*, vol. 30, pp. 265–83.

Henham, R. 2005, *Punishment and Process in International Crime Trials*, Ashgate, Aldershot.

Henham, R. 2007a, 'International sentencing in the context of collective violence', *International Criminal Law Review*, vol. 7, pp. 449-468

Henham, R. 2007b, 'Some reflection on the legitimacy of international trial justice', *International Journal of the Sociology of Law*, vol. 35, no. 2, pp. 75–95.

Henham, R. and Findlay, M. 2005, *Transforming International Criminal Justice: Retributive and Restorative Justice in the Trial Process*, Willan, Cullompton.

Hier, S. 2003, 'Risk and panic in late modernity: implications of the converging sites of social anxiety', *The British Journal of Sociology*, vol. 54, no. 1, pp. 3–20.

Hills, A. 2000, 'Research note: revisiting institutional resilience as a tool in crisis management', *Journal of Contingencies and Crisis Management*, vol. 8, no. 2, pp. 109–118.

Hochschild, A. 1999, *King Leopold's Ghost: A Story of Greed, Terror, and Heroism in Colonial Africa*, Houghton Mifflin Company, Boston.

Hochschild, A. 2009, 'The trial of Thomas Lubanga', *The Atlantic*, December, accessed 11 June 2011, www.theatlantic.com/magazine/archive/2009/12/the-trial-of-thomas-lubanga/7762.

Holligan, A. 2012, 'Invisible Children's Kony Campaign gets support of ICC prosecutor', *BBC News*, 8 March, accessed 5 April 2012, www.bbc.co.uk/news/world-africa-17303179.

HRW (Human Rights Watch) 2001, *Uganda in Eastern DRC: Fuelling Political and Ethnic Strife*, 1 March, accessed 12 June 2011, www.unhcr.org/refworld/docid/3ae6a87e8.html

HRW 2002, *The War Within the War: Sexual Violence Against Women and Girls in the Eastern Congo*, accessed 12 June 2011, www.hrw.org/reports/2002/drc/Congo0602.pdf.

HRW 2003a, *Briefing on Bilateral Immunity Agreements*, June 20, accessed 6 October 2010, www.hrw.org/sites/default/files/related_material/2003.06_US_Bilateral_Immunity_Agreements.pdf.

HRW 2003b, *Ituri: 'Covered in Blood': Ethnically Targeted Violence in Northeastern DR Congo*, accessed 12 June 2011, www.hrw.org/sites/default/files/reports/DRC0703.pdf.

HRW 2005, *The Curse of Gold: Democratic Republic of Congo*, accessed 10 June 2011, www.hrw.org/sites/default/files/reports/drc0505_0.pdf.

HRW 2006a, *UPC Crimes in Ituri (2002–2003): Summary*, accessed 11 June 2011, www.hrw.org/reports/2006/11/08/upc-crimes-ituri-2002-2003.

HRW 2006b, 'DR Congo: ICC arrest first step to justice', *Human Rights Watch News*, accessed 13 June 2011, www.hrw.org/news/2006/03/17/dr-congo-icc-arrest-first-step-justice.

HRW 2008, 'ICC: Congo ruling victory for justice', *Human Rights Watch News*, 18 November, accessed 15 June 2011, www.hrw.org/en/news/2008/11/18/icc-congo-ruling-victory-justice.

HRW 2009a, *Soldiers Who Rape, Commanders Who Condone: Sexual Violence and Military Reform in the Democratic Republic of Congo*, accessed 15 June 2011, www.hrw.org/sites/default/files/reports/drc0709web.pdf.

HRW 2009b, *Selling Justice Short: Why Accountability Matters for Peace*, accessed 19 January 2010, www.hrw.org/sites/default/files/reports/ij0709webwcover_3.pdf.

HRW 2010a, *Trial of Death: LRA Atrocities in Northeastern Congo*, accessed 15 June 2011, www.hrw.org/sites/default/files/reports/drc0310webwcover_0.pdf.

HRW 2010b, *Always on the Run: The Vicious Cycle of Displacement in Eastern Congo*, accessed 21 June 2011, www.hrw.org/sites/default/files/reports/drc0910webwcover.pdf.

HRW 2011a, *Course Correction: Recommendations to the ICC Prosecutor for a More Effective Approach to 'Situations Under Analysis'*, accessed 27 September 2011, www.hrw.org/sites/default/files/related_material/HRW%20Course%20Correction_0.pdf.

HRW 2011b, *International Justice: Unfinished Business Closing Gaps in the Selection of ICC Cases*, accessed 20 December 2011, www.hrw.org/sites/default/files/reports/icc0911webwcover.pdf.

HRW 2012a, *Unacknowledged Deaths: Civilian Causalities in NATO's Air Campaign in Libya*, accessed 15 November 2012, www.hrw.org/sites/default/files/reports/libya0512webwcover_0.pdf.

HRW 2012b, 'UN Security Council: address inconsistency in ICC referrals', *Human Rights Watch News*, 16 October, accessed 6 November 2012, www.hrw.org/news/2012/10/16/un-security-council-address-inconsistency-icc-referrals-0.

HRW 2012c, *Death of a Dictator: Bloody Vengeance in Sirte*, accessed 20 December 2012, www.hrw.org/reports/2012/10/16/death-dictator-0.

HRW 2012d, 'DR Congo: M23 rebels committing war crimes', *Human Rights Watch News*, 11 September, accessed 19 November 2012, www.hrw.org/news/2012/09/11/dr-congo-m23-rebels-committing-war-crimes.

HRW 2012e, 'DR Congo: US should urge Rwanda to end M23 support', *Human Rights Watch News*, 20 November, accessed 22 November 2012, www.hrw.org/news/2012/11/20/dr-congo-us-should-urge-rwanda-end-m23-support.

HRW 2012f, 'ICC: landmark verdict a warning to rights abusers', *Human Rights Watch News*, 14 March, accessed 14 March 2012, www.hrw.org/news/2012/03/14/icc-landmark-verdict-warning-rights-abusers.

HRW 2012g, 'ICC: Congolese rebel leader gets 14 years', *Human Rights Watch News*, 10 July, accessed 10 July 2012, www.hrw.org/news/2012/07/10/icc-congolese-rebel-leader-gets-14-years-0.

Hudson, B. 2003a, *Understanding Justice: An Introduction to Ideas, Perspectives and Controversies in Modern Penal Theory*, 2nd ed., Open University Press, Maidenhead, Berkshire.

Hudson, B. 2003b, *Justice in the Risk Society: Challenging and Re-affirming 'Justice' in Late Modernity*, Sage, London.

ICC (International Criminal Court) 2004, 'President of Uganda refers situation concerning the Lord's Resistance Army (LRA) to the ICC', Press release, ICC 20040129-43, 29 January.

ICC 2006a, 'Warrant of arrest', *Situation in the Democratic Republic of the Congo, The Prosecutor v Thomas Lubanga Dyilo,* ICC-01/04-01/06, 10 February, accessed 18 June 2010, www.icc-cpi.int/iccdocs/doc/doc191959.PDF.

ICC 2006b, 'Warrant of arrest', *Situation in the Democratic Republic of the Congo, The Prosecutor v Bosco Ntaganda*, ICC-01/04-02/06, 22 August, accessed 29 October 2011, www.icc-cpi.int/iccdocs/doc/doc305330.PDF.

ICC 2007, *Situation Democratic Republic of Congo, The Prosecutor v Thomas Lubanga Dyilo,* Transcript ICC-01/04-01/06-T-48-EN, 29 January, accessed 8 June 2011, www.icc-cpi.int/iccdocs/doc/doc232035.PDF.

ICC 2008a, 'Urgent warrant of arrest for Jean-Pierre Bemba Gombo', *Situation in the Central African Republic, The Prosecutor v Jean-Pierre Bemba Gombo,* ICC-01/05-01/08, 23 May, accessed 13 June 2011, www.icc-cpi.int/iccdocs/doc/doc504390.PDF.

ICC 2008b, 'The trial in the case of Thomas Lubanga Dyilo will commence on 23 June 2008', Press release, ICC-CPI-20080313-PR297.

ICC 2008c, 'Decision on the consequences of non-disclosure of exculpatory materials covered by Article 54(3)(e) agreements and the application to stay the prosecution of the accused, together with certain other issues raised at the Status Conference on 10 June 2008', *Situation in the Democratic Republic of the Congo, The Prosecutor v Thomas Lubanga Dyilo,* ICC-01/04-01/06, 13 June, accessed 4 August 2010, www1.umn.edu/humanrts/instree/ICC/Stay_the_Proceedings.html.

ICC 2008d, 'Decision on the release of Thomas Lubanga Dyilo', *Situation in the Democratic Republic of the Congo, The Prosecutor v Thomas Lubanga Dyilo,* ICC-01/04-01/06, 2 July, accessed 4 August 2010, www.icc-cpi.int/NR/rdonlyres/0108F157-B2F7-4A99-81E5-4AC34365022A/277765/ICC010401061418ENG.pdf.

ICC 2008e, 'Judgment on the appeal of the Prosecutor against the Decision of Trial Chamber I entitled "Decision on the Release of Thomas Lubanga Dyilo"', *Situation in the Democratic Republic of the Congo, The Prosecutor v Thomas Lubanga Dyilo*, ICC-01/04-01/06 OA 12, 21 October, accessed 7 August 2010, www.icc-cpi.int/iccdocs/doc/doc578365.pdf.

ICC 2008f, 'Decision on the confirmation of charges in the case of The Prosecutor v. Germain Katanga and Mathieu Ngudolo Chui', Press release, ICC-CPI-20080926-PR357.

ICC 2009a, 'Judgment on the appeals of Mr Lubanga Dyilo and the Prosecutor against the Decision of Trial Chamber 1 of 14 July 2009', *Situation in the Democratic Republic of the Congo, The Prosecutor v Thomas Lubanga Dyilo*, ICC-01/04-01/06 OA15, 8 December, accessed 13 July 2010, www.icc-cpi.int/iccdocs/doc/doc790147.pdf.

ICC 2009b, 'Office of the Prosecutor', *Fact Sheet*, ICC-PIDS- FS-03- 002/09_Eng, accessed 2 August 2010, www.icc-cpi.int/iccdocs/PIDS/femalecounsel/OTPEng.pdf.

ICC 2009c, *Situation in the Democratic Republic of the Congo, The Prosecutor v Thomas Lubanga Dyilo*, Transcript ICC-01/04-01/06-T-ENG ET WT, 26 January, accessed 10 June 2011, www.icc-cpi.int/iccdocs/doc/doc623638.pdf.

ICC 2009d, 'Prosecution's Application for Leave to Appeal the "Decision giving notice to the parties and participants that the legal characterisation of the facts may be subject to change in accordance with Regulation 55(2) of the Regulations of the Court"', *Situation in the Democratic Republic of the Congo, The Prosecutor v Thomas Lubanga Dyilo*, 12 August, accessed 2 August 2010, www.icc-cpi.int/iccdocs/doc/doc725647.pdf.

ICC 2010a, *The Review Conference of the Rome Statute*, accessed 21 August 2012, www.kampala.icc-cpi.info.

ICC 2010b, 'Redacted decision on intermediaries', *Situation in the Democratic Republic of the Congo, The Prosecutor v Thomas Lubanga Dyilo*, ICC-01/04- 01/06, 31 May, accessed 16 August 2012, www.worldcourts.com/icc/eng/decisions/2010.05.31_Prosecutor_v_Lubanga.pdf.

ICC 2010c, 'Redacted decision on the prosecution's urgent request for variation of the time-limit to disclose the identity of intermediary 143 or alternatively to stay proceedings pending further consultations with the VWU', *Situation in the Democratic Republic of the Congo, The Prosecutor v Thomas Lubanga Dyilo*, 8 July, accessed 16 August 2012, www.icc-cpi.int/iccdocs/doc/doc906146.pdf.

ICC 2010d, *Project to Define Policies Governing Relations Between the ICC and Intermediaries*, draft, accessed 21 June 2011, www.scribd.com/doc/33127686/Draft-ICC-Policy-on-Intermediaries- 2010-En-1.

ICC 2010e, 'Prosecution's urgent provision of further information following consultation with the VWU, to supplement the request for variation of the time-limit or stay', *Situation in the Democratic Republic of the Congo, The Prosecutor v Thomas Lubanga Dyilo*, ICC-01/04-01/06, 7 July, accessed 16 August 2012, www.icc-cpi.int/iccdocs/doc/doc905825.pdf.

ICC 2011a, 'ICC Pre-Trial Chamber III authorises the Prosecutor to launch an investigation in Côte d'Ivoire', Press release, ICC-CPI-201111003-PR730, 3 October.

ICC 2011b, 'Widespread or systematic killings in Cote d'Ivoire may trigger OTP investigation', ICC statement, 6 April, accessed 3 August 2012, www.icc-cpi.int/menus/icc/structure%20of%20the%20court/office%20of%20the%20prosecutor/comm%20and%20ref/c%C3%B4te%20divoire/otpstatement060411.

ICC 2011c, 'Initial appearance hearing', *Situation in the Democratic Republic of the Congo, The Prosecutor v Callixte Mbarushimana*, Transcript ICC-01/04-01/10-T-1, 28 February, accessed 1 March, www.icc-cpi.int/iccdocs/doc/doc1009117.pdf.

ICC 2011d, 'Decision on the confirmation of charges', *Situation in the Democratic Republic of the Congo, The Prosecutor v Callixte Mbarushimana*, Transcript ICC-01/04-01/10-465-Red, 16 December, accessed 25 January 2012, www.icc-cpi.int/iccdocs/doc/doc1286409.pdf.

ICC 2011e, 'Callixte Mbarushimana is released from the ICC custody', Press release, ICC-CPI-20111223-PR760, 23 December, accessed 10 August 2015, www.icc-cpi.int/en_menus/icc/press%20and%20media/press%20releases/press%20releases%20(2011)/Pages/pr760.aspx.

ICC 2011f, 'ICC Prosecutor to open an investigation in Libya', Press release, 2 March, accessed 3 March 2012, www.icc-cpi.int/en_menus/icc/situations%20and%20cases/situations/icc0111/press%20releases/Pages/statement%20020311.aspx.

ICC 2011g, 'Statement ICC Prosecutor press conference on Libya 16 May 2011', Press release, 16 May, accessed 17 May 2012, www.icc-cpi.int/en_menus/icc/structure%20of%20the%20court/office%20of%20the%20prosecutor/reports%20and%20statements/statement/Pages/statement%20icc%20prosecutor%20press%20conference%20on%20libya%2016%20may%202011.aspx.

ICC 2011h, 'Pre-Trial Chamber I issues three warrants of arrest for Muammar Gaddafi, Saif Al-Islam Gaddafi and Abdualla Al-Senussi', Press release, ICC-CPI-20110627-PR689, 27 June, accessed 28 June 2012, www.icc-cpi.int/en_menus/icc/situations%20and%20cases/situations/icc0111/press%20releases/Pages/pre_trial%20chamber%20i%20issues%20three%20warrants%20of%20arrest%20for%20muammar%20gaddafi_%20saif%20al.aspx.

ICC 2011i, 'Initial appearance hearing', *Situation in the Democratic Republic of the Congo the Prosecutor v Callixte Mbarushimana*, Transcript ICC-01/04-01/10- T-1-ENG ET WT 28-01-2011 1-13 NB PT, 28 January, accessed 10 August 2015, www.icc-cpi.int/en_menus/icc/situations%20and%20cases/situations/situation%20icc%200104/related%20cases/icc01040110/transcripts/pre%20trial%20chamber%20i/pages/1.aspx.

ICC 2012a, 'Judgment pursuant to Article 74 of the Statute', *Situation in the Democratic Republic of the Congo, The Prosecutor v Thomas Lubanga Dyilo*, ICC-01/04-01/06, 14 March, accessed 20 March 2012, www.icc-cpi.int/iccdocs/doc/doc1379838.pdf.

ICC 2012b, 'Decision on sentence pursuant to article 76 of the statute Situation in the Democratic Republic of Congo', *Situation in the Democratic Republic of the Congo, The Prosecutor v Thomas Lubanga Dyilo*, ICC-01/04-01/06, 10 July, accessed 23 July 2012, www.icc-cpi.int/iccdocs/doc/doc1438370.pdf.

ICC 2012c, 'Hearing pursuant to Article 76(2)', *Situation in the Democratic Republic of the Congo, The Prosecutor v Thomas Lubanga Dyilo*, ICC-01/04- 01/06, 13 June, accessed 16 June 2012, www.icc-cpi.int/iccdocs/doc/doc1436881.pdf.

ICC 2012d, 'ICC Trial Chamber II acquits Mathieu Ngudjolo Chui', Press release, 18 December, accessed 21 December 2012, www.icc-cpi.int/en_menus/icc/press%20and%20media/press%20releases/news%20and%20highlights/Pages/pr865.aspx.

ICC 2012e, 'Victims and witnesses', International Criminal Court website, accessed 21 December 2012, www.icc-cpi.int/en_menus/icc/structure%20of%20the%20court/victims/Pages/victims%20and%20witnesses.aspx.

ICC 2012f, 'Permanent Premises', International Criminal Court website, accessed 22 November 2012, www.icc-cpi.int/en_menus/icc/about%20the%20court/permanent%20premises/Pages/permanent%20premises.aspx.

ICC 2015, 'Situations and cases', International Criminal Court website, accessed 10 August 2015, www.icc-cpi.int/en_menus/icc/situations%20and%20cases/Pages/situations%20and%20cases.aspx.

ICC Assembly of States Parties (ICC ASP) 2006, *Strategic Plan of the International Criminal Court*, International Criminal Court, The Hague, accessed 20 July 2010, www.icc-cpi.int/NR/rdonlyres/D6B4058F-2C5D-415E-A85F-64A305C81DF0/0/ICCASP56_English.pdf.

ICC ASP 2014, *Report on Budget Performance of the International Criminal Court as at 30 June 2014*, International Criminal Court, The Hague, accessed 12 June 2015, www.icc-cpi.int/iccdocs/asp_docs/ASP13/ICC-ASP-13-8-ENG.pdf.

ICC Office of the Prosecutor (OTP) 2003a, *Paper on Some Policy Issues Before the Office of the Prosecutor*, accessed 12 December 2012, www.icc-cpi.int/NR/rdonlyres/1FA7C4C6-DE5F-42B7-8B25-60AA962ED8B6/143594/030905_Policy_Paper.pdf.

ICC OTP 2003b, 'The Prosecutor on the co-operation with Congo and other States regarding the situation in Ituri, DRC', Press release, ICC-OTP-20030926-37, 26 September.

ICC OTP 2004a, 'Prosecutor receives referral of the situation in the Democratic Republic of Congo', Press release, ICC-OTP-20040419-50.

ICC OTP 2004b, 'The Office of the Prosecutor opens its first investigation', Press release, ICC-OTP-20040623-59.

ICC OTP 2004c, 'Prosecutor of the International Criminal Court opens an investigation into Northern Uganda', Press release, ICC-OTP-20040729-65.

ICC OTP 2006a, *Statement by Luis Moreno-Ocampo*, Press conference in relation with the surrender to the Court of Mr Thomas Lubanga Dyilo, The Hague, 18 March, accessed 12 August 2011, www.icc-cpi.int/NR/rdonlyres/699D1671-4841-4AAC-BFF4-1F1BF3F9DFEC/143842/LMO_20060318_En1.pdf.

ICC OTP 2006b, *Report on Prosecutorial Strategy*, accessed 16 September 2010, www.icc-cpi.int/NR/rdonlyres/D673DD8C-D427-4547-BC69-2D363E07274B/143708/ProsecutorialStrategy20060914_English.pdf.

ICC OTP 2006c, 'Child soldier charges in the first International Criminal Court case' Press release, ICC-OTP-20060828-157.

ICC OTP 2008, *OTP statement in relation to events in Kenya*, The Hague, 5 February, accessed 4 November 2012, www.icc-cpi.int/NR/rdonlyres/1BB89202-16AE-4D95-ABBB-4597C416045D/0/ICCOTPST20080205ENG.pdf.

ICC OTP 2009a, 'ICC Prosecutor reaffirms that the situation in Kenya is monitored by his office', 11 February, accessed 4 November 2012, www.icc-cpi.int/NR/rdonlyres/06455318-783E-403B-8C9F-8E2056720C15/279793/KenyaOTPpubliccommunication200902 11.pdf.

ICC OTP 2009b, 'Opening Statement', *Situation in the Democratic Republic of the Congo, The Prosecutor v Thomas Lubanga Dyilo*, ICC-01/04-01/06, 26 January, accessed 23 November 2010, www.icc-cpi.int/NR/rdonlyres/82809488-9418-4AA9-BCF4-5FE3D609CBA7/279630/ICCOTPSTLMO20090126ENG2.pdf.

ICC OTP 2010, *Prosecutorial strategy 2009–2012*, accessed 16 September 2011, www.icc-cpi.int/NR/rdonlyres/66A8DCDC-3650-4514-AA62-D229D1128F65/281506/OTPProsecutorialStrategy20092013.pdf.

ICC OTP 2012a, 'ICC Prosecutor's address on the sentencing of Thomas Lubanga', Press release, ICC-OTP-20120613-PR809, 13 June, accessed 10 August 2015, www.icc-cpi.int/en_menus/icc/press%20and%20media/press%20releases/Pages/pr809.aspx.

ICC OTP 2012b, 'Statement: Office of the Prosecutor on Lubanga sentence', International Criminal Court website, 10 July, accessed 13 July 2012, www.icc-cpi.int/en_menus/icc/press%20and%20media/press%20releases/news%20and%20highlights/Pages/otp-statement100712.aspx.

ICC OTP 2013a, *Situation in Mali: Article 53(1) Report*, 16 January, accessed 18 January 2013, www.icc-cpi.int/en_menus/icc/situations%20and%20cases/situations/icc0112/Documents/SASMaliArticle53_1PublicReportENG16Jan2013.pdf.

ICC OTP 2013b, 'ICC prosecutor opens investigation into war crimes in Mali: "the legal requirements have been met. We will investigate"', Press release, 16 January, accessed 18 January 2013, www.icc-cpi.int/en_menus/icc/press%20and%20media/press%20releases/Pages/pr869.aspx.

Inder, B. 2011, *Reflection: Gender Issues and Child Soldiers the Case of Prosecutor v Thomas Lubanga Dyilo*, accessed 12 December 2012, www.iccnow.org/documents/Gender-Issues-and-Child-Soldiers.pdf.

International Bar Association (IBA) 2012, 'IBA welcomes conclusion of ICC's first trial; despite procedural hurdles, the Lubanga case is a symbolic achievement for the ICC', IBA website, 14 March, accessed 15 March 2012, www.ibanet.org/Article/Detail.aspx?ArticleUid=189e7801-4c18-41f9-978d-825dc6f6e5fc.

International Centre for Transitional Justice Situation 2008, *Brief: Thomas Lubanga and the ICC*, accessed 10 August 2015, www.ictj.org/sites/default/files/ICTJ-DRC-Lubanga-Trial-2009-English.pdf.

International Crisis Group 2012, 'Kenya: Impact of the ICC Proceedings', *Africa Briefing*, no. 84.

International Rescue Committee 2007, *Mortality in the Democratic Republic of Congo*, accessed 23 August 2012, www.rescue.org/special-reports/special-report-congo-y.

IRIN 2005, 'DRC: Another key Ituri leader arrested', IRIN website, 22 March, accessed 23 August 2012, www.irinnews.org/Report/53537/DRC-Another-key-Ituri-leader-arrested.

IRIN 2006, 'DRC: Kabila wins presidential election', IRIN website, 16 November, accessed 15 August 2012, www.irinnews.org/Report/61572/DRC-Kabila-wins-presidential-election.

IRIN 2011, 'Jury still out on the ICC trials in DRC', News From Africa website, 21 January, accessed 6 February 2012, www.newsfromafrica.org/newsfromafrica/articles/art_12244.html.

Jabre, L. and Moni, J. 2012, 'Is Africa on trial? The role of the ICC examined', *New African* online, 27 July, accessed 26 September 2012, www.newafricanmagazine.com/features/politics/is-africa-on-trial-the-role-of-the-icc-examined.

Jackson, R. H. 1946, 'The case against the Nazi war criminals: opening statement for the United States of America', Alfred A. Knopf, New York, accessed 12 June 2015 (online The Avalon Project, Yale Law School), http://avalon.law.yale.edu/imt/11-21-45.asp.

Jain, N. 2005, 'A separate law for peacekeepers: the clash between the Security Council and the International Criminal Court', *European Journal of International Law*, vol. 16, no. 2, pp. 239–54.

James, R. 2009, 'Sudanese President Omar Hassan al-Bashir', *Time* online, accessed 25 April 2010, www.time.com/time/world/article/0,8599,1883213,00.html.

Jianping, L. and Zhixiang, W. 2005, 'China's attitude towards the ICC', *International Criminal Justice*, vol. 3, no. 3, pp. 608–20.

Johnstone, D. 2011, 'Gaddafi's Libya as demon', *CounterPunch* online, 31 August, accessed 15 October 2012, www.counterpunch.org/2011/08/31/gaddafis-libya-as-demon.

Jones, T. and Newburn, T. 2002, 'The transformation of policing? Understanding current trends in policing systems', *British Journal of Criminology*, vol. 42, no. 1, pp. 129–46.

Kafka, F. 1956, *The Trial*, Secker and Warburg, London.

Kalivretakis, E. 2001, 'Are nuclear weapons above the law? A look at the International Criminal Court and the prohibited weapons category', *Emory International Law Review*, vol. 15, pp. 683–732.

Kambale, P. 2012, 'The ICC and Lubanga: missed opportunities', *African Futures Essays*, March 16, accessed 29 April 2012, http://forums.ssrc.org/african-futures/2012/03/16/african-futures-icc-missed-opportunities.

Kant, I. 1991, *Kant: Political Writings*, ed. H. Riess, Cambridge University Press, Cambridge.

Kearney, M. 2012, 'Why statehood now: a reflection on the ICC's impact on Palestine's engagement with international law', in C. Meloni and G. Tognonim (eds), *Is There a Court for Gaza? A Test Bench for International Justice*, T.M.C. Asser Press, The Hague, pp. 391–408.

Kegoro, G. 2011, 'AU hostility threatens international justice', *The Kenyan Section of the International Commission of Jurists, Commentary*, 31 May, accessed 15 October 2012, www.icj-kenya.org/index.php/media- centre/press-releases/commentary.

Keller, L. 2007, 'Seeking justice at the International Criminal Court: victims' reparations', *Thomas Jefferson Law Review*, vol. 29, no. 2, pp. 189–217.

Kennedy, D. 2002, 'The international human rights movement: part of the problem?', *Harvard Human Rights Journal*, vol. 15, pp. 101–26.

Kennedy, D. 2004, *The Dark Sides of Virtue*, Princeton University, New Jersey.

Keppler, E. 2011, 'Managing setbacks for the International Criminal Court in Africa', *Journal of African Law*, vol. 56, no. 1, pp. 1–14.

Kinley, D. 2009, *Civilising Globalisation: Human Rights and the Global Economy*, Cambridge University Press, Cambridge.

Kirsch, P. and Holmes, J. 1999, 'The Rome Conference on an International Criminal Court: the negotiating process', *The American Journal of International Law*, vol. 93, no. 1, pp. 2–12.

Kleingeld, P. (2006) 'Cosmopolitanism', *The International Encyclopaedia of Ethics, Stanford Encyclopedia of Philosophy*, accessed 10 August 2015, www.rug.nl/research/portal/files/14454370/plato.stanford.pdf, pp. 1–24.

Köhler, L. and Saner, H. (eds) 1993, *Correspondence: Hannah Arendt and Karl Jaspers 1926–1969*, Harcourt Brace, New York.

Koskenniemi, M. 2002, *The Gentle Civiliser of Nations: The Rise and Fall of International Law 1870–1960*, Cambridge University Press, Cambridge.

Koskenniemi, M. and Leino, P. 2002, 'Fragmentation of International Law? Postmodern anxieties', *Leiden Journal of International Law*, vol. 15, no. 3, pp. 553–79.

Kramer, R. and Michalowski, R. 2005, 'War, aggression and state crime: a criminological analysis of the invasion and occupation of Iraq', *British Journal of Criminology*, vol. 45, no. 4, pp. 446–69.

Kramer, R. and Michalowski, R. 2011, 'Empire and exceptionalism: the Bush Administration's criminal war against Iraq', in D. Rothe and C. Mullins (eds), *State Crime: Current Perspectives*, Rutgers, US, pp. 94–121.

Kramer, R., Michalowski, R., and Rothe, D. 2005, '"The supreme international crime": how the U.S. war in Iraq threatens the rule of law', *Social Justice*, vol. 32, no. 2, pp. 52–81.

Kramer, S. 2012, 'Deconstructing Lubanga, the ICC's first case: the trial and conviction of Thomas Lubanga Dyilo', American Non-Governmental Organizations Coalition for the International Criminal Court (AMICC) website, accessed 1 December 2012, www.amicc.org/docs/Deconstructing_Lubanga.pdf.

Kress, C. 2003, 'The procedural law of the International Criminal Court in outline: anatomy of a unique compromise', *Journal of International Criminal Justice*, vol. 1, pp. 603–17.

Kristafer, A. 2000, 'Why the United States should be wary of the International Criminal Court: concerns over sovereignty and constitutional guarantees', *Washburn Law Journal*, vol. 39, pp. 80–105.

Kvale, S. and Brinkmann, S. 2009, *Interviews: Learning the Craft of Qualitative Research Interviewing*, 2nd ed., Sage, Thousand Oaks.

Landry, B. 2012, 'The Church abuse scandal: prosecuting the Pope before the International Criminal Court', *Chicago Journal of International Law*, vol. 12, pp. 341–73.

Lash, S. 2000, 'Risk culture', in B. Adam, U. Beck, and J. Van Loon (eds), *The Risk Society and Beyond: Critical Issues for Social Theory*, Sage, London, pp. 47–62.

Laughland, J. 2008 'International justice is power without responsibility', *The Independent*, 29 July.

Liamputtong, P. and Ezzy, D. 2005, *Qualitative Research Methods*, Oxford University Press, South Melbourne.

Lint, W. de, and Virta, S. 2004, 'Security in ambiguity: towards a radical security politics', *Theoretical Criminology*, vol. 8, no. 4, pp. 465–89.

Lint, W. de, Marmo, M., and Chazal, N. 2013, *Crime and Justice in International Society*, Routledge, Oxon.

Lippens, R. 1998, 'Alternatives to what kind of suffering? Towards a border-crossing criminology', *Theoretical Criminology*, vol. 2, pp. 311–43.

Loader, I. 2000, 'Plural policing and democratic governance', *Social Legal Studies*, vol. 9, no. 3, pp. 323–45.

Lofland, J. and Lofland, L. 1995, *Analyzing Social Settings: A Guide to Qualitative Observation and Analysis*, Wadsworth, Belmont,

Lopes, C., Rodrigues, L., and Sichieri, R. 1996, 'The lack of selection bias in a snowball sampled case-control study on drug abuse', *International Journal of Epidemiology*, vol. 25, no. 6, pp. 1267–70.

Lyotard, J. 1984, *The Postmodern Condition: A Report on Knowledge*, University of Minnesota Press, Minneapolis.

McCarthy, C. 2009 'Reparations under the Rome Statute of the International Criminal Court and reparative justice theory', *Transitional Justice*, vol. 3, no. 2, pp. 250–71.

McConville, M. 2000, 'A global war on drugs: why the United States should support the prosecution of drug traffickers in the International Criminal Court', *American Criminal Law Review*, vol. 37, pp. 75–102.

McCulloch, J. 2003, '"Counter-terrorism", human security and globalisation—from welfare to warfare state?', *Current Issues in Criminal Justice*, vol. 14, no. 3, pp. 283–98.

McCulloch, J. and Pickering, S. 2009, 'Pre-Crime and counter-terrorism: imagining future crime in the "war on terror"', *British Journal of Criminology*, vol. 49, no. 5, pp. 628–45.

McGreal, C. 2008, 'War in Congo kills 45,000 people each month', *The Guardian* online, 23 January, accessed 12 June 2012, www.guardian.co.uk/world/2008/jan/23/congo.international.

Mackenzie, S. 2006, 'Systematic crimes of the powerful: criminal aspects of the global economy', *Social Justice*, vol. 33, no. 1, pp. 162–82.

Mackenzie, S. 2010, 'Counterfeiting as corporate externality: intellectual property crime and global insecurity', *Crime, Law and Social Change*, vol. 54, pp. 21–38.

McKeon, P. 1997, 'An international criminal court: balancing the principle of sovereignty against the demands for international justice', *St John's Journal of Legal Commentary*, vol. 12, pp. 535–64.

McVeigh, K. 2011, 'Pope accused of crimes against humanity by victims of sex abuse', *The Guardian* online, 13 September, accessed 20 December 2012, www.guardian.co.uk/world/2011/sep/13/pope-crimes-humanity-victims-abuse.

Mamdani, M. 2001, *When Victims Become Killers: Colonialism, Nativism, and the Genocide in Rwanda*, Princeton University Press, New Jersey.

Manning, S. 2013, 'Kenya's 2013 presidential election: recurring violence or a peaceful transition', *The Northeastern University Political Review*, accessed 10 August 2015, www.nupoliticalreview.com/?p=1989.

Mason, M. 2010, 'Sample size and saturation in PhD studies using qualitative interviews', *Forum: Qualitative Social Research*, vol. 11, no. 3, pp. 1–13.

Meek, D. 2012, 'YouTube and social movements: A phenomenological analysis of participation, events and cyberplace', *Antipode*, vol. 44, no. 4, pp. 1429–48.

Melandri, M. 2009, 'The relationship between state sovereignty and the enforcement of international criminal law under the Rome Statute (1998): a complex interplay', *International Criminal Law Review*, vol. 9, no. 3, pp. 531–45.

Mennecke, M. 2007, 'Punishing genocidaires: a deterrent effect or not?' *Human Rights Review*, vol. 8, no. 4, pp. 319–39.

Michalowski, R. 2009, 'Power, crime and criminology in the new imperial age', *Crime, Law & Social Change*, vol. 51, pp. 303–25.

Middle East Monitor 2012, 'Abbas does not rule out going to International Criminal Court', Memo Middle East Monitor website, 12 December, accessed 13 December 2012, www.middleeastmonitor.com/news/middle-east/4804-abbas-does-not-rule-out-going-to-international-criminal-court.

Minca, C. and Vaughan-Williams, N. 2012, 'Carl Schmitt and the concept of the border', *Geopolitics*, vol. 17, no. 4, pp. 756–72.

Moffett, L. 2009, 'Ending the cycle of violence in the Congo: is peace possible in the heart of darkness?', *Journal of Peace, Conflict and Development*, vol. 13, February 2009.

Moreno-Ocampo, L. 2009, 'The International Criminal Court: seeking global justice', *Case Western Reserve Journal of International Law*, vol. 40, pp. 215–26.

Moreno-Ocampo, L. 2010, 'Prosecutor of the ICC, statement', *Review Conference—General Debate*, Kampala, 31 May, accessed 19 November 2010, www.icc-cpi.int/iccdocs/asp_docs/RC2010/Statements/ICC-RC-statements-LuisMorenoOcampo-ENG.pdf.

Morse, J. 1995, 'Editorial: the significance of saturation', *Qualitative Health Research*, vol. 5, pp. 147–49.

Moy, A. 2006, 'The International Criminal Court's arrest warrants and Uganda's Lord's Resistance Army: renewing the debate over amnesty and complementarity', *Harvard Human Rights Journal*, vol. 19, pp. 267–74.

Moynier, G. 1872, 'Note sur la création d'une institution judiciaire internationale propre à prévenir et à réprimer les infractions à la Convention de Genève', *Bulletin International des Sociétés de Secours aux Militaires Blessés*, Comité international, no. 11, April.

Moyser, G. 1987, *Research Methods for Elite Studies*, Allen & Unwin, London.

Moyser, G. 2006, 'Elite interviewing', in V. Jupp (ed.), *The SAGE Dictionary of Social Research Methods*, Sage, London, pp. 85–86.

Mulcahy, L. 2007, 'Architects of justice: the politics of courtroom design', *Social Legal Studies*, vol. 16, no. 3, pp. 383–403.

Mullins, C., Kauzlarich, D., and Rothe, D. 2004, 'The International Criminal Court and the control of state crime: prospects and problems', *Critical Criminology*, vol. 12, pp. 285–308.

Mullins, C. and Rothe, D. 2008a, *Blood, Power and Bedlam: Violations of International Criminal Law in Post-Colonial Africa*, Peter Lang Publishing, New York.

Mullins, C. and Rothe, D. 2008b, 'Gold, diamonds and blood: international state-corporate crime in the Democratic Republic of the Congo', *Contemporary Justice Review: Issues in Criminal, Social, and Restorative Justice*, vol. 11, no. 2, pp. 81–99.

Mullins, C. and Rothe, D. 2010, 'The ability of the International Criminal Court to deter violations of international criminal law: a theoretical assessment', *International Criminal Law Review*, vol. 10, pp. 771–86.

Mundis, D. 2001, 'From "common law" towards "civil law": the evolution of the ICTY rules of procedure and evidence', *Leiden Journal of International Law*, vol. 14, no. 2, pp. 367–82.

Murumba, G. 2012, 'Indict Museveni for war crimes—says lawyer', *Uganda Correspondent*, 30 April, accessed 12 September 2012, www.ugandacorrespondent.com/articles/2012/04/indict-museveni-for-war-crimes-says-lawyer.

Mutua, M. 1996, 'The ideology of human rights', *Virginia Journal of International Law*, vol. 36, pp. 589–658.

Mutua, M. 2001, 'Savages, victims, and saviors: the metaphor of human rights', *Harvard International Law Journal*, vol. 42, no. 1, pp. 201–46.

Mutua, M. 2010, *The International Criminal Court in Africa: Challenges and Opportunities*, Noref Working Paper, Norwegian Peacebuilding Centre, September 2010, accessed 30 October 2011, www.peacebuilding.no/var/ezflow_site/storage/original/application/d5dc6 870a40b79bf7c1304f3befe0b55.pdf.

Mythen, G. and Walklate, S. 2006, 'Introduction: thinking beyond the risk society', in G. Mythen and S. Walklate (eds), *Beyond the Risk Society: Critical Reflections on Risk and Human Security*, Open University Press, Berkshire, pp. 1–7.

Natarajan, M. 2005, *Introduction to International Criminal Justice*, McGraw-Hill Custom Publishing, Boston.

Neimeyer, G. J. (ed.) 1993, *Constructivist Assessment: A Casebook*, Sage, Newbury Park.

Nesi, G. and Politi, M. (eds) 2004, *The International Criminal Court and the Crime of Aggression*, Ashgate, Aldershot.

Neuman, L. and Wiegand, B. 2000, *Criminal Justice Research Methods: Qualitative and Quantitative Approaches*, Allyn and Bacon, Boston.

Ngolet, F. 2011, *Crisis in the Congo: The Rise and Fall of Laurent Kabila*, Palgrave Macmillan, New York.

Nietzsche, F. 1997, *Beyond Good and Evil: Prelude to a Philosophy of the Future*, Dover Publications, Mineola, Dover Thrift Edition (republication of Helen Zimmern translation of original *The Complete Works of Friedrich Nietzsche*, 1919–1913).

No Peace Without Justice (NPWJ) 2012, 'NPWJ welcomes milestone of first ICC judgment in the Lubanga case and landmark decision for the protection of children', NPWJ website's International Criminal Justice Program, 14 March, accessed 15 March 2013, www.npwj.org/ICC/NPWJ-welcomes-milestone-first-ICC-judgment-Lubanga-case-and-landmark-decision-protection-childre.

Norton-Taylor, R. 2011, 'Libya: a new breed of military intervention', *The Guardian* online, 25 August, accessed 23 September 2012, www.guardian.co.uk/commentis free/2011/aug/25/libya-military-intervention.

Notar, S. 2006, 'Peacekeepers as perpetrators: sexual exploitation and abuse of women and children in the Democratic Republic of Congo', *American University Journal of Gender, Social Policy and the Law*, vol. 14, pp. 413–30.

Nouwen, S. and Werner, G. 2011, 'Doing justice to the political: the International Criminal Court in Uganda and Sudan: a rejoinder to Bas Schotel', *European Journal of International Law*, vol. 21, no. 4, pp. 941–65.

Nowlin, J. 2012, 'The ICC unfair in the eyes of the African Union', *International Institute for Justice and Development Blog*, 8 August, accessed 14 September 2012, http://iijd.org/blog/entry/the-international-criminal-court-unfair-in-the-eyes-of-the-african-union.

Nuremberg Human Rights Centre 2007, *From Nuremberg to The Hague: The Road to the International Criminal Court*, accessed 5 August 2009, www.iccnow.org/documents/FromNurembergtoHague_07july_eng.pdf.

Nussbaum, M. 1997, 'Capabilities and human rights', *Fordham Law Review*, vol. 66, pp. 273–300.

Nzongola-Ntalaja, G. 2002, *The Congo from Leopold to Kabila: A People's History*, Zed Books, London.

Nzongola-Ntalaja, G. 2004, *From Zaire to the Democratic Republic of the Congo*, 2nd ed., Nordiska Afrikainstituttet, Sweden.

Obokata, T. 2006, 'Trafficking of human beings as a crime against humanity: some implications for the international legal system', *International and Comparative Law Quarterly*, vol. 54, pp. 445–58.

O'Donohue, J. 2005, 'The 2005 budget of the International Criminal Court: contingency, insufficient funding in key areas and the recurring questions of the independence of the prosecutor', *Leiden Journal of International Law*, vol. 18, no. 3, pp. 591–603.

Odora, O. 2012, 'Kony2012 opens Pandora's box: Uganda government's own role in "dirty War" now exposed', *Black Star News*, 4 April, accessed 10 August 2015, www.blackstarnews.com/others/extras/kony2012-opens-pandoras-box-uganda-governments-own-role-in-dirty-war-now-exposed.html.

Oisel, M. 2000, *Mass Atrocity, Collective Memory and the Law*, Traction Publishers, New Jersey.

Oisel, M. 2009, *Making Sense of Mass Atrocity*, Cambridge University Press, Cambridge.

O'Malley, P. 1999, 'Volatile and contradictory punishment', *Theoretical Criminology*, vol. 3, no. 2, pp. 175–96.

O'Malley, P. 2006, 'Criminology and risk' in G. Mythen and S. Walklate (eds), *Beyond the Risk Society: Critical Reflections on Risk and Human Security*, Open University Press, Berkshire, pp. 43–59.

O'Malley, P. 2010, 'Resilient subjects: uncertainty, warfare and liberalism', *Economy and Society*, vol. 39, no. 4, pp. 488–509.

O'Malley, P. 2011, 'Security after risk: security strategies for governing extreme uncertainty', *Current Issues in Criminal Justice*, vol. 23, no. 1, pp. 5–15.

Open Society Justice Initiative 2012, 'Open Society Justice Initiative welcomes ICC Lubanga judgment', Press release, 14 March, accessed 14 March 2012, www.opensocietyfoundations.org/press-releases/open-society-justice-initiative-welcomes-icc-lubanga-judgment.

Orentlicher, D. 2003, 'Judging global justice: assessing the International Criminal Court', *Wisconsin International Law Journal*, vol. 21, pp. 495.

Pace, W. and Schense, J. 2004, '"International lawmaking of historic proportions": civil society and the International Criminal Court, in P. Gready (ed.), *Fighting for Human Rights*, Routledge, London, pp. 104–116.

Packer, H. L. 1964, 'Two models of the criminal process', *University of Pennsylvania Law Review*, vol. 113, no. 1, pp. 1–68.

Packer, H. L. 1968, *The Limits of the Criminal Sanction*, Stanford University Press, Stanford.

Papaioannou, A. M. 2006, 'The illegal exploitation of natural resources in the Democratic Republic of Congo: a case study in corporate complicity in human rights abuses', in *Symposium—Transnational Corporations and Human Rights* (Global law working paper 01/05), NYU School of Law, New York.

Paris, R. 2001, 'Human security: paradigm shift or hot air?', *International Security*, vol. 26, no. 2, pp. 87–102.

Patton, M. 2002, *Qualitative Research and Evaluation Methods*, 3rd ed., Sage, Thousand Oaks.

Pepinsky, H. and Quinney, R. 1991, *Criminology as Peacemaking*, Indiana University Press, Indiana.

Peskin, V. 2005, 'Beyond victor's justice? The challenge of prosecuting the winners at the International Criminal Tribunals for the Former Yugoslavia and Rwanda', *Journal of Human Rights*, vol. 4, no. 2, pp. 213–31.

du Plessis, M. and Louw, A. 2011, 'Justice and the Libyan crisis: the ICC's role under Security Council Resolution 1970, Institute for Security Studies briefing paper, accessed 21 December, www.issafrica.org/pgcontent.php?UID=30878.

Poynting, S. 2003, 'Bin Laden in the suburbs: attacks on Arab and Muslim Australians before and after 11 September', *Current Issues in Criminal Justice*, vol. 14, pp. 43–64.

PR Newswire 2008, 'At September 25 rally outside United Nations, Amnesty International to send message to UN Security Council on Darfur: reject efforts to block war crimes investigation against Sudanese President al-Bashir', PR Newswire (US), 24 September.

Proulx, V. J. 2004, 'Rethinking the jurisdiction of the International Criminal Court in the post-September 11th era: should acts of terrorism qualify as crimes against humanity?' *American University International Law Review*, vol. 19, pp. 1009–90.

Prunier, G. 2004, 'Rebel movements and proxy warfare: Uganda, Sudan and the Congo (1986-99), *African Affairs*, vol. 103, pp. 359–83.

Prunier, G. 2009, *Africa's World War: Congo, the Rwandan Genocide, and the Making of a Continental Catastrophe*, Oxford University Press, Oxford.

Pruthi, P. 2012, 'In a historic judgment, the International Criminal court convict Thomas Lubanga Dyilo of recruiting children into armed conflict', Unicef website, 14 March, accessed 15 March 2012, www.unicef.org/protection/57929_62002.html.

Quinney, R. 1970, *The Social Reality of Crime*, Little Brown, Boston.

Rabinow, P. (ed) 1991, *The Foucault Reader: An Introduction to Foucault's Thought*, Penguin, London.

Rakisits, C. 2008, 'Child soldiers in the East of the Democratic Republic of the Congo', *Refugee Survey Quarterly*, vol. 27, no. 4, pp. 108–22.

Ralph, J. 2007, *Defending the Society of States: Why America Opposes the International Criminal Court and its Vision of World Society*, Oxford University Press, Oxford.

Ratner, S. 1998, 'The schizophrenias of international criminal law', *Texas International Law Journal*, vol. 33, pp. 237–56.

Ratner, S., Abrams, J., and Bischoff, J. 2009, *Accountability for Human Rights Atrocities in International Law: Beyond the Nuremberg Legacy*, Oxford University Press, Oxford.

REDRESS 2008, 'ICC prosecutor leaves unfinished business in Ituri, DRC', Press statement, 13 February, accessed 23 May 2012, www.redress.org/downloads/news/08-

02-20%20ICC%20DRC%20-%20REDRESS%20Press%20Statement%20-%20Final%20-CORRECTED.pdf.

REDRESS 2009, 'War victims in DRC shocked at ICC decision to release Lubanga', Press release, 3 July, accessed 23 May 2012, www.coalitionfortheicc.org/documents/REDRESS_3_July_Release.pdf.

REDRESS 2010, 'Victims express relief at decision to resume first war crimes trial at the International Criminal Court', Press release, 8 October, accessed 23 May 2012, www.redress.org/Lubanga%20case%20resumed%20-%20REDRESS%20stmt%208%20Oct%202010.pdf.

REDRESS 2012, 'Lubanga's verdict only first step towards justice for victims', Press release, 14 March, accessed 16 March 2012, www.redress.org/downloads/REDRESS Lubangastatement-140312.pdf.

Reinold, T. 2012, 'Constitutionalization? Whose constitutionaliszation? Africa's ambivalent engagement with the International Criminal Court', *International Journal of Constitutional Law*, vol. 10, no. 4, pp. 1076–105.

Renton, D., Seddon, D., and Zeilig, L. 2007, *The Congo: Plunder and Resistance*, Zed Books, London.

Reynolds, P. 2008 'Bashir move bold but problematic', *BBC News* online, accessed 14 July 2011, http://news.bbc.co.uk/go/pr/fr/-/2/hi/africa/7500437.stm.

Reyntjens, F. 1999, 'Briefing: the second Congo war: more than a remake', *African Affairs*, vol. 98, no. 391, pp. 241–50.

Reyntjens, F. 2001, 'Briefing: the Democratic Republic of Congo, from Kabila to Kabila', *African Affairs*, vol. 100, pp. 311–17.

Risse, T. 1999, 'International norms and domestic change: arguing and communicative behaviour in the human rights area', *Politics Society*, vol. 27, pp. 529–59.

Roach, K. 1999, 'Four models of the criminal process', *Journal of Criminal Law and Criminology*, vol. 89, no. 2, pp. 671–716.

Roberts, P. and McMillan, N. 2003, 'For criminology in international criminal justice', *Journal of International Criminal Justice*, vol. 1, pp. 315–38.

Robertson, G. 2006, *Crimes Against Humanity: The Struggle for Global Justice*, Penguin, London.

Robertson, G. 2010, 'Put the pope in the dock', *The Guardian* online, 2 April, accessed 12 November 2012, www.guardian.co.uk/commentisfree/libertycentral/2010/apr/02/pope-legal-immunity-international-law.

Robinson, D. 1999, 'Defining "crimes against humanity" at the Rome Conference', *The American Journal of International Law*, vol. 93, no. 1, pp. 43–57.

Robinson, D. 2008, 'The identity crisis of international criminal law', *Leiden Journal of International Law*, vol. 21, pp. 925–63.

Roche, D. 2005, 'Truth commission amnesties and the International Criminal Court', *British Journal of Criminology*, vol. 45, pp. 565–81.

Roche, M. 2000, *Mega-events and Modernity*, Routledge, London.

Rome Statute of the International Criminal Court (1998), accessed 23 January 2013, www.icc-cpi.int/nr/rdonlyres/ea9aeff7-5752-4f84-be94-0a655eb30e16/0/rome_statute_english.pdf.

Rose, N. 1999, *Powers of Freedom: Reframing Political Thought*, Cambridge University Press, Cambridge.

Rosenbloom, J. 1998, 'Social ideology as seen through courtroom and court-house architecture', *Columbia Journal of Law and the Arts*, vol. 22, pp. 463–523.

Ross, J. (ed.) 2000, *Varieties of State Crime and its Control*, Willow Tree Press, Monsey, NY.

Roth, K. 2012, 'Time to abandon the autocrats and embrace rights: the international response to the Arab Spring', *Human Rights Watch World Report*, accessed 10 August 2015, www.hrw.org/sites/default/files/reports/wr2012.pdf.

Rothe, D. 2010, 'Shedding the blanket of immunity: a commentary on the global principle of ending impunity, realpolitik and legal precedent', *Crime, Law and Social Change*, vol. 53, pp. 397–412.

Rothe, D., Kramer, R., and Mullins, C. 2009, 'Torture, impunity, and open legal spaces: Abu Ghraib and international control', *Contemporary Justice Review: Issues in Criminal, Social, and Restorative Justice*, vol. 12, no. 1, pp. 27–43.

Rothe, D. and Mullins, C. 2006a, *Symbolic Gestures and the Generation of Global Social Control: The International Criminal Court*, Lexington Books. Lanham.

Rothe, D. and Mullins, C. 2006b, 'The International Criminal Court and United States opposition: a structural contradictions model', *Crime, Law and Social Change*, vol. 45, pp. 201–26.

Rothe, D. and Mullins, C. 2010, 'Beyond the juristic orientation of international criminal justice: the relevance of criminological insight to international criminal law and its control, a commentary', *International Criminal Law Review*, vol. 10, pp. 97–110.

Rothe, D., Muzzatti, S., and Mullins, C. 2006, 'Crime on the high seas: crimes of globalization and the sinking of the Senegalese ferry Le Joola', *Critical Criminology*, vol. 14, no. 2, pp. 159–80.

Rothe, D. and Shoultz, I. 2013 'International criminal justice: law, courts and punishment as deterrent mechanisms', in W. de Lint, M. Marmo, and N. Chazal, (eds), *Crime and Justice in International Society*, Routledge, Oxon.

Rowe, P., McGoldrick, D., and Donnelly, E. 2004, *The Permanent International Criminal Court: Legal and Policy Issues*, Hart Publishers, Oxford.

RT 2011, 'Gaddafi son wants to surrender to The Hague—NTC', *RT*, 26 October, accessed 25 September 2012, http://rt.com/news/gaddafi-son-hague-ntc-815.

Rudolph, C. 2001, 'Constructing an atrocities regime: the politics of war crimes tribunals', *International Organization*, vol. 55, no. 3, pp. 655–91.

Ruggie, J. 1998, *Constructing the World Polity: Essays on International Institutionalization*, Routledge, London.

Ryngaert, C. 2009, 'The International Criminal Court and universal jurisdiction: a fraught relationship?', *New Criminal Law Review*, vol. 12, pp. 498–512.

Sadat, L. N. 2002, *The International Criminal Court and the Transformation of International Law: Justice for the New Millennium*, Transnational, New York.

Sadat, L N. and Carden, S. R. 2000, 'The new International Criminal Court: an uneasy revolution', *Georgetown Law Journal*, vol. 88, pp. 381–474.

Salecl, R. 2004, *On Anxiety*, Routledge, New York.

Salecl, R. 2010, *Choice*, Profile, London.

Samset, I. 2002, 'Conflict of interests or interests in conflict? Diamonds and war in the DRC', *Review of African Political Economy*, vol. 29, no. 93–94, pp. 463–80.

Sander, B. 2012, 'Case Summary: Application 004/2011 African Commission on Human and Peoples' Rights v. The Great Socialist People's Libyan Arab Jamahiriya', ARC Project Blog, accessed 10 August 2015, http://arcproject.co.uk/wp-content/uploads/2013/04/CSW-004-2011.pdf.

Sands, P. 2013, 'Referring Syria to the International Criminal Court is a justified gamble', *The Guardian* online, 16 January, accessed 17 January 2013, www.guardian.co.uk/commentisfree/2013/jan/16/syria-international-criminal-court-justified-gamble.

Sarre, R. 2012 'The Criminal Process', in M. Marmo, W. de Lint, and D. Palmer (eds) *Crime and Justice: A Guide to Criminology*, 4th ed., Law Book Co, Pyrmount, pp. 345–454.

Sawyer, I. 2013, 'Ending the cycle of abuse in Congo', *Human Rights Watch*, accessed 10 January 2014, www.hrw.org/news/2013/01/02/ending-cycle-abuse-congo.

Scarf, M. 1994, 'Getting serious about an international criminal court', *Pace International Law Review*, vol. 6, no. 1, pp. 103–19.

Schabas, W. 2004, 'United States hostility to the International Criminal Court: it's all about the Security Council', *European Journal of International Law*, vol. 15, no. 4, pp. 701–20.

Schabas, W. 2006, 'International justice for international crimes: an idea whose time has come', *European Review*, vol. 14, no. 4, pp. 421–39.

Schabas, W. 2007a, '"Complementarity in practice": some uncomplimentary thoughts', *Criminal Law Forum*, vol. 19, pp. 5–33.

Schabas, W. 2007b, *An Introduction to the International Criminal Court*, Cambridge University Press, Cambridge.

Schabas. W. 2008, 'Prosecutorial discretion v. judicial activism at the International Criminal Court', *Journal of International Criminal Justice*, vol. 6, pp. 731–61.

Schaefer, B. and Groves, S. 2011, 'The motivation for the referral of Libya to the ICC: political pressure or justice?', *The Heritage Foundation Web Memo*, 4 March, No. 3180, accessed 29 November 2012, www.heritage.org/research/reports/2011/03/the-motivation-for-the-referral-of-libya-to-the-icc-political-pressure-or-justice.

Scheffer, D. 2010, 'Whose lawfare is it, anyway?', *Case Western Reserve Journal of International Law*, vol. 43, pp. 215–28.

Schiff, B. 2008, *Building the International Criminal Court,* Cambridge University Press, Cambridge.

Schmitt, C. 1996, *The Concept of the Political*, translated by George Schwab, The University of Chicago Press, Chicago.

Shklar, J. 1986, *Legalism: Law, Morals and Political Trials*, Harvard University Press, Cambridge.

Silverman, D. 2010, *Doing Qualitative Research*, 3rd ed., Sage, London.

Simon, J. 1995, 'They died with their boots on: the boot camp and the limits of modern penality', *Social Justice*, vol. 22, no. 1, pp. 25–49.

Simpson, G. 2004a, *Great Powers and Outlaw States: Unequal Sovereigns in the International Legal Order*, Cambridge University Press, Cambridge.

Simpson, G. 2004b, 'Politics, sovereignty, remembrance', in D. McGoldrick, P. Rowe, and E. Donnelly (eds), *The Permanent International Criminal Court: Legal and Policy Issues*, Hart Publishing, Portland, Oregon, pp. 47–60.

Simpson, G. 2007, *Law, War and Crime*, Polity Press, Cambridge.

Simpson, G. 2008, 'One among many: the ICC as a tool of justice during transition', in N. Waddell and P. Clark (eds), *Courting Conflict? Justice, Peace and the ICC in Africa*, The Royal African Society, pp. 73–79.

Simpson, G. 2011, 'Gaddafi warrants expose the limits of global justice', *The Sydney Morning Herald* online, 29 June, accessed 13 June 2012, www.smh.com.au/opinion/politics/gaddafi-warrants-expose-the-limits-of-global-justice-20110629-1gpt1.html.

Smart, C. 1984, *The Ties That Bind: Law, Marriage and the Reproduction of Patriarchal Relations*, Routledge & Kegan Paul, London.

Smeulers, A. and Haveman, R. (eds) 2008, *Supranational Criminology: Towards a Criminology of International Crimes*, Intersentia, Oxford.

Smeulers, A. and van Niekerk, S. 2009, 'Abu Ghraib and the war on terror—a case against Donald Rumsfeld', *Crime, Law & Social Change*, vol. 51, no. 3–4, pp. 327–49.

Smith, D. 2012a, 'Hunting the terminator: Congo continues search for Bosco Ntaganda', *The Guardian* online, 28 November, accessed 29 November 2012, www.guardian.co.uk/world/2012/nov/28/terminator-search-bosco-ntaganda-congo.

Smith, D. 2012b, 'Congo child army leader Thomas Lubanga found guilty of war crimes', *The Guardian* online, 14 March, accessed 16 March 2012, www.guardian.co.uk/law/2012/mar/14/congo-warlord-thomas-lubanga-icc.

Smith, A. 2012c, 'The Emergence of International Justice as Coercive Diplomacy: Challenges and Prospects', Harvard Human Rights Program Working Paper Series, May 2012, accessed 28 July 2015, www.brandeis.edu/ethics/pdfs/internationaljustice/biij/BIIJ2013/smith.pdf.

Song, S. H. 2012, *10th Anniversary of the Court,* Speech of ICC President Judge Sang-Hyun Song, 14 November, accessed 1 December 2012, www.icc-cpi.int/NR/rdonlyres/B8042F7D-AF32-4B1B-BEA292D57DE5603/0/121114RidderzaalSpeech.pdf.

Sriram, C. L. and Ross, A. 2007, 'Geographies of crime and justice: contemporary transitional justice and the creation of 'zones of impunity', *The International Journal of Transitional Justice*, vol. 1, pp. 45–65.

Ssenyonjo, M. 2005, 'Accountability of non-state actors in Uganda for war crimes and human rights violations: between amnesty and the International Criminal Court', *Journal of Conflict and Security Law*, vol. 10, no. 3, pp. 405–34.

Stahn, C. 2007, 'Complementarity: a tale of two notions', *Criminal Law Forum*, vol. 19, pp. 87–113.

Stahn, C. 2012, 'Libya, the International Criminal Court and complementarity: a test for "shared responsibility"', *Journal of International Criminal Justice*, vol. 10, pp. 325–49.

Stahn, C., El Zeidy, M., and Olásolo, H. 2005, 'The International Criminal Court's ad hoc jurisdiction revisited', *The American Journal of International Law*, vol. 99, no. 2, pp. 421–31.

Stake, R. 1998, 'Case studies', in N. Denzin (ed.), *Strategies of Qualitative Research*, Sage, Thousand Oaks, pp. 86–109.

Stammers, N. 1999, 'Social Movements and the social construction of human rights', *Human Rights Quarterly*, vol. 21, no. 4, pp. 980–1008.

Stearns, S. 2011, 'African Union says ICC prosecutions are discriminatory', Voice of America website, 5 July, accessed 1 May 2012, www.voanews.com/english/news/africa/-African-Union-Says-ICC-Prosecutions-Are-Discriminatory-125012734.html.

Steele, S. 2005, 'Victim-witnesses in the International Criminal Court: justice for trauma, or the trauma of justice?', *Australian International Law Journal*, vol. 12, pp. 99–108.

Steidle, B. 2007, *The Devil Came on Horseback: Bearing Witness to the Genocide in Darfur*, Public Affairs, New York.

Stein, M. 2006, 'The Security Council, the International Criminal Court and the crime of aggression: how exclusive is the Security Council's power to determine aggression?', *Indiana International and Comparative Law Review*, vol. 16, pp. 1–36.

Stenning, P. 2013, 'The politics of prosecution: the role of the prosecutor of the International Criminal Court', in W. de Lint, M. Marmo, and N. Chazal (eds), *Crime and Justice in International Society*, Routledge, Oxon.

Stenson, K. 2001, 'The new politics of crime control', in K. Stenson and R. Sullivan (eds), *Crime, Risk and Justice: The Politics of Crime Control in Liberal Democracies*, Willan Publishing, Devon, pp. 15–28.

Stover, E. and Weinstein, H. M. 2004, *My Neighbour, My Enemy: Justice and Community in the Aftermath of Mass Atrocity*, Cambridge University Press, Cambridge.

Strapatsas, N. 2003, 'Universal jurisdiction and the International Criminal Court', *Manitoba Law Journal*, vol. 29, no. 1, pp. 1–32.

Strauss, A. and Corbin, J. 1998, *Basics Of Qualitative Research: Techniques and Procedures for Developing Grounded Theory*, 2nd ed., Sage, Thousand Oaks.

Stronach, I. 2006, 'Enlightenment and the "heart of darkness": (neo)imperialism in the Congo, and elsewhere', *International Journal of Qualitative Studies in Education*, vol. 19, no. 6, pp. 757–68.

Sudan Tribune 2012, 'Sudan is backing Joseph Kony's LRA, says Uganda', *Sudan Tribune*, 30 April, accessed 25 June 2012, www.sudantribune.com/spip.php?article42451.

Sullivan, R. 2001, 'The schizophrenic state: neoliberal criminal justice', in K. Stenson and R. Sullivan (eds), *Crime, Risk and Justice: The Politics of Crime Control in Liberal Democracies*, Willan Publishing, Devon, pp. 29–48.

Swart, A. H. J., Zahar, A., and Sluiter, G. 2011, *The Legacy of the International Criminal Tribunal for the Former Yugoslavia*, Oxford University Press, Oxford.

Takemura, H. 2007, 'Big fish and small fish debate—an examination of the prosecutorial discretion', *International Criminal Law Review*, vol. 7, pp. 667–85.

Takemura, H. 2012, 'Reconsidering the meaning and actuality of the legitimacy of the International Criminal Court', *Amsterdam Law Forum*, vol. 4, pp. 3–15.

Tallgren, I. 1998, 'Completing the "international criminal order": the rhetoric of international repression and the notion of complementarity in the draft statute for an international criminal court', *Nordic Journal of International Law*, vol. 67, pp. 107–37.

Tallgren, I. 1999, 'We did it? The vertigo of law and everyday life at the diplomatic conference on the establishment of an international criminal court', *Leiden Journal of International Law*, vol. 12, pp. 683–707.

Tallgren, I. 2002, 'The sensibility and sense of international criminal law', *European Journal of International Law*, vol. 13, no. 3, pp. 561–95.

Teitel, R. 2002, 'Humanity's law: rule of law for the new global politics', *Cornell International Law Journal*, vol. 35, pp. 355–87.

Terdiman, R. 1987, 'The force of law: toward a sociology of the juridical field: translator's introduction', *Hastings Law Journal*, vol. 38, pp. 805–13.

Thijssen, H. 2012, 'The African Union and the International Criminal Court', *Peace Palace Library International Law Blog*, 22 June, accessed 15 September 2012, www.peacepalacelibrary.nl/2012/06/the-african-union-and-the-international-criminal-court.

Tochilovsky, V. 2003, 'Globalizing criminal justice: challenges for the International Criminal Court', *Global Governance*, vol. 9, pp. 291–99.

Totani, Y. 2008, *The Tokyo War Crimes Trials: The Pursuit of Justice in the Wake of World War II*, Harvard University Press, Cambridge.

Trust Fund for Victims 2012, Trust Fund for Victims website, accessed 21 December, www.trustfundforvictims.org.

Turner, T. 2007, *Congo Wars: Conflict, Myth And Reality*, Zed Books, London.

Tuzmukhamedov, B. 2005, 'The ICC and Russian constitutional problems', *Journal of International Criminal Justice*, vol. 3, no. 3, pp. 621–26.

Trahan, J. 2011, 'The Rome Statute's amendment on the crime of aggression: negotiations at the Kampala Review Conference', *International Criminal Law Review*, vol. 11, pp. 49–104.

TRIAL 2012, 'The victim's role before the International Criminal Court', TRIAL website, 6 September, accessed 9 October 2012, www.trial-ch.org/index.php?id=997&L=5.

UN (United Nations) 1998, *United Nations Diplomatic Conference of Plenipotentiaries on the Establishment of an International Criminal Court,* Official records, vol. 2, accessed 14 January 2010, http://legal.un.org/diplomaticconferences/icc-1998/vol/english/vol_II_e.pdf.

UN 1999, Rome Statute of the International Criminal Court overview, accessed 10 August 2015, http://legal.un.org/icc/general/overview.htm.

UN 2010, 'An age of accountability', Secretary-General's address to the Review Conference on the International Criminal Court, Kampala, Uganda, 31 May, accessed 5 April 2011, www.un.org/sg/statements/?nid=4585.

UN 2015, Member States of the United Nations page, United Nations website, accessed 12 June 2015, www.un.org/en/members/index.shtml.

UN General Assembly 1994, *Report of the International Law Commission on the Work of its Forty-Sixth Session*, 1 September, accessed 19 October 2010, www.iccnow.org/documents/ILCDraftRomeStatute94.pdf.

UN High Commissioner for Human Rights 1998, Opening remarks of the high commissioner for human rights at NGO meeting on the establishment of an international criminal court, 15 June, accessed 10 August 2015, www.unhchr.ch/huricane/huricane.nsf/f161d566b36240f8802566100031b4c0/ea0266ea290bbcb8802567c1003257c6?OpenDocument.

UNHRC (Human Rights Council) 2010, *Democratic Republic of the Congo, 1993–2003*, Report of the mapping exercise, accessed 26 July 2011, http://repositories.lib.utexas.edu/bitstream/handle/2152/11732/DRC10_06_xx_Report_Draft_Democratic_Republic_of_the_Congo_1993-2003.pdf?sequence=2.

UNHRC 2011, *Report of the International Commission of Inquiry to Investigate All Alleged Violations of International Human Rights Law in the Libyan Arab Jamahiriya*, A/HRC/17/441, accessed 8 August 2012, www2.ohchr.org/english/bodies/hrcouncil/docs/17session/A.HRC.17.44_AUV.pdf.

UNHRC 2012, *Report of the United Nations High Commissioner for Human Rights on the Situation of Human Rights and the Activities of her Office in the Democratic Republic of Congo*, accessed 3 February 2012, www2.ohchr.org/english/bodies/hrcouncil/docs/19session/A-HRC-19-48_en.pdf.

UN Information Service 2002, '"Exciting but challenging journey" lies ahead, says Secretary-General on fourth anniversary of adoption of ICC statute', Press release, SG/SM/8309 L/3011, 18 July, accessed 26 September 2009, www.unis.unvienna.org/unis/pressrels/2002/sgsm8309.html.

UN News Service 2012a, 'Ban discusses Libya with Obama; urges punishment of those responsible for violence', UN News Centre website, accessed 10 August 2015, www.un.org/apps/news/story.asp?NewsID=37647&Cr=libya&Cr1.

UN News Service 2012b, 'In landmark ruling, ICC finds Congolese warlord guilty of recruiting child soldiers', UN News Centre website, 14 March, accessed 15 March 2012, www.un.org/apps/news/story.asp?NewsID=41537&Cr=ICC&Cr1.

UN News Service 2013, 'General Assembly grants Palestine non-member observer State status at UN', UN News Centre website, 29 November, accessed 1 December 2013, www.un.org/apps/news/story.asp?NewsID=43640.

UNSC (United Nations Security Council) 1999a, *Lusaka Ceasefire Agreement*, accessed 28 August 2011, http://peacemaker.un.org/sites/peacemaker.un.org/files/CD_990710_LusakaAgreement.pdf.

UNSC 1999b, *Resolution 1273*, Adopted by the Security Council at its 4060th meeting, S/RES/1273, 5 November, accessed 18 August 2009, www.unhcr.org/refworld/docid/3b00f1aa14.html.

UNSC 2003, Report on the Panel of Experts on the Illegal Exploitation of Natural Resources and Other Forms of Wealth of the Democratic Republic of Congo, accessed 10 August 2015, http://daccess-dds-ny.un.org/doc/UNDOC/GEN/N03/567/36/IMG/N0356736.pdf?OpenElement.

UNSC 2011, *Resolution 1970*, Adopted by the Security Council at its 6491st meeting, 26 February, accessed 26 July 2012, www.icc-cpi.int/NR/rdonlyres/081A9013-B03D-4859-9D61-5D0B0F2F5EFA/0/1970Eng.pdf.

UNSC 2014, *Final report of the group of experts on the Democratic Republic of the Congo*, accessed 10 August 2015, www.securitycouncilreport.org/atf/cf/%7B65BFCF9B-6D27-4E9C-8CD3-CF6E4FF96FF9%7D/s_2014_42.pdf.

Urry, J. 2003, *Global Complexity*, Polity Press, Oxford.

US Department of State 2003, *International Criminal Court, Article 98, Agreement between the United States of America and Uganda*, Treaties and other international acts series 03-1023, accessed 5 May 2012, www.state.gov/documents/organization/152670.pdf.

Vaus, D. de, 2001, *Research Designs in Social Research*, Sage, London.

Vinck, P. et al. 2008, *Living with fear: a population-based survey on attitudes about peace, justice and social reconstruction in Eastern Democratic Republic of Congo*, accessed 5 February 2010, http://ictj.org/sites/default/files/ICTJ-DRC-Attitudes-Justice-2008-English.pdf.

Virilio, P. 2006, *Speed and Politics*, Semiotext(e), Los Angeles.

Voice of America 2011, 'World powers agree to military intervention in Libya', *Voice of America* website, 18 March, accessed 19 December 2012, www.voanews.com/content/world-powers-agree-to-military-intervention-in-libya-118298724/157707.html.

Van der Vyver, J. 2011, 'Prosecuting the President of Sudan: a dispute between the African Union and the International Criminal Court', *African Human Rights Law Journal*, vol. 11, pp. 683–98.

Walt, V. 2012, 'Why Libya—and not The Hague—will try Gaddafi's son', *Time World*, 10 October, accessed 15 October 2012, http://world.time.com/2012/10/10/why-libya-and-not-the-hague-will-try-gaddafis-son.

Weber, L. 2005, 'The detention of asylum seekers as a crime of obedience', *Critical Criminology*, vol. 13, no. 1, pp. 89–109.

Weber, L. and Bowling, B. 2008, 'Valiant beggars and global vagabonds: select, eject, immobilise', *Theoretical Criminology*, vol. 12, no. 3, pp. 355–75.

Weber, L. and Pickering, S. J. 2011, *Globalization and Borders: Death at the Global Frontier*, Palgrave Macmillan, Hampshire.

Weissman, S. 2010, 'New evidence shows U.S. role in Congo's decision to send Patrice Lumumba to his death', All Africa website, 1 August, accessed 2 February 2012, http://allafrica.com/stories/201008010004.html.

Wenaweser, C. 2010, 'Reaching the Kampala compromise on aggression: the chair's perspective', *Leiden Journal of International Law*, vol. 23, no. 4, pp. 883–87.

Wendt, A. 1992, 'Anarchy is what states make of it: the social construction of power politics', *International Organization*, vol. 46, no. 2, pp. 391–425.

Wendt, A. 1995, 'Constructing international politics', *International Security*, vol. 20, no. 1, Summer, pp. 71–81.

Women's Initiatives for Gender Justice 2007, *Statement by the Women's Initiatives for Gender Justice on the Arrest of Germain Katanga,* accessed 10 August 2015, www.iccwomen.org/documents/ArrestKatanga_Statement_2007.pdf.

Women's Initiatives for Gender Justice 2012, 'First sentencing judgement by the ICC: *The Prosecutor v Thomas Lubanga Dyilo*', Press statement, 11 July, accessed 12 July 2012, www.coalitionfortheicc.org/documents/Press-Statement-on-Lubanga-Sentencing.pdf.

Wonders, N. 2006, 'Global flows, semi-permeable borders and new channels of inequality', in S. Pickering and L. Weber (eds), *Borders, Mobility and Technologies of Control,* Springer, The Netherlands, pp. 63–86.

Wonders, N. 2007, 'Globalisation, border reconstruction projects, and transnational crime', *Social Justice*, vol. 34, no. 2, pp. 33–46.

Wong, M. 2009, *In the Footsteps of Mr. Kurtz: Living on the Brink of Disaster in Mobutu's Congo*, Harper Collins, New York.

Yair, G. 2007, 'Ambivalence', in G. Ritzer (ed.), *Blackwell Encyclopaedia of Sociology,* Blackwell Reference Online, accessed 28 November 2011, www.sociologyencyclopedia.com/subscriber/tocnode?id=g9781405124331_chunk_g97814051243317_ss1-45.

Yates, P. 2003, *The Reckoning: the Battle for the International Criminal Court*, Skylight Pictures/International Centre for Transitional Justice.

Yin, R. 2003, *Applications of Case Study Research,* 3rd ed., Sage, Thousand Oaks.

Yin, R. 2009, *Case Study Research: Design and Methods*, Sage, Thousand Oaks.

Young, E. 2006, 'DRC war crimes suspect Lubanga formally charged by ICC', All Africa website, 29 August, accessed 8 June 2011, http://allafrica.com/stories/200608291014.html.

Young, J. 1999, *The Exclusive Society: Social Exclusion, Crime and Difference in Late Modernity*, Sage, London.

Young, J. 2007, *The Vertigo of Late Modernity*, Sage, London.

Zapata, M. 2011, 'Congo: the first and second wars, 1996–2003', Enough website, accessed 15 July 2012, www.enoughproject.org/blogs/congo-first-and-second-wars-1996-2003.

Zedner, L. 1994, 'Reparation and retribution: are they reconcilable?', *The Modern Law Review,* vol. 57, no. 2, pp. 228–50,

Zedner, L. 2007, 'Pre-crime and post-criminology', *Theoretical Criminology*, vol. 11, pp. 261–81.

Zolo, D. 2009, *Victors' Justice from Nuremberg to Baghdad*, Verso, London.

Zwartz, B. 2012, 'Church taken to ICC', *The Age* online, 27 November, accessed 20 December 2012, www.theage.com.au/national/church-taken-to-icc-20121126-2a3wx.html.

Index

www.ingramcontent.com/pod-product-compliance
Ingram Content Group UK Ltd.
Pitfield, Milton Keynes, MK11 3LW, UK
UKHW011017180926
475701UK00004B/792
9781138614598